T0213519

Lecture Notes in Computer Science 10368

Commenced Publication in 1973
Founding and Former Series Editors:
Gerhard Goos, Juris Hartmanis, and Jan van Leeuwen

Jonathan Anderson · Vashek Matyáš
Bruce Christianson · Frank Stajano (Eds.)

Security Protocols XXIV

24th International Workshop
Brno, Czech Republic, April 7–8, 2016
Revised Selected Papers

 Springer

Editors

Jonathan Anderson
Memorial University
St. John's, NL
Canada

Bruce Christianson
University of Hertfordshire
Hertfordshire
UK

Vashek Matyáš
Faculty of Informatics
Masaryk University
Brno
Czech Republic

Frank Stajano
University of Cambridge
Cambridge
UK

ISSN 0302-9743   ISSN 1611-3349   (electronic)
Lecture Notes in Computer Science
ISBN 978-3-319-62032-9   ISBN 978-3-319-62033-6   (eBook)
DOI 10.1007/978-3-319-62033-6

Library of Congress Control Number: 2017945734

LNCS Sublibrary: SL4 – Security and Cryptology

Printed on acid-free paper

This Springer imprint is published by Springer Nature
The registered company is Springer International Publishing AG
The registered company address is: Gewerbestrasse 11, 6330 Cham, Switzerland

Preface

The 24th International Security Protocols Workshop was held in April 2016 at the Mendel Museum of Masaryk University in Brno, Czech Republic. This former Augustinian abbey is where Gregor Mendel presented his seminal *Versuche ber Pflanzenhybriden* (Experiments on Plant Hybridization); in keeping with this location, the theme of the workshop was "Evolving Security."

Security protocols evolve with their changing requirements, their changing mechanisms, and attackers' changing agendas and capabilities. We saw examples of this presented at the workshop: Llewellyn-Jones, Jenkinson, and Stajano described how the Pico authentication system is evolving to support more flexible delegation mechanisms, while Pieczul and Foley brought a qualitative approach to the workshop in their longitudinal consideration of how security-sensitive software has evolved over time in one open-source software project. Sometimes, however, the evolution we see is not in security software but in the attacks against it. Jonker, Mauw, and Trujillo-Rasua described for the workshop how middleperson attacks have evolved over the years but models of them have not, while Kang, Gligor, and Sekar showed us the evolution of DDoS attacks against core Internet infrastructure. With an even more explicit Mendel connection, Ošťádal, Švenda, and Matyáš made use of genetic algorithms in the context of ad hoc network protocols to better model wireless attackers.

As is often the case, many papers and discussions did not fit the theme but were challenging and thought-provoking. We hope that all of these papers and transcripts — edited both by authors and by ourselves — will provoke further debate as our protocols and our understanding of them continue to evolve.

April 2017

Jonathan Anderson
Bruce Christianson
Vashek Matyáš
Frank Stajano

Previous Proceedings in This Series

The proceedings of previous International Security Protocols Workshops are also published by Springer as *Lecture Notes in Computer Science* and are occasionally referred to in the text:

23rd Workshop (2015)	LNCS 9379	ISBN 978-3-319-26096-9
22nd Workshop (2014)	LNCS 8809	ISBN 978-3-319-12399-8
21st Workshop (2013)	LNCS 8263	ISBN 978-3-642-41716-0
20th Workshop (2012)	LNCS 7622	ISBN 978-3-642-35693-3
19th Workshop (2011)	LNCS 7114	ISBN 978-3-642-25866-4
18th Workshop (2010)	LNCS 7061	ISBN 978-3-662-45920-1
17th Workshop (2009)	LNCS 7028	ISBN 978-3-642-36212-5
16th Workshop (2008)	LNCS 6615	ISBN 978-3-642-22136-1
15th Workshop (2007)	LNCS 5964	ISBN 978-3-642-17772-9
14th Workshop (2006)	LNCS 5087	ISBN 978-3-642-04903-3
13th Workshop (2005)	LNCS 4631	ISBN 3-540-77155-7
12th Workshop (2004)	LNCS 3957	ISBN 3-540-40925-4
11th Workshop (2003)	LNCS 3364	ISBN 3-540-28389-7
10th Workshop (2002)	LNCS 2845	ISBN 3-540-20830-5
9th Workshop (2001)	LNCS 2467	ISBN 3-540-44263-4
8th Workshop (2000)	LNCS 2133	ISBN 3-540-42566-7
7th Workshop (1999)	LNCS 1796	ISBN 3-540-67381-4
6th Workshop (1998)	LNCS 1550	ISBN 3-540-65663-4
5th Workshop (1997)	LNCS 1361	ISBN 3-540-64040-1
4th Workshop (1996)	LNCS 1189	ISBN 3-540-63494-5

No published proceedings exist for the first three workshops.

Introduction: Evolving Security
(Transcript of Discussion)

Vashek Matyáš

Masaryk University, Brno, Czech Republic

Good morning everybody, my name is Vashek Matyáš, I'm a local from Masaryk University and I'd like to welcome you to a monastary that does not belong to the University. [laughter]

Ground rules for the discussions: don't hesitate to ask questions. However, when you ask, you must say your name clearly. All discussions, including your names, will be recorded. Then, transcripts will follow. Of course, you will get audio and transcripts for your revision. For your revisions, you can edit them and give instructions accordingly. The transcription will actually happen in Canada, where in Newfoundland — and partly outsourced — the transcripts will be transformed from audio into text. The text and the audio you'll get to revise as soon as possible. So, anybody with any questions, first let everybody know who you are, especially for the recording. Raise your questions at any time you'd like, just raise your hand.

Now it's my pleasure to introduce the first speaker, Giampaolo Bella.

Contents

Invisible Security

Giampaolo Bella[1]([✉]), Bruce Christianson[2], and Luca Viganò[3]

[1] Dipartimento di Matematica e Informatica, Università di Catania, Catania, Italy
giamp@dmi.unict.it
[2] School of Computer Science, University of Hertfordshire, Hatfield, UK
[3] Department of Informatics, King's College London, London, UK

Abstract. In the last decades, digital security has gone through many theoretical breakthroughs, practical developments, worldwide deployments and subtle flaws in a continuous loop. It is mainly understood as a property of a technical system, which is eventually built as a tangible piece of technology for common people to use. It has therefore been assessed in terms of its correctness because it may easily go wrong, of its usability because it may be difficult to interact with, and of its economics because it may be inconvenient to deploy, maintain or re-deploy.

In line with the theme "Evolving Security" of this year's Security Protocols Workshop, our view is that the shape of security as outlined above is in fact getting more and more multifaceted as we write. It was at the same event last year when we depicted an additional facet of security that is its being beautiful [1], namely inherently desirable for its users. Here, we further observe that security should be invisible in the sense that the user's perceived burden of complying with it be negligible. Through a few past, present and (advocated) future examples, this position paper supports invisibility as yet another desirable facet of security.

1 Position

A number of works have advocated that digital security suffers limitations during its practical use and that consequently it should be implemented through a number of defences in depth. By contrast, the current Millennium has taught us that innumerable people consider security an annoying burden and a fastidious waste of time. It is difficult to tell whether this is due, among other reasons, to the adoption of mobile computing devices by a constantly increasing number of people, perhaps with a low attitude towards technology in general, or in haste while on the move.

In this recent, empirically instated setting, we dare contradict the literature (though only apparently, as we shall see) by postulating that the depth of the security mechanisms should be as thin as possible, so that people would not perceive security as an overhead and, rather, would comfortably comply with it. Upon these observations, this position paper poses the extreme question of whether that depth can be reduced so much that people would not notice it at all, and therefore security would become intangible, i.e., invisible to the users

J. Anderson et al. (Eds.): Security Protocols XXIV, LNCS 10368, pp. 1–9, 2017.
DOI: 10.1007/978-3-319-62033-6_1

of the technology to be secured. We shall demonstrate that *invisible security* is possible over some applications and, as such, qualifies as yet another facet of the shape of security.

It must be emphasised that we can shed some light on this new facet of the shape of security only if we take a *socio-technical view* at it, namely a view that accounts for the users as much as it does for the technology; this expands the more traditional *technical view* that saw many defences in depth. Arguably, the interrelation between these two points of view resolves the apparent contradiction hinted at above.

It would be an exaggeration to imagine that invisible security makes sense for every possible application, namely that security can always be made invisible and yet remain as effective as in "Minority Report" [2]. For example, user authentication should arguably be not invisible when the user is authenticating in order to operate a safety-critical application. Invisible security is for mass-use, non safety-critical applications such as those executed on a mobile device, whose users cannot be generally assumed to be security experienced *and* at the same time security aware.

Invisible security is coherent with the facet of beautiful security we introduced last year [1]. It stated that even security can be made beautiful and, by leveraging on some sort of Bettinelli's assumption that people tend to beauty [3], technology users would somewhat instinctively feel comfortable with it and avoid creative attempts at circumventing it. Beautiful security was found to enjoy at least three attributes: to be a primary system feature, not to be disjoint from the system functions, and to be ambassador of a positive user experience. The examples of invisible security found so far may see the security defence well integrated with some system function, thus sometimes meeting the second of the three attributes. Therefore, we can currently logically conclude that invisible security may also contribute to beautiful security.

This paper outlines four possible scenarios prescribing the integration of a security defence with other features of the technical system (Sect. 2). These could be a useful system function that the system users may desire, or an existing security defence that the system users can be assumed to be already happy with. Four examples of such defences are introduced, one per scenario, and their design is discussed and justified as an incarnation of invisible security; an additional, fifth example is advanced as a proposal to make thinner yet more robust the flight boarding protocol that is executed at the airport between a hostess and a passenger (Sect. 3). Remarkably, not only does the novel protocol make security more invisible for the users than the current protocol does, but the novel protocol also is more robust against potential distraction or neglect by the hostess in checking the passenger's boarding card. This is due to the fact that thinner checks are required to prevent an attack whereby two passengers exchange their destinations. Some conclusions terminate the presentation (Sect. 4).

2   Scenarios

This section begins by outlining four possible scenarios supporting the making of security more invisible than it used to be. Each scenario either sees a new security defence become intertwined with existing system features, or an existing security defence become simpler internally.

Scenario 1 *A new security defence is integrated into an existing function of the technical system.* In this scenario, an existing function that users are already used to is assumed.

Scenario 2 *A new security defence is integrated into a new function of the technical system.* A new system function is assumed to be useful and desirable for the system users.

Scenario 3 *A new security defence is integrated into an existing security defence.* A security defence is assumed to be already in place and at the same time to be well received by the system users.

Scenario 4 *An existing security defence is thinned.* An existing security defence is collapsed internally, hence made more invisible and less of a burden.

The next section will provide five example *ceremonies* within the given scenarios, where the term "ceremony" is used to describe a security defence and its human users [4–8].

3   Ceremonies

This section describes four ceremonies as they currently are. We shall see that their design can be considered an application of our principle of invisible security because the security defences are somewhat integrated and thinned with respect to an original design. The section concludes with a proposal to apply the same principle to a fifth example, derived from the flight boarding ceremony.

All our example ceremonies insist on a number of common roles. The following roles can be identified.

Prover (or P for brevity) is the principal who intends to prove his/her identity in order to obtain a service. It is traditionally played by a human being, namely a user who wants to get authenticated to the verifier through some technical system.

Technical system (or TS for brevity) is any piece of technology that may support the prover's authentication, e.g., a computer, a network of computers, a tablet, a smartphone or a smartwatch.

Verifier (or V for brevity) is the principal who intends to verify the identity of the prover. Depending on the application, it may either be played by a human being or coincide with the technical system.

Equipment$_1$, ..., Equipment$_n$ (or $E_1, \ldots, E_n$ for brevity) are each an additional tangible item, ranging from a dedicated piece of technology to paper documents, that the prover may appeal to in support of his/her authentication case.

We remark that the principle of invisible security is successfully applied to the following example ceremonies because the resulting security defences, though made more invisible than they were, are not generally weakened.

3.1 iPhone Authentication

Roles and Principals. P = iPhone user, TS = iPhone, V = TS. Example of Scenario 1.

Protocol Outline. The current protocol whereby a user authenticates to his/her iPhone can be seen as a successful attempt at making the user authentication protocol invisible. The protocol can be represented simply as follows:

$$1.\ P \longrightarrow V : press(button(V))$$
$$2.\ V \longrightarrow P : ack$$

In particular, by leveraging on the fingerprint reading technology of iPhones, the authentication protocol was integrated with the screen-activation protocol, which originally involved pressing the home button, and indeed the *ack* is simply the granted access to the home screen. Therefore, this design practice is an example of Scenario 1.

Security Analysis. It seems fair to claim that authentication to an iPhone (or a similar smartphone or device equipped with a fingerprint reader) is now seamless, as opposed to more traditional devices without a fingerprint reader, on which the traditional user's quest at simplicity may result in the removal of every authentication procedure.

3.2 ICRTouch EPoS

Roles and Principals. P = waiter, TS = network of distributed tills, V = TS, E_1 =waiter's swipe card. Example of Scenario 2.

Protocol Outline. ICRTouch is a company producing solutions for restaurants. Its latest Electronic Point of Sale (EPoS) system relies on networked, distributed tills. It forces each waiter to authenticate to a till to be able to operate on an order and its bill. To support and facilitate authentication, a prover may swipe a personal card and enter a PIN number on any instance of the technical system, namely on any till. The protocol can be represented as follows:

$$1.\ P \longrightarrow instance(1, V) \qquad : swipe(E_1, instance(1, V))$$
$$2.\ instance(1, V) \longrightarrow P \qquad : ack$$
$$\vdots$$
$$2m - 1.\ P \longrightarrow instance(m, V) : swipe(E_1, instance(m, V))$$
$$2m.\ instance(m, V) \longrightarrow P \qquad : ack$$

The card swiping was initially received as extra burden through the routine operations; however, it came coupled with an innovative function that turned out to be very useful: the ability to view a standing order from any till in the shop, which here we have simply abbreviated as the *ack* that is provided by each till *instance*(i, V). Therefore, this design practice is an example of Scenario 2.

Security Analysis. ICRTouch EPoS is arguably more secure than traditional order management systems not just because it enforces authentication before sensitive operations can be carried out, but because it does so by offering the prover something useful and desirable, namely a new function. In consequence, authentication works well in practice because the prover does not perceive it as useless overhead but, rather, as an add-on that dissolves into a wonderful function.

3.3   Hard-Disc Decryption

Roles and Principals. P = computer user, TS = computer, $V = TS$. Example of Scenario 3.

Protocol Outline. To thwart the risks of data leaks following computer thefts, users may encrypt their home folders using free programs. Traditionally, data at rest must first be decrypted before it can be profitably used. As a consequence, the user should enter a password to run the decryption service, followed by another one to pass the O.S.'s login procedure. Most hard-disc decryption programs integrate the two passwords, so that users do not notice any extra burden. The protocol can be represented as follows:

1. $P \longrightarrow V : insert\_password(P, V)$
2. $V \longrightarrow P : ack$

Here, the *ack* is simply the granted access to the home directory. This choice of internal integration assumes that users are currently happy to enter one password, as multi-user systems have made them become used to through the years. This means that one security defence, that is to enter a password at login time, belongs to the users' normal routine; by contrast, any extra effort to decrypt the home space does not. Therefore, this design practice is an example of Scenario 3.

Security Analysis. It is clear that if all home folders are protected by encryption, then users' security and privacy gain a great lot. Meeting the precondition is greatly facilitated if the security defence dissipates into one that is already well received, such as entering one password at login, and a user perceives no extra hassle.

3.4   Remote Car-Alarming

Roles and Principals. P = car owner, TS = car, $V = TS$, E_1 = car owner's remote control. Example of Scenario 4.

Protocol Outline. Historically, the power-door locks of cars were first operated by the car key and then by a dedicated remote control. In addition to the standard locking mechanism, a user could have a car alarm installed to counter theft, and this alarm ultimately came with its own remote control. At some point were the two technologies integrated over a single remote control, resulting in the following protocol:

1. $P \longrightarrow V : signal\_from\_pressing(E_1)$
2. $V \longrightarrow P : ack$

Here, the *ack* could be the locking or opening of the doors, possibly accompanied by a flash of the car's lights and/or a toot by its horn. As a consequence, the user is currently able to lock the door and at the same time set the alarm remotely. Therefore, this design practice is an example of Scenario 4.

Security Analysis. We can assume that the two technologies, namely remote power-door locks and remote alarm, existed for some time based upon two separate remote controls. Yet, it is clear that their integration makes them more reliable for the simple fact that the chances of operating one system while forgetting the other one get zeroed.

3.5 Flight Boarding

Roles and Principals. P = passenger, TS = computer with checked-in passenger database, V = hostess, E_1 = passenger's electronically readable identifier, E_2 = passenger's boarding card. Example of Scenario 4.

Current Protocol Outline. The current protocol sees the passenger hand over two things to the hostess who stands at a gate: the passenger's identifier (passport or ID card) and boarding card (printed or displayed on a hand-held device). The hostess is called to check that the passenger's face matches the picture on the identifier, and that the details on the identifier match those on the boarding card; this is a customary, three-valued authentication check. The hostess also scans the boarding card in order to check that the passenger is authorised to fly to the particular destination currently set at the gate. The passenger will be allowed through the gate only if all these checks succeed. The hostess will ultimately return the two documents to the passenger. The protocol can be represented as follows:

1. $P \longrightarrow V : E_1, E_2$

    $V\,checks(E_1, E_2, P);$
    $V\,scans(E_2);$
    if $OK(all\_checks)$ then $admitted(V)$
2. $V \longrightarrow P : E_1, E_2$

Novel Protocol Outline. We suggest a novel boarding protocol that disposes entirely with the boarding card, in the sole assumption that the passenger's identifier can be read electronically, for example by NFC technology. The protocol is obtained from the previous one by merely pruning out any reference to the boarding card. Therefore, it can be described as follows:

1. $P \longrightarrow V : E_1$

   $V\,checks(E_1, P);$
   $V\,scans(E_2);$
   if $OK(all\_checks)$ then $admitted(V)$

2. $V \longrightarrow P : E_1$

It can be seen that the manual checks that the hostess has to do get simplified. In particular, the authentication checks reduce to a traditional, two-valued check between the passenger's face and their identifier. Scanning the identifier on the computer will then tell the hostess whether that passenger is allowed on that flight. Therefore, this design practice is an example of Scenario 4.

Security Analysis. Our novel boarding protocol works equally well as the currently known boarding protocol. This is possible because the passenger details can be read electronically from the identifier rather than from the boarding card via a QR code. In return, the passenger gets the bonus of the removal of the need to carry a boarding card, be it paper based or electronic on a smartphone.

From a security standpoint, the novel protocol seems more secure than the current one because the burden on the hostess is lightened, hence reducing the room for human error or distraction. The hostess may read the passenger details mechanically from the identifier rather than from the boarding card. Additionally, the hostess now only needs to check the passenger identifier to match the passenger. This simple check may ultimately thwart an attack whereby two accomplices pass security successfully and then attempt to exchange destinations at the gates; this attack could realistically succeed in the present setting where a passenger was able to board the wrong plane [9] and the issue hit the press perhaps only because the passenger denounced it. This attack is likely to have derived from distraction or negligence in checking also the boarding card, a need that our novel protocol removes.

Note that some airports enforce security procedures in which the boarding card is actually checked several times, e.g., before the passenger is admitted to the security control (where bags and people are scanned) and at the "border" control, before being admitted to the gate to board a flight to an international destination. If these additional procedures are in place, the protocol we discuss will of course require a modification not only of the boarding ceremony but also of the security check and passport control, but also these procedures would actually benefit from the simplified, more invisible security.

4   Conclusions

This paper advances the position that digital security comes with the yet vastly unexplored facet that we call "invisible security". It outlines four possible scenarios in which security has been made effectively more invisible than it was, namely less tangible as a burden for its users and yet perfectly working. It is clear that invisible security makes sense only upon the precondition of looking at security from a socio-technical standpoint, otherwise we would be content with the more traditional rule of thumb of stacking up more and more defences in depth. Those are likely to look like requiring unjustified effort to the layman, who will therefore engage into finding ways to get around them in practice. This is how a whole stack of security defences may collapse in the real world.

The examples of security ceremonies discussed in relation to each scenario support the claim that invisible security has somewhat been up in the air without, we conjecture, being recognised as a useful facet of security and hence as a working principle to apply. As a result, users perhaps do not even realise that today they are authenticating to a smartphone without remembering a PIN, operating an advanced EPoS without wanting to sellotape their swipe cards to each and every till, decrypting their home space on their computer seamlessly, and locking and alarming their cars with a single press.

Leveraging on our notion as on a fully-fledged principle, we set out to simplify the flight boarding ceremony. The motivation for this choice was multiple. It is a tremendously common ceremony and it would seem desirable to eliminate the need to carry a boarding card and yet keep the ceremony secure. Also, the fact that a passenger recently boarded to the wrong flight shows room for a practical attack that sees two accomplices exchange destinations. Because this is likely to derive from error or distraction of the hostess who is at the gate, we set out to make the security of this ceremony more invisible. This was possible in the sole assumption that the passenger's identifier is electronically readable as it was done with a traditional boarding card. As a result, the checks that the hostess is called to operate are reduced.

We understand that some passengers may feel more relaxed by continuing to carry a boarding card, and of course this may be optionally issued at check-in time. Also, it is clear that our protocol may raise some negative business considerations, and some airline companies may not be happy with it. Quite a considerable percentage of their income comes from charging the passenger even 40 or 50 Euros to print a boarding card at a check-in desk. Since this is generally perceived as an unfair charge by the passengers, we believe that our novel boarding protocol will actually enhance the user experience, ultimately benefiting the airline company as well.

In terms of research, our boarding protocol demonstrates that the current technology makes it possible to effectively simplify such a widespread security ceremony so that a traditional textbook contradiction is subverted: not only security enhances but at the same time also the user experience improves.

References

1. Bella, G., Viganò, L.: Security is beautiful. In: Christianson, B., Švenda, P., Matyáš, V., Malcolm, J., Stajano, F., Anderson, J. (eds.) Security Protocols 2015. LNCS, vol. 9379, pp. 247–250. Springer, Cham (2015). doi:10.1007/978-3-319-26096-9_25
2. Minority Report: A movie directed by Steven Spielberg and starring Tom Cruise. The screenplay was written by Scott Frank and Jon Cohen, quite loosely based on a short story by Philip K. Dick (2002)

3. Bettinelli, S.: Tomo secondo che contiene l'Entusiasmo. Dalle Stampe Zatta (1780)
4. Bella, G., Coles-Kemp, L.: Layered analysis of security ceremonies. In: Gritzalis, D., Furnell, S., Theoharidou, M. (eds.) SEC 2012. IAICT, vol. 376, pp. 273–286. Springer, Heidelberg (2012). doi:10.1007/978-3-642-30436-1_23
5. Bella, G., Curzon, P., Lenzini, G.: Service security and privacy as a socio-technical problem. J. Comput. Secur. **23**, 563–585 (2015)
6. Ellison, C.M.: Ceremony design and analysis. IACR Cryptology ePrint Archive 2007: 399 (2007)
7. Martina, J.E., dos Santos, E., Carlos, M.C., Price, G., Custódio, R.F.: An adaptive threat model for security ceremonies. Int. J. Inf. Sec. **14**, 103–121 (2015)
8. Radke, K., Boyd, C., Gonzalez Nieto, J., Brereton, M.: Ceremony analysis: strengths and weaknesses. In: Camenisch, J., Fischer-Hübner, S., Murayama, Y., Portmann, A., Rieder, C. (eds.) SEC 2011. IAICT, vol. 354, pp. 104–115. Springer, Heidelberg (2011). doi:10.1007/978-3-642-21424-0_9
9. Smith, R.: Ryanair passenger gets on wrong plane and flies to Sweden instead of France (2012). http://www.mirror.co.uk/news/uk-news/ryanair-passenger-gets-on-wrong-plane-946207

Invisible Security
(Transcript of Discussion)

Giampaolo Bella[✉]

University of Catania, Catania, Italy
giamp@dmi.unict.it

I'm presenting joint work with Luca Viganò and Bruce, and it's all going to be about what I like to call *invisible security*. This concept tries to make the very security mechanisms and stakeholders that we have to go through in our everyday's lives less of a burden for ourselves, for the user. But before I dig into it, let me ask you a hopefully thought-provoking question. We are all used to fly, and therefore we all have to use boarding cards to board a flight: that's the protocol we have to go through. We have various versions of boarding cards, the most traditional version up here on the slide, then the printout version and the mobile version, but the question is, why do we need a boarding card in the first place, what are boarding cards there for? If you don't mind, I leave this question open, and I'll get back to it later on.

The current security baseline, the way we can look at security today, consists essentially of these two views. As a student I was taught the defense-in-depth principle, so don't just use one security mechanism, use many in a row because you have all sorts of limitations in the real world. Things may go wrong in practice when you implement the mechanisms, so use many in a row in such a way that if one breaks down, you still have all the other security mechanisms to make the attacker's life difficult hopefully. Well, this makes perfect sense for highly security-sensitive services or applications, such as military applications, or for example, industrial control systems (are they secure nowadays?) but it doesn't work equally well for our day-to-day applications.

I imagine a user who is doing security-sensitive transactions such as accessing her bank account while she is using a mobile phone hopping on the tube, and I'm not sure whether this user would like to have many security defenses to go through. So, when we take the socio-technical standpoint, a very interesting question would be whether we can compress the security mechanisms together and make them as thin as possible, and ultimately invisible to the user's eyes, to the user's perception. Of course, we would love them to be yet effective.

To answer this question, we have at least four approaches. Approach one says: assume there is a wonderful system function that the users tremendously like to have, like to use; if we manage to integrate the security defense to the system function, and I'll have examples of such integration, then the user, who is typically goal-oriented and wants that system function, will probably not realize the burden of having to go through the security defense. And you can do quite the same, approach two, if you have a new system function that turns out to be tremendously useful as well, and if you integrate the security defense to this new

© Springer International Publishing AG 2017
J. Anderson et al. (Eds.): Security Protocols XXIV, LNCS 10368, pp. 10–18, 2017.
DOI: 10.1007/978-3-319-62033-6_2

system function, then you may get the same result that the user doesn't really realize that he's going through some hassle, or some security defense, simply because he wants the new system function.

Approach three says that you can do something very similar by conjugating two security defenses together. Suppose there is one mechanism that's well-established, well-accepted, either because it's very thin, very light, or because it's been there for many years so people accept it nowadays; for example, I'm thinking that we all have to enter a password when we switch on our laptop. If you integrate a new security defense with this old, previously well-established, security defense, then the burden of having to go through the new one will probably be compressed, and the user won't realize he's actually going through two security defenses tied together. Approach four says: let's compress a security defense internally, let's simplify it, let's make it thinner so that security will become ultimately more invisible.

I have examples of all these approaches, namely scenarios in which these approaches have been taken already or could be taken. The best example about approach one is the iPhone 5S's idea of integrating the fingerprint scan to the screen activation function. I think this was a cool idea, because we're all used to the fact that we need to somehow activate the screen of our phone before using it, in order to wake it up. Nowadays, when you press the button, you won't probably realize that you are actually going through a security defense because you just wanted to press the button, you had to press the button, you knew this beforehand. This is a clear example of integration of a security defense with a system function in such a way that they security defense will become more invisible.

Approach two can be exemplified easily as well. I remember that at last year's event Bruce put forward the example of an Electronic Point Of Sale system by ICRTouch which would ask each waiter to authenticate to the till by swiping a card and inserting a code. You may imagine that at the very beginning this was not very well received, we have a busy restaurant, waiters are running around, and they still have to authenticate, swipe, insert the PIN every time they need to use a till. But there may be many tills in a restaurant, and the waiters might find it nice, easy and ultimately convenient to be able to login to different tills depending on where they are in the restaurant. The new function that Bruce was describing last year is that they could find their standing orders inside any till they would login to. Very quickly was this found to be a useful function, and so the burden of swiping the card and then entering the PIN number was kind of forgotten because of this integration with a useful system function.

We now come up to the approach of integrating two security defenses together. If you really want to apply the defense-in-depth principle to your laptop, you would have to have a boot password, namely a BIOS/EFI password, then a password to decrypt your hard disk, then a user password. I wonder if we really use three passwords to operate our laptops. But here's a screen that comes from the Ubuntu installation routine: you may choose to encrypt your home folder, it's asking the user password here. What happens in practice is that, after the installation, when you login by inserting that password, you're actually decrypting the home folder first, and then doing the routine user access procedure. The second and third passwords that I was describing earlier have been integrated together. You insert one password, but you still are activating two security mechanisms. Here's another example of approach three: with one remote control you activate the power-door locks of your car and you also activate an alarm system, but I remember many years ago people actually holding two remote controls, one for the car door locks, and one for the alarm system. These two mechanisms have been integrated together, and everything is much easier to actually use.

What about approach four? Here comes my question about why we need boarding cards in the first place. I'm showing you my personal distillation of the flight boarding protocol that is executed at the gate before you actually step on the aircraft. Essentially, the passenger will hand over to the gate attendant three pieces of information: face, an ID such as a passport, and the boarding card. What the attendant does is normally, check A, match your face to the picture on the passport in such a way to make sure that the passport really belongs to you. Then, check B, check if the passport has been tampered with. The attendant also uses the ID as a source of important information, your name and surname, which then, check C, the attendant will match to the name and surname on the boarding card. Ultimately, check D, she will scan the boarding card and use its information to query a database of all the people who are checked-in for that particular flight, and will be able to check that the information is correct, namely this name and surname is registered to board the very flight that is sitting at her back, behind the gate.

Finally, if everything is successful, the attendant will tell you go through, or else stop for further scrutiny. A few observations can be made. Check A and B could be swapped, you could first check the passport and then match it to the face. Check C and D can be equally swapped, but I guess the crucial check is check C, because authentication here is based on the passport and authorization is based on the boarding card. Therefore, the attendant needs to make sure that the same person she's authenticating is also authorized to board the flight.

I guess this is an important security protocol for the simple fact that boarding a flight is a security-sensitive service, and particularly security-sensitive perhaps nowadays. The question I was asking myself: is it secure? Does it work in practice? We would call it a human scale protocol, because it involves a lot of human checks and so on and so forth. Humans may make mistakes, so I wouldn't call this 100% secure, at least for what we read from the news, that a passenger taking off from Stansted ended up being in Sweden rather than in France as he would have wanted. Then he complained with Ryanair that he really wanted to go to France.

Is this an attack? Perhaps not, but we can see the same scenario as a threat, because you may imagine for example that I may like to buy a cheap ticket to fly somewhere, and then try to use the boarding card to go to a different place whose airfare was much more expensive. Or you may imagine that two accomplices with two valid tickets and boarding cards pass security, and then they try to swap destinations at the gates. And I'm afraid we should also worry about other terrorism-based scenarios I can't see at the moment. I think this is an important issue, I think we need to look at this protocol with much criticism, and we really want to make sure it is secure. Now, let me recall that my main point originally was whether I can make this security defense more invisible to the user, but obviously I still want it to be effective.

Hugo Jonker: I've seen other stories about people who boarded the wrong plane, I've never seen a story about an attack in the sense that you described, so deliberately boarding the wrong plane. Do you have an example?

Reply: No, I don't, I was just conjecturing it, and well, perhaps there has been an attack where the attacker went unspotted. We don't know, I'm saying that if this is possible you may easily turn into a threat and open up new attack scenarios.

Hugo Jonker: I was wondering that because people made mistakes here, but that doesn't necessarily imply that you can count on those mistakes being made when you want them to be made.

Reply: Of course, but if this passenger didn't complain with Ryanair afterwards, and was happy to have gone to Sweden instead of France, then you would've called this an attack, but perhaps we wouldn't have known because he wouldn't have reported the issue.

Bruce Christianson: Indeed, if the person gets on the plane, and they're detected, "You're on the wrong flight!", then they're not going to say, "Oh, my attack has been foiled".

Reply: That's what I meant.

Bruce Christianson: "Oh, that's a good thing you spotted that." Almost by definition, there's going to be no example of a detected unsuccessful attack.

Reply: And who knows how many examples of undetected successful attacks there are. So, I think that this protocol can be simplified and made more invisible to the humans who have to go through it by using an electronic passport.

Hugo Jonker: You're looking at it from a very, I would say, European or like perspective. In India, my favorite example, they follow a completely different procedure, and with different goals. I don't believe in the simplification in the sense of simplifying overall the boarding card without fully considering what the protocols about the use of the boarding pass actually are.

Reply: I couldn't agree more, but in fact you'll probably agree with me that the main goal of the boarding card, or one of the main ones, is authorization. Here I'm precisely questioning this very goal, then I would ask you what other goals you are thinking about: memorizing, perhaps memorizing the seat number? But that's not a security goal as such.

Ross Anderson: Well, one would be reassuring the passenger. 25 years ago if you bought a plane ticket it was a fancy multi-part thing with red carbon paper, you went and checked in, you got a boarding card that was fancy. It had a mag stripe on this side, it had a tear-off bit and printing, it looked official, you were reassured you were holding something that might actually get you on the plane. Nowadays, you can dispense with your boarding card, you can have something on your mobile phone. I don't do that because I'm nervous that my mobile phone will run out of battery and I will end up being charged by Ryanair for an extra 45 quid to print another boarding card. I would say that a boarding card is actually pure security theater, whether or not you get on the plane depends on whether your name and passport number are entered against that flight number on the Amadeus computer at the end of the runway in Munich airport. If some jumbo crashes on takeoff, nobody's going to fly for months, and months, and months.

Reply: Yeah, I think I'm in line with that comment. I'm not saying that I want to dispose with this whole reassurance thing, you still have to go through check-in, for example, for the overbooking story and the like, but you might easily just get a printout to memorize the seat after you went through check-in. Here I'm only talking about the authorization goal as such.

Ross Anderson: Well, now you need seat numbers, three years ago Easyjet didn't, but now they give you seat numbers so they can charge you an extra 13 pounds.

Reply: Exactly.

Frank Stajano: In a previous slide you had something that said "20 years ago". In fact, 20 years ago what happened, especially in America with all these inside-the-US flights, so you basically bought a ticket and all that matters was someone paid for the ticket, and they can basically exchange, nobody would even check your name, all that mattered was the seat was paid for, that was pre-9/11, now after 9/11 there's all this business about security and this and that to which airlines latch on because it means that you cannot resell your ticket, you cannot give your ticket to someone else, they would have to buy a new one which is very neat for them because this trading of tickets of course can be useful. I don't know to what extent the fact that someone has had their name entered is any more authorization than the fact that they have paid, I don't know if they have how many background checks, or this guy was a terrorist before, or something like that, and I don't know how effective they are. One goal is just to extract more money by preventing the recirculation of tickets that have already been paid.

Reply: Yeah. I'm not trying to rule out the business considerations of course, so I agree with you. But what I'm saying is that from a security standpoint today, it is important to match the authentication with the authorization, the piece of information that authentication is based upon with the piece of information that authorization is based upon, at least because as you are saying, you want the same person who bought the tickets under their name to be the one who is flying.

Jonathan Anderson: I think that actually, from a security perspective, we don't care very much that the person who paid is the person who gets on board, but I think what we really care about is that the person who gets on board has been checked not to have any bombs, and that somebody paid for the seat, and that somebody is now sitting in the seat, and there is a mapping of no more than one person per seat. The other thing that airlines really care about is the penalty that they pay if they get to the other country, and then somebody gets turned back from the border, and they have to ship them back because they let someone on the airplane who shouldn't have been allowed on the plane because they didn't have their passport, or something silly like that. I think that, that pressure is the only reason. And even then it's not so much about matching the name on the passport to the boarding pass, it's just that this person has a passport that will let them into Austria, and they also have a boarding card that says somebody paid for the seat. I think the airline, except for all of the no-fly or whatever that the regulators impose, the airline doesn't actually care, and from a security perspective, I'm not sure it really matters.

Reply: Right, but still they do care because as Frank was saying, they want to make sure that who flies is precisely who bought the ticket under the name so that if this is not the case they may charge you. You can't just give your ticket to someone else because that's convenient.

Jonathan Anderson: Again, that's a business resale consideration.

Reply: I guess also a security consideration because as you said, they need to check that you have a valid passport, so they really want to check the person who's flying to have a valid passport. Perhaps they could do that without checking that name is the same name as the one printed on the ticket, so I concede that the current protocol aims at a mix of security and business goals.

Brian Kidney: That actually pre-supposes that requires a passport. To fly within Canada you do not actually need a photo ID, you can either have a government issued photo ID, or two other pieces of government issued ID, one of which has your address on it. An actual picture is not a requirement for flying within Canada. It's a little old man and he goes, "Well, do you have a license?" I know because my mother-in-law doesn't, so she doesn't actually have a government issued photo ID.

Reply: Right, so I'm not sure how they make sure that the ID really belongs to you.

Brian Kidney: They don't.

Reply: They don't, they don't care?

Brian Kidney: As long as the name and address matches the ticket, you can get on the plane.

Reply: So the identity is just attested there, it's not really linked to you as a physical person. I find that a bit surprising, and especially these days, in terms of both security and safety.

Bruce Christianson: It relies on the ID being hard to forge and the person holding it having an incentive not to let it out of their sight.

Hugo Jonker: It's also hard for a terrorist to enter the country on an in-country flight.

Ross Anderson: Well there's also the point that, as a practical matter, people cannot recognize a human person in front of them against a photo ID. There's a famous study on this by University of Westminster about 20 years ago, a double-blind study, half a dozen Sainsbury's checkout people, forty-odd students, each with and without photos, basically people cannot identify people from photos.

Reply: And that's why people can fly to the wrong destinations.

Bruce Christianson: The protocols that have been mentioned where you're getting stamped on your boarding card... the reason those stamps are going on your boarding card is because you already have a boarding card, it's convenient to do that. In other places, what they will do is give you a piece of plastic and say, "don't lose this or you're not getting on the plane", thereby aligning your incentives with theirs. The threat is an insider attack, the threat is someone in a position of trust with the airline smuggling a passenger on a plane.

Audience: They do that because it's convenient. Maybe a boarding card is not really needed for security today but to help people not to get lost because people get lost in the airport.

Reply: Are you sure?

Audience: I can imagine lots of people confusing their planes.

Reply: I can imagine the opposite scenario, I live in Sicily, which is quite far, at least it is far because to come here, you always need to go through Rome. For some time Alitalia decided that they would allow printout boarding cards, and you would have to have two sheets of paper, two sheets of boarding card literally for each single leg of flight. To go to Vienna I had to have four sheets of paper with me, then my mobile phone of course because we all want that, and the ID, and let me tell you, I didn't really like that. Now I have a QR code on my phone, I still have a boarding card literally speaking, but I'm much happier that way.

Audience: It may be much easier for operating the services of the aircraft if it's known that everybody has a piece of paper at the airport to help you find your plane and so on, you wouldn't get lost, and "I don't really know, which flight is it?" and people would need to go and query a database based on their IDs to find their flight. Having that, maybe, it is one of your cases, maybe it's easier to build security on top of that, providing that people already have their boarding cards.

Ross Anderson: There is another incentive to put the boarding card on the phone, which is that a big cost for airlines, it is that people are late at the gate. They're sitting in the bar, or they're sitting in the duty-free shop, and there's always one sot who's ten minutes late and the plane misses its departure slot. Now, if everybody had to have their boarding card on the phone, you could send the heavy squad into the bar to fetch Mister Smith and drag him to the Stockholm flight. That would be a value-add for the airlines.

Jonathan Anderson: Well, that's assuming that the airlines don't *want* you to miss your flight so that they don't get dinged for overbooking.

Reply: I still only see two different types of passengers: a passenger who memorizes the flight details so he knows where to go, looks it up on the screen and finds out the gate, and that's it; and a passenger who doesn't. For the first passenger, I don't see the need of a boarding card, not even as a memo. And simply for the second passenger I see the need of a boarding card *merely* as a memo, but not for authorization purposes. In fact, this revision I'm presenting here of the boarding protocol tries to make sure that the passenger is both authenticated and authorized simply by means of, say, an electronic passport.

You see that checks B and C have been emptied completely, you see that what is scanned here is the electronic passport, and the resulting protocol is lighter, the security mechanisms are thinner. I would argue that this protocol's security is more invisible than the original protocol's. The question is, is it as effective as the original protocol? I guess so, in terms of authentication and authorization, and let me argue, perhaps it's even more secure than the original protocol, because the amount of human intervention here is reduced. You may even think that the passport has a scan of your fingerprint, and so you just go through even without a human attendant there, you just go through, scan your passport, scan your finger, and you would be let in or not. Doesn't it work like that to enter the UK if you have an electronic passport nowadays?

Ross Anderson: Yes, but it takes ten seconds, fifteen seconds at the gate.

Reply: Yes, but tomorrow it will take three seconds. The question is, would a human attendant take less than ten seconds? That was certainly not the case with my last flight.

Ross Anderson: Well, with people checking you in at the gate, it will typically take one or two seconds if they are rushing through a big queue. There's another reason why you may want a boarding card, which is when you are on top of the airplane steps, she has a quick look at your boarding card, and most of the time if you're trying to go to Dublin and the plane's for another city, she'll say, "Excuse me sir, you are on the wrong plane". Do you want to dispense with that entirely? Perhaps the occasional person will go to the wrong city. Perhaps civilization can survive that.

Reply: I'm arguing from a security/safety standpoint, I don't really like that.

Ross Anderson: Why? A terrorist on one plan blows up one plan instead of another plan, the same number of casualties, the same difference. Who cares whether it's a flight to Sweden or to Dublin?

Reply: Well, which plane it is may matter to me!

Brian Kidney: There's a question there as well about the actual security, because we use no-fly lists to keep people off planes that we don't actually want on there, but a big problem with the no-fly list is that there is no picture attached, and there are lots of people with the same name who don't have a piece of ID. I think that the protocol is thinner and more invisible, however I don't think that the original protocol is much more than security theatre.

Reply: All I'm saying is that if we have any passport, and we have the infrastructure, namely a database with the details of who's flying to that particular flight, all the stakeholders could be mechanized, and by merely authenticating yourself through your electronic passport, I guess that these various security problems of authentication of authorization could be solved.

Jonathan Anderson: However, one unique thing about the boarding card that's different from your ID, and that's different from your face, is that it is under the control of the airlines, that they can put whatever they want on it, and the atomic transaction involved from when you purchase the ticket to when you get on the plane, those two discrete events are bound by this boarding card, whereas, if I buy a flight three months in advance to save on the cost, and then I get a new passport, I have to renew my passport in the meantime, I go and look and say, "Oh, my passport's expired" after I buy the flight. Well then, what happened in this protocol, if you are authenticating just the name, well that's not really more secure, however you need a strong binding between the passport itself, and getting on the flight, well then, we need an additional protocol for me to transfer my ticket from my old passport to my new passport, and I think that is where the vulnerabilities are likely to lie in the new protocol.

Reply: It looks like I haven't got time to give you a full answer, but let me just say that Ryanair asked me the details of my passport *when* I purchased my ticket to Pisa. Isn't that more problematic than having my revised protocol in place? I believe so.

Jonathan Anderson: Not all airlines do that though. We should not substitute "Ryanair" for "an airline"! [laughter].

Reply: True, no, but logically the claim I'm making here is that the problems that you fear my protocol would be introducing are already in place at least for one airline that is very popular.

Man-in-the-Middle Attacks Evolved... but Our Security Models Didn't

Hugo Jonker[1(✉)], Sjouke Mauw[2], and Rolando Trujillo-Rasua[2]

[1] Open University of the Netherlands, Heerlen, The Netherlands
hugo.jonker@ou.nl
[2] University of Luxembourg, Luxembourg City, Luxembourg
{sjouke.mauw,rolando.trujillo}@uni.lu

Abstract. The security community seems to be thoroughly familiar with man-in-the-middle attacks. However, the common perception of this type of attack is outdated. It originates from when network connections were fixed, not mobile, before 24/7 connectivity became ubiquitous. The common perception of this attack stems from an era before the vulnerability of the protocol's context was realised. Thanks to revelations by Snowden and by currently available man-in-the-middle tools focused on protocol meta-data (such as so-called "Stingrays" for cellphones), this view is no longer tenable. Security protocols that only protect the contents of their messages are insufficient. Contemporary security protocols must also take steps to protect their context: who is talking to whom, where is the sender located, etc.

In short: the attacker has evolved. It's high time for our security models and requirements to catch up.

1 Introduction

Man-in-the-Middle (MitM) attacks are well-known to the security protocols community. Indeed, a security protocol will typically be proved secure against a Dolev-Yao [7] attacker, a powerful definition of man-in-the-middle from 1983. However, the use of systems has evolved since 1983 – as have threats against systems. The current use of MitM models by the security protocols community does not account for this evolution and, as such, is outdated. Two key ways in which systems and their use have evolved are:

- Ubiquitous usage coupled with a dependence on connectivity,
- Personalisation of the connection.

This has led to numerous MitM attacks on deployed protocols such as SSL/TLS and GSM (cf. Sect. 2). Such attacks are generally treated as individual occurrences. In this paper, we advocate that such attacks are part of a larger pattern: the current notion of man-in-the-middle as used in security research no longer matches real world MitM-attacks. We propose to address this by evolving the notion of man-in-the-middle to account for a protocol's context, that is, those

© Springer International Publishing AG 2017
J. Anderson et al. (Eds.): Security Protocols XXIV, LNCS 10368, pp. 19–25, 2017.
DOI: 10.1007/978-3-319-62033-6_3

data that influence the protocol or are inherently used or disclosed by the protocol (cf. Sect. 2). We distinguish two classes of solutions, based on whether or not the communication partner is trusted. We call these classes *context agreement* and *context verification*, which are discussed in Sects. 3.1 and 3.2, respectively. We illustrate how context may be leveraged to strengthen protocols by showing a simplified extension for GSM/UMTS in Sect. 4.

2   How Man-in-the-Middle Attacks Outgrew Security Models

As mentioned, networks and the use of networks has evolved. The dependence on connectivity ensures that most protocols have fallbacks to ensure backwards compatibility. The mobility of the endpoints means that the context is no longer fully known a priori. Moreover, as connected devices have become small and capable, the connection has become far more personal.

2.1   Backwards Compatibility

Computers have become ubiquitous, and are used in many if not most jobs in the western world. Moreover, computers have become vastly interconnected: a button pressed here affects a display there, a file saved here is updated there, a withdrawal here changes a balance sheet there, etc. Nowadays, many systems even depend on such interconnectivity. This interconnectivity is only possible if the computers on either end understand each other - computers must be using the same communication protocol.

As our understanding of security increased, flaws in communication protocols were found and repaired. Since systems depend on interconnectivity, there inevitably has to be a fallback mechanism to communicate with computers that are not yet updated. Typically, this leads to an initialisation phase, during which the computers agree on version, cipher suite, and other parameters of the protocol. However, in general, this phase is not considered part of the protocol and omitted from security proofs. This has already caused multiple vulnerabilities, e.g. the DROWN [2], LOGJAM [1], FREAK [4], and POODLE [10] attacks on TLS.

The solutions for such attacks are typically rather ad hoc, in that the solution addresses the attack and little beyond that. However, we should learn more from these attacks than just how to prevent one instance.

2.2   Personalisation of the Connection

With the rise of the smart phone and wireless connectivity, users no longer need to be stationary to communicate. Connections have become mobile. As such, the user's context is no longer fixed. Moreover, the small form factor, ubiquitous connectivity and the mature capabilities of current devices allow users to take their personal computing platform with them at all times, and communicate at any time using wireless communication. Thereby, these devices have become far more intwined with personal life than any computing platform that came before. Of course, the wireless communication signals can be picked up by any nearby antenna, and so security protocols can ensure that the contents of their communication remains confidential from an eavesdropper. However, an eavesdropper can still learn information, such as the approximate location of the communicating party. Since the communication endpoint has become far more personal, determining the location of the communicating device has become synonymous with determining a person's location. Nowadays, there exist commercially-available MitM devices for intercepting and tracking GSM devices[1] and WiFi/Bluetooth devices[2]. These devices perform typical man-in-the-middle attacks, yet such attacks are not considered when proving security of the protocol.

Existing solutions against such tracking are based on detecting the trackers, for instance by analysing protocol properties of the communication signal. Currently, research into detecting cell site simulators has just begun (e.g. [6]), and a few smart phone apps claim to detect such shenanigans. These all rely on particular details of the used protocol (e.g., base station parameter fingerprinting, network operator fingerprinting, etc.), and the simulator's imperfection in replicating such details. However, we hold the view that this will only lead to an arms race, while not addressing the crucial underlying point: that there is, indeed, a man-in-the-middle. A more thorough, generic solution must be developed.

3   How to Determine Context

Remark that all these attacks arise from the outdated perception of man-in-the-middle as currently held by the security community. While the aforementioned attacks are all classified as MitM attacks once discovered, our current design processes and evaluation tools are insufficient to prevent these attacks. We argue that the security community must start researching contextual physical properties in a formal way as to make it part of the protocol. An example of such a property is signal strength.

We distinguish two categories of possible solutions:

- **context verification:** without a trusted communication partner,
- **context agreement:** with a trusted communication partner.

If there exists a trusted communication partner for the user (e.g., a trusted base station), the user and her partner can exchange their observations on the perceived context, and determine whether their combined observations indicate an anomaly. Thus, user and partner agree on some properties of the context, which is reminiscent of the security requirement "data agreement". Hence we label this *context agreement.*

If the user does not trust any communication partner, she is determining the validity of the context by herself. We label this *context verification.*

---

[1] For an overview, see EFF's cell site simulator FAQ.

[2] E.g. the Navizon indoor triangulation system.

3.1   Context Verification

Security claims are proven based on assumptions on the adversary capabilities. An important assumption is whether the adversary is able to decrypt an encrypted message without knowing the encryption key, also known as perfect cryptography, without which it is impossible to prove security in current security protocols. Such assumption is based on computationally hard problems and our inability to solve them. It is thus apparent that physical claims can also be proven based on physical laws that constrain the capabilities of the adversary.

So, what do a secret key and the speed of light have in common? The theory of relativity states that a message or a signal cannot travel at a speed faster than the speed of light. Thus, an adversary cannot manipulate a message traveling at the speed of light without inevitably causing a delay, just as he cannot forge a signature without knowing the secret key. This provides a means for context verification, in particular for proximity verification, which has been studied since 1993 when Brands and Chaum introduced *distance bounding* protocols [5].

Distance bounding protocols are cryptographic protocols that exchange messages at (nearly) the speed of light. By measuring the round-trip-time (RTT) of a message exchange, a verifier can securely compute a tight upper bound on its distance to a prover. Therefore, the verifier can ensure that the prover is within a given radius.

While there exists a rich literature in distance bounding protocols [3], the secure verification of other physical properties (e.g. location and signal strength) is still an open challenge. There exist heuristics approaches, such as [6], which measures the deviation of the attacker's signal from the expected signal. The challenge is thus how to bring this heuristic approaches into a formal framework that allows for security proofs.

Definition 1 (Context verification). *A party A achieves* context verification *of her observation $obs_A(C_B)$ of the context C_B of party B if, whenever A completes a run of the protocol (apparently with B) then $obs_A(C_B)$ is correct with respect to C_B.*

In contrast to standard security properties, context verification relies on properties that may change with time, e.g., location and meteorological conditions. Remark that context verification does not require B to execute the protocol with A. As such, it captures contextual information about the context of the communication partner that can be verified without his involvement.

3.2   Context Agreement

We introduce context agreement as a notion weaker than context verification. To formalise it, we build on the notion of *data agreement* in security protocols, whereby two parties securely agree on the values of a set of variables [8]. This is used, for example, to secretly agree on a session key for subsequent communications.

Definition 2 (Context agreement). *A party A achieves* context agreement *with another party B on B's context C_B if, whenever A completes a run of the protocol (apparently with B) then B has been previously running the protocol (apparently with A) and the observation of A on B's context is the same as B's observation of his context in that run, that is: $obs_A(C_B) = obs_B(C_B)$.*

Note that in context agreement the trusted parties agree on the *observed* context, not on the actual context. A sufficiently powerful attacker or a lying party can ensure that a fake context is agreed to. For example, a device B may determine its location based on a fake GPS signal. Upon agreement on B's location, neither A nor B are aware that a false location has been agreed upon.

We observe that context agreement has already been used to prevent downgrade attacks. Downgrade attacks are a type of MitM attack that exploit backward compatibility. For example, a renegotiation vulnerability[3] was uncovered in some implementations of SSL/TLS.

Note that context verification requires that the context observed by A is indeed B's actual context, while context agreement may be an agreement on a context that is different from B's actual context. Therefore these properties are incomparable.

4   An Illustration: Detecting a GSM/UMTS MitM

A recent hot topic is the availability of simulators [9] (also known as IMSI catchers or Stingrays). These devices act as plug-and-play man-in-the-middle devices for GSM/UMTS traffic. As phones favor towers with strong signal strength, reducing security is simple for this device: just ensure that the lowest-security base station has the best signal, or impersonate a base station and switch to low-security mode. In some cases, the cell-site simulator itself can easily turn off encryption completely. A cell-site simulator can thus collect identifying information such as the International Mobile Subscriber Identity (IMSI), metadata about calls like the telephone number dialed, the date, time, and duration of the call, or even learn the content of the calls if none or weak encryption is used.

There exist several underlying security protocols in the UMTS/GSM standard. Figure 1 shows a simplification (omitting most details) of the standard handshake in UMTS. Every phone shares its own long term secret key[4] k with a dedicated home network. To further simplify the depiction, we let this key be known to the base station. Once connected to a base station, the phone sends its identity. The base station then uses the secret key to authenticate the phone.

Note that the protocol in Fig. 1 does not perform context authentication. Therefore, this protocol is unable to prevent MitM attacks as the one in [9].

---

[3] CVE-2009-3555.

[4] In the GSM standard, the tower may choose unilaterally to stop encryption, and the client has to follow. An attacker can therefore simply shut down encryption (e.g. by using a downgrading attack to fall back to the old standard, and then to stop encryption). Thus, this shared key alone cannot ensure secure communication.

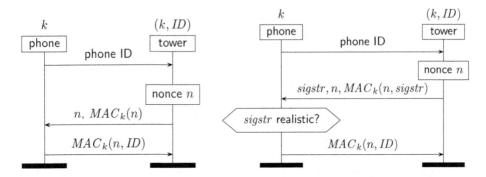

Fig. 1. Simplified UMTS protocol.   **Fig. 2.** Inclusion of context.

We propose to leverage this shared key in order to achieve context agreement as follows: The phone and the tower communicate securely on the tower's signal strength (*sigstr* in Fig. 2). Using the authenticated value of signal strength, the phone can determine whether the perceived signal strength is "realistic", and not far higher or lower than the rest of the communication warrants. This is depicted in Fig. 2. Obviously, this approach can be strengthened by including further details of the context. An obvious extension is inclusion of the tower's GPS coordinates, as this will allow the phone to determine a much narrower range of acceptable values of the signal strength.

The point of the sketched solution is to illustrate how context can be leveraged to detect a man-in-the-middle. A MitM attacker can either relay encrypted messages from the client, or drop them. If messages are dropped, after the tower has announced its capability to engage in this exchange (which will be nothing more than announcing supported protocols), then clearly there is a MitM attacker. If the messages do come encrypted, but the tower finds the client's perceived signal strength unrealistic, then likely there is a MitM attacker.

5   Conclusions

In this paper, we highlighted that more and more man-in-the-middle attacks are of a type that are not addressed by current security models. The overall principle is that security models do not take sufficient context into account. Context includes details such as the setup/initialisation phase, in which protocol parameters are decided, but also physical parameters, such as location.

We presented examples of either case where the lack of consideration of context led to attacks. To address this, we advocated research of contextual physical properties in a formal way. Finally, we sketched two solution directions for considering contextual properties. In future research, we will look deeper into context:

- Context can be both subjective and objective. The possession of a secret key can be regarded as an objective contextual information, either you have it or not. Location however can be both objective and subjective. A fixed communication tower has an objective view on its location, but a mobile phone does not. This distinction between subjective or objective contextual data requires further clarification and formalization.
- Context may change. Therefore, distinguishing between older context and current context can provide a way to satisfy security properties. For example, if a phone is communicating with a fixed base station, it is sufficient to verify whether the (observation of the) current context of the base station matches the previously determined context, as this context should not change.

References

1. Adrian, D., Bhargavan, K., Durumeric, Z., Gaudry, P., Green, M., Halderman, J.A., Heninger, N., Springall, D., Thomé, E., Valenta, L., VanderSloot, B., Wustrow, E., Béguelin, S.Z., Zimmermann, P.: Imperfect forward secrecy: how Diffie-Hellman fails in practice. In: Proceedings of 22nd Conference on Computer and Communications Security (CCS 2015), pp. 5–17. ACM (2015)
2. Aviram, N., Schinzel, S., Somorovsky, J., Heninger, N., Dankel, M., Steube, J., Valenta, L., Adrian, D., Halderman, J.A., Dukhovni, V., Ksper, E., Cohney, S., Engels, S., Paar, C., Shavitt, Y.: DROWN: Breaking TLS using SSLv2 (2016)
3. Avoine, G., Mauw, S., Trujillo-Rasua, R.: Comparing distance bounding protocols: a critical mission supported by decision theory. Comput. Commun. **67**, 92–102 (2015)
4. Beurdouche, B., Bhargavan, K., Delignat-Lavaud, A., Fournet, C., Kohlweiss, M., Pironti, A., Strub, P.-Y., Zinzindohoue, J.K.: A messy state of the union: taming the composite state machines of TLS. In: Proceedings of 36th Symposium on Security and Privacy (S&P 2015), pp. 535–552. IEEE Computer Society (2015)
5. Brands, S., Chaum, D.: Distance-bounding protocols. In: Helleseth, T. (ed.) EURO-CRYPT 1993. LNCS, vol. 765, pp. 344–359. Springer, Heidelberg (1994). doi:10.1007/3-540-48285-7_30
6. Dabrowski, A., Pianta, N., Klepp, T., Mulazzani, M., Weippl, E.R.: IMSI-catch me if you can: IMSI-catcher-catchers. In: Proceedings of 30th Annual Computer Security Applications Conference (ACSAC 2014), pp. 246–255. ACM (2014)
7. Dolev, D., Yao, A.C.: On the security of public key protocols. IEEE Trans. Inf. Theor. **29**(12), 198–208 (1983)
8. Lowe, G.: A hierarchy of authentication specifications. In: Proceedings of 10th Workshop on Computer Security Foundations (CSFW 1997), pp. 31–43. IEEE Computer Society (1997)
9. Meyer, U., Wetzel, S.: A man-in-the-middle attack on UMTS. In: Proceedings of 3rd Workshop on Wireless Security (WiSE 2004), New York, NY, USA, pp. 90–97. ACM (2004)
10. Möller, B., Duong, T., Kotowicz, K.: This POODLE bites: exploiting the SSL 3.0 fallback (2014)

Man-in-the-Middle Attacks Evolved...
but Our Security Models Didn't
(Transcript of Discussion)

Hugo Jonker[(✉)]

Open University of the Netherlands, Heerlen, The Netherlands
hugo.jonker@ou.nl

Hugo Jonker: Hi everyone. My name is Hugo Jonker. I'm from the Open University in the Netherlands.

Although we've known man-in-the-middle attacks for a very long time, we suck at them. We, security protocol people, think we understand man-in-the-middle attacks and then we find out there are all sorts of them.

You've probably seen Needham-Schroeder and you've seen Needham-Schroeder-Lowe. This is a typical man-in-the-middle attack. There's a man and he's in the middle. There are many examples of this in academic literature and we are aware of this attack. The original Diffie-Helmann key exchange is basically about establishing a cryptographic key such that a man-in-the-middle wouldn't know the key. In 1976, they were already basically thinking of man-in-the-middles. Lowe's attack on Needham-Schroeder's protocol is from 1995. That's really a long time ago.

There's quite a few things happening in practice as well. Just one example I put on the slide, Moxy Marlinspike. He's a guy making practical attacks. He has presentations often on BlackHat. He made a tool SSLsniff in 2002. This tool attacks Internet Explorer 5.5. We're currently past Internet Explorer 10. Internet Explorer is dead. This is how long we have known man-in-the-middle attacks. We know this. We understand that this is happening.

Let's see. Can we stop it? Well, we have distance bounding. The first theoretical approach to distance bounding is from 1993. Distance bounding means making sure that something is within a certain distance of something else. It's like when you have a smartcard to pass a door, for example, you don't want to be at the other end of the hallway. Nowadays, you have bank cards that you can pay contactlessly with. I'm still looking for a student to make sure that I can have my lunches paid for by my colleagues. This is exactly what distance bounding prevents.

Model checking. This is what Lowe did in 1995. I'm assuming everyone knows, but this is how Lowe found the attack on Needham-Schroeder. He model checked and then out pops an attack. We know how to find these attacks. Tagging, making sure that messages in protocols are used for exactly that one version of that one protocol and not somewhere else. Tool support, model checkers all over the place. There's a gazillion more.

In practice, we have certificate authorities, DNS certificate pinning. We've got this. Man-in-the-middle, ha, forget it. This ain't happening anymore, right?

© Springer International Publishing AG 2017
J. Anderson et al. (Eds.): Security Protocols XXIV, LNCS 10368, pp. 26–34, 2017.
DOI: 10.1007/978-3-319-62033-6_4

Meanwhile in reality, anyone here heard of the POODLE attack? Yeah. That's a man-in-the-middle. It forces a downgrade of the protocol. That's not good. The FREAK attack, maybe also known to a few people here. It forces TSL – which is like *the* security protocol of the internet, the one thing that keeps the internet secure for most normal people – It forces it to use weak crypto. The Logjam attack, that's actually the same thing, downgrading to Diffie-Helmann export instead of to RSA export.

The DROWN attack. This is 2016. Basically, this is a bit more intricate but it's again an attack on TLS, the one thing keeping the internet secure, banking secure, anything secure on the internet for average people. Again attacked by a man-in-the-middle. All these are from the last 18 months. Four major practical attacks in the last 18 months and I didn't even look hard into it, all of them relying on a man-in-the-middle.

What happened? Seriously, we know how to do this since 1995. How can we have in 2015, 2016, how can we look back on 18 months of four major attacks that actually break, 10–20% of the servers on the internet? Where did we go wrong? How do we stop going wrong?

You might say these are all academic, in a sense. The attacks are genuine and they do break TLS. You can argue this is researched by academics. There are very clever cryptographers figuring out how to actually exploit certain cryptographic weaknesses using hundreds or thousands of cipher texts and they put it all together. This is not something your average Joe does, right? You're right. An average Joe just buys a man-in-the-middle device for cellphones.

This just blows my mind. We think we understand how a man-in-the-middle attack works. We think we can automatically detect man-in-the-middle. If you're a law enforcement agency in the US, you can buy for 20,000 euros, something that performs an automated man-in-the-middle attack on cellphones. Not only do we not really have this, we've gotten to a point where there is a commercial industry selling man-in-the-middles. We've really dropped the ball – enormously. I think this is a problem that people are making money out of the things that we're trying to make sure can't happen. I think that's a problem. It's not all that bad, I hope. Feel free to interrupt me if you completely disagree. Yes?

Jonathan Anderson: In terms of the economics of the protocol, the people who are most in control of the protocol are the telcos. I think as long as routine man-in-the-middle is only done by authorized law enforcement agencies under national remits, those national telcos have absolutely no incentive to prevent man-in-the-middle. Their customers might like it or might not like it, but it's not like the customers have any say in it. They're not going to say, "Well, I'm going to switch to somebody who is not using UMTS." When this starts to happen routinely, like it's common knowledge that this is happening routinely outside of a law enforcement context, well in that case, the telcos might want to act. This slide, I don't think the telcos care that the law enforcement can man-in-the-middle them because if law enforcement did not man-in-the-middle them here, they would just go look at things on the back end anyway, so the telcos are quite cozy with that.

Reply: I can agree with that. But: the stuff that these things are man-in-the-middling wasn't thought up in 1995. That was later. When we had the tools. People started talking about "let's make protocols for 3G, for 4G" and then these things were invented from scratch. There were technical committees. We care about this – we should've been there. Somehow, we didn't make sure that man-in-the-middle cannot happen. I agree, now that we are in a situation where there are man-in-the-middle attacks, the business interest is going to say, "Do we care about this type of man-in-the-middle attacks? No." Unless we somehow make it a terrorist plot, businesses are going to say, "I don't care." Completely true.

We need to make sure we never get there again. We need to make sure that if a protocol is developed then it's not open for a man-in-the-middle attack. That's my view and that was my point with this slide. However, there are some things happening to mitigate part of this, fairly recently.

There's a recent paper at ACSAC14 about detecting these man-in-the-middle devices for cellphones. What they do here is they use specific non-security aspects, properties of the protocol. They're saying it's a cellphone. Cellphones have a nice feature where they say, here's a list of neighbor cellphone towers. They use all sorts of aspects like this. There is a neighbor list. You can request a neighbor list. You can request this sort of property. It has another function. Then they made a detection mechanism based on using these properties and seeing if they're consistent with what was expected.

This is one approach to do it. I like it. It gives a good answer. My problem with this is, if we were to do this then for every single protocol, we need to figure out, what are the extra properties. What in TLS are extra options you can support or not and how can we then establish a fingerprint of that and match that, every single time? There's a man-in-the-middle in between. He's in between. Why can't we figure that out? Why can't we make the protocol such that when there's a man-in-the-middle, he's in between, we see that he's in between so we're not talking to him, irrespective of the protocol used. Not relying on specific particulars of TLS or UMTS or whatever.

Another recent paper just appeared in February on the arXiv and that was looking into distance bounding for cellphone payments. The point here was they were looking into can you use a telephone sensor to actually verify at the moment of paying that the cellphone is very close to the payment terminal. Not that the cellphone is sitting there and the payment terminal is at the lunch register, paying for my lunch and not your lunch. In a nutshell the conclusion is: No. The error rates are horrendous for an individual sensor. For one individual sensor, this is nowhere near realistic.

This is a strong limit. The sensors such as gyroscope, light sensors, microphone, accelerometer, that sort of thing: if you use any of those to ask the question, "Am I close? Yes or no.", then it's not good enough.

There are some specific examples but what I want to propose here is that we would move more towards a generic solution. There's a man, he's in the middle. He's in a place where we don't want him. That affects the protocol, not the specific properties but that affects the communication. Can we detect how it affects the communication?

If we look at the problems I've sketched, we've seen these attacks on TLS and they were sort of all targeted at the initialization. These cellphone man-in-the-middle devices, they attack a completely different thing. They attack new properties. They attack things that we didn't think of that we wanted to keep secret but now that they're suddenly being exposed, we're looking at the protocol and saying, "we should have taken care of that". Something like call duration, contacts, location. That sort of thing.

In both cases, this underlying protocol is not claiming that they will prevent this sort of attack. The security claims of the protocol do not cover these attacked properties. In a sense these are not attacks. They do not violate security requirements. We need to start accounting for these security requirements. I think this is where we went wrong. That there are security requirements that we did not make explicit and we did not incorporate into our protocols and therefore we were not checking for them. We can check for them.

We see two types of contexts. We have a protocol context, like initialization but also protocol metadata: signal strength, for example. We also see a different context, the context of the user. For example, location. This is something I would not like the protocol to leak, but it might. What we figured is we want to embed this type of context into formal security proofs. Based on the notion of agreement, data agreement, we have an initial formalization of something we call context agreement where two parties agree on the context. You can also do this without a trusted partner, which is a stronger requirement, harder to achieve and then you are sure about context. This is more like verification.

What is context agreement? Basically, it means, that you and your partner have the same observation about the context. This still allows a man-in-the-middle. It allows a man-in-the-middle who is strong enough to make sure that A's observation about B's context, is the same as B's observation about B's context. If someone is strong enough to fake both of that at the same time, then you can have context agreement, both parties agreed that the context looks like something, when in reality it doesn't.

Frank Stajano: I think that previously you had grievances about the fact that, "Ah we were stupid because we didn't consider all these things when we defined protocols." Now in here, when we look at the observed context, we will define what we are observing and so there will always be a case where the crook will do something which has not been in the definition of what we observed.

Reply: Yes, true. This is the point where I'm saying, we need to account for these things. Protocol context and user context. You're right that there is a risk that we might be overlooking specifically new properties, but right now I see a whole new class of new properties, namely those relevant to a user.

Frank Stajano: What I was saying, the complaints that, "Ah, we were stupid because we didn't think about that." is too general, for anything to be done now. Whatever you put in the context, there will be things that haven't been thought of. So they could be smarter, they could exploit those next time.

Reply: Yes. I will agree with you on this. However, I will not agree that we will get to a situation like this, where we have people, commercial institutions selling their services for man-in-the-middling. I agree that this is an arms race. You have people trying to man-in-the-middle and you have us, stalwart champions of mankind and we're trying to defend people. Here we are really losing very much and I'm not sure that we are aware.

Ross Anderson: Many of these protocols were designed 20 or 30 years ago and in fact, in 1994, I believe at the workshop and also in my thesis of the same year, I argued that robust security was about explicitness. That is about putting all the even possibly relevant context on the face of the protocol so that it would be authenticated by both parties and bound to current freshness in some way or another. My observation was that doing this eliminated essentially all the attacks that we knew about at the time. I still think that that's a reasonable principle and its violation by GSM, TLS et cetera and it just keeps on being violated.

Reply: Yup. Essentially I can but agree and just note that apparently your warning in '94 wasn't caught well enough so I'm here repeating you.

Jonathan Anderson: If you think about the evolution of TLS. For instance if we said, the next version of TLS, we will require that you authenticate the list of protocols that you negotiated. You sent this, I sent this. Then we said let's change to this version of the protocol then we downgraded to this. Then we downgraded to that. Then we have to authenticate that record. That of course, will only exist in the next version of the protocol. By definition if you have a protocol downgrade attack, then you won't see that. Do you see this as something that, when we have to deal with the evolution of existing protocols that... Are you proposing another layer that can maybe be placed on top of this? Or are you talking about when we get an opportunity to start from scratch now on?

Reply: No. Actually, neither. You're right that if there is a protocol downgrade attack, then you get into insecure territory. We upgraded them for a reason. If we make a new protocol, we should make sure that a new protocol does not allow a protocol downgrade attack. It allows protocol downgrade and not the attack.

Bill Roscoe: In a sense, how do you do this? If I downgrade to get to an insecure level, then the protocol is very likely to be able to manipulate the data to be able to justify the downgrade to our side. In other words, two people are going to see different data from the other one. But they will not be able to agree on the downgrade activity because the protocol was attacked, so they basically will get...

Reply: I don't have a particular solution but I see a direction for a solution: in the protocol context we should also consider all previous versions of the protocol. This is something we have to account for and we should also account for whether or not someone is trying to cheat us.

Bill Roscoe: It seems to me that, if the protocol gets downgraded to the extent that we could reasonable expect insecurities (such as those of the examples that you gave us earlier on in your talk), then that basically shouldn't be allowed; the user should be warned.

Reply: Yes indeed, I agree. That's also a partial reply to Jon's question. There should be a point where we just say okay, this we toss out. I think browsers should be doing things like that and it is actually happening. I recently was surfing the Web and suddenly my browser said, you're not going to that website. It's insecure. You're not allowed to use https to go to that website. We're getting to that point, I think.

Context verification. The idea is that your observation of the other person's context, for example the cellphone tower, you as a cellphone user have an observation signal strength and all sorts of other variables about this cellphone tower that you're talking to. Your observation is correct. How do you define correct? That's tricky. On the other hand, I think we can do better than we are doing now, without having to rely on the fact that it is cellphones that we're talking about. So for wireless communication we have signal strength.

We have an example, just to wrap up. How does cellphone communication work? The phone and the tower share a secret key. Technically the tower doesn't but it asks the backend. What happens if you want to talk? You send your ID to the tower. The tower generates a nonce. It sends the nonce and a message authentication code using the key of that. Hash using the key of the nonce and you reply back with a message authentication code using the key of the nonce and your identity. This is the basic thing we have now. This is a gross oversimplification of the basic thing we have now and this is where man-in-the-middle attacks can happen.

Ross Anderson: You're suggesting that, just as Google will now give you a Gmail warning if it thinks that the local government is trying to man-in-the-middle your email, that someone should sell you a cellular phone which will similarly give you a warning if it thinks that the local police force is trying to stingray you.

Reply: Yup.

Ross Anderson: Well, that's an interesting idea. I wonder how many governments there are that will actually permit the unlicensed sale of such equipment to civilians.

Reply: My point is actually, it doesn't have to be equipment. This other paper that I pointed out that already does this, this one. These people made an app. You can download it. You can install it and it gives you colors. Green, yellow, red. Green is we have information and the information is okay. Yellow is we have information, it's a bit weird. We're not sure. Red is definitely wrong and then it has gray for saying we're lacking information. We've never seen this tower before in my life. We don't know anything about it.

This is just an app. You can download it. By now, it's two years since, it's kind of hard for governments to stop this since the internet doesn't forget.

This is the oversimplification. What we are proposing, to give you one example, is to use signal strength. The idea would be that the tower tells you the signal strength it is broadcasting at and you determine if the signal strength that is claimed is realistic compared to what you're receiving. You have an observation of the signal strength. This is context agreement. You are receiving a certain signal and you can determine the signal strength there and you have a claim by the cellphone tower of the signal strength it is emitting at. Your cellphone then has to determine: is this claim realistic given the signal strength I am receiving, given my observation of the signal strength? Therefore, you can add in a check at this point. If yes you can go on; and if no, you're worried about a man-in-the-middle. That's one example of how we can actually start using this sort of ideas.

Conclusions, man-in-the-middle attacks not only exist, they've actually become commercially viable. They are preventable, I think. You pointed out the extent to which needs to be understood. As Ross said, if we just put everything that we care about in a protocol line it is genuinely everything that we care about, and we make sure the protocol secures that, then that won't leak.

Prevention, we should account for context. Context of the protocol, context of the user and this can be done with or without trusted partner.

Brian Kidney: Question about your example with signal strength. I wonder how easy it is to actually determine whether or not the context is reasonable because signal strength depends on distance which would be the easiest... approximately how far it is from the tower so based on normal losses it should be this, but then you have buildings and different building materials and different antennas and different phones. I could be here sitting next to Jon and we could have totally different signal strengths and has to do with sort of the properties of the phone plus everything that's in between us and the tower.

Reply: Well, so the properties of the phone, this is something your phone should be aware of. This is something local that can be determined. The variations between two phones for neighbors, based on the physical properties of the phone, this is something that you should be able to bake into the phone.

Brian Kidney: Yeah. There are other things that could come in place like different phone cases. The original antenna problem with the iPhone with the hand in the wrong way so that the signal strength drops.

Reply: You do have a valid point. My example was not meant to suggest that just based on signal strength we will have a unique way of determining, this is exactly that one tower, there's no man-in-the-middle. Our idea here is more similar to distance bounding and distance bounding they use the speed of light, which we know is a hard upper limit, and then they say: "Okay, the speed of light would have given us this much distance, so this means this item is within 300 m or 10 Km of the other item." Same thing here. If we correlate what we observe plus what is claimed, then we could say, "Hey. Are you standing next to the tower? Because I'm observing ten watts and the tower claims it's emitting at ten watts so you must sort of be standing next to the tower." Then you look around, and can decide "No".

It's not perfect but it is a piece of information that will limit an attackers ability somewhat. Using more of these, my hope is that we can actually limit it so that it becomes actually functional.

Frank Stajano: There's a classic problem here: the technology is giving a somewhat ambiguous warning to the user and the user, who has something that they want to do, has to decide how to respond to the warning. What is the user supposed to do, when they get the yellow warning? Well, maybe the tower is a bit suspicious... Ignore that. I have to get on WiFi because I need to get my email. What's the response that the user should have? Should they just abort and not get their WiFi which is what they really care about? They don't care about this "Maybe man-in-the-middle. Maybe." Even the technology is not sure if there's a man-in-the-middle.

Ross Anderson: What maybe your laptop should do is turn your screen saver into Jaws. Just be careful about what you type. The NSA might be listening.

Reply: I think it's a good question.

Frank Stajano: If it gives a warning that doesn't really have a definite yes or no, then it's just dumping all the responsibility on the users. It may be or may not be a man-in-the-middle but now it's your fault if you get man-in-the-middle'd. It's not the protocol's fault anymore, it's your fault for deciding to go ahead.

Reply: I think our first step should be to actually know that there's a man-in-the-middle.

Frank Stajano: You don't know. You're just giving a yellow warning. You're not giving a red warning.

Reply: Right now, we're not giving a warning at all. Right now we have no idea. If we're giving a red warning, which is what the other paper is doing.

Frank Stajano: If you're confident about red warning, you should just shut it off. You should not let them proceed if you want to warn of man-in-the-middle. If you're just giving the ambiguity then the person says, "Well, if they can't figure it out, how can I figure it out?"

Ross Anderson: But Frank, ambiguity may be good. In the real world that we live in, there are many analog cues. People's body language, are they relaxed or aggressive, their tone of voice. What sort of neighborhood is it? Is anybody painting the window frames, fixing the windows around here? Or should I maybe go with three big friends and some guns in our pocket? We are used as a species to dealing with many analog signals but in the digital world we have completely cut them out. Another digital device has become evermore complex and evermore difficult to secure. Your mobile phone with, what, 50 different CPU's in it? Who knows where all of the code comes from? Perhaps, we need a studied shift towards more constructed ambiguity, so that we know when we should be slightly skeptical.

Frank Stajano: I object. I object to technology giving an ambiguous warning to the user. I'm dumping on the user the responsibility for taking a crap decision. If even the technology can't tell whether there's an attack or not, how can the grandmother?

Bruce Christianson: I think Ross' point is, is that in the real world, we rely on the environment to give us the cues and then our judgement to make a decision. We don't want this box to make the decision for us. We want to say, "Well, am I comfortable doing this particular transaction in this context or not? Or do I need more nuanced information about the context, rather than binary yes or no".

Ross Anderson: The problem with most digital devices is that they're built and operated by companies whose incentives are not ours. Facebook's incentive is to give you the impression that you're in a private walled garden with friends so that you'll give over as much private information as you possibly can, so that they can throw it to the spammers. That's the problem. There shouldn't be a shiny, private walled garden: it should have deep shadows around the edges that makes me very, very aware of all the lurking, menacing things out there. Of course Facebook doesn't want that to happen because then there would be less information for them to sell to the spammers.

Reply: I completely agree with Ross and to take Ross' example: would I count my money in the street? That's my decision. If I do that somewhere, you know, in broad daylight, where I can clearly see that I'm in a secluded corner but in open view, there's no one threatening around, I might feel comfortable doing that. If I'm in a rundown, graffiti stricken, needle stricken part of town around midnight and I see all sorts of people cloaking their faces walking by and making shady deals in the corner, I might feel differently about it, but I might still do it. It's up to me, it's not up to my wallet.

The Price of Belief: Insuring Credible Trust?

Paul Wernick and Bruce Christianson[✉]

University of Hertfordshire, College Lane, Hatfield, Herts AL10 9AB, England
{p.d.wernick,b.christianson}@herts.ac.uk

Abstract. Today, the majority of distributed system users are not systems programmers, nor do they aspire to be. The problem with existing access control mechanisms is not that they don't work, it is that users despise them and will not interact with them in the way the security model requires. We argue that this is not primarily a user-education issue; instead the user interface needs to be re-factored in a way that will involve a radical change to the way security is modelled.

Twenty years ago, Chuang and Wernick [3] proposed a mechanism for distributed systems security which attempted to put aside the formulaic binary yes/no outcome of traditional authentication mechanisms in favour of a system of sufficient authentication for a particular purpose built up from a number of supporting credentials, much as lenders take out appropriate references before lending money. In this position paper we revisit this idea in a more general form, seeking to move from modelling 'trust' as a binary absolute rarely if ever found in the real world, to a more realistic, nuanced approach, based on balancing the risk taken by accepting particular credentials against some cost if the risk is not accepted.

There are at least two reasons for moving from an absolute to a risk-based approach. The first is that this better reflects the real-world idea of an information source or service taking a risk when deciding to allow a client user or process to access or use the resource; and the client bearing the cost (such as loss of business, including repeat business) if access is denied. Increasingly the decisions whether to grant access are not actually taken by the party bearing the risk of granting access, nor do the decisions directly involve the party that will bear the cost if access is denied. More and more access control is being mediated by what are effectively third-parties, ostensibly in order to provide increased 'efficiency', reduced 'cost', and better 'security'[1]. It is therefore desirable to have a model for access control that incorporates such outsourcing of security, and which in particular may allow the access outcome to depend upon the explicit arbitrage of risk and cost. For example, this could be reflected by charging some (not necessarily financial) cost to the requester as a condition of access[2].

---

[1] Thus meeting Roger Needham's definition of optimization as replacing something good that works by something better that almost works.

[2] This idea is not new, see [7]. However, it is worth pointing out that the variance of an anticipated loss is at least as important to model as its expectation – people buy both insurance and lottery tickets. See Clarke et al. [4].

© Springer International Publishing AG 2017
J. Anderson et al. (Eds.): Security Protocols XXIV, LNCS 10368, pp. 35–38, 2017.
DOI: 10.1007/978-3-319-62033-6_5

An often unstated assumption underlying many modern computer security mechanisms is that the "safe" thing to do is to refuse access unless absolutely sure that the other party is authenticated and authorised; this may not be the correct attitude. When, for example, the medical history of a patient is needed to plan urgent treatment, a life-endangering failure to provide information to medical staff might be a potentially greater problem than unauthorised (but at least partially controlled) leakage of this information [5].

A further motivation for our approach is that a risk-based information security mechanism opens the possibility of making systems easier for users to configure and interact with securely, as advocated by Bella and Viglan [2], because such an approach better reflects the way in which non-security specialists make decisions about insecure situations.

In the real world, retailers rationally decide to accept a certain level of loss due to shoplifting rather than searching each customer as they leave for articles not paid for; and to attach security tags only to items which are of comparatively high value or easy to conceal, in order to save cashiers from having to remove them from other items and waste both their – and their customers' – time. Similarly, contactless credit/debit card providers deliberately permit offline authentication for low-value transactions in order to facilitate faster operation, in exchange for the cost of accepting some low value transactions from stolen cards even after the issuer has been informed of the theft[3].

In a similar way, a risk-based security mechanism might be based on reformulating access control decisions as insurance problems[4]. A server considering an access request could be presented with the option to insure itself against a particular risk, in exchange for a premium. The server could choose to pass the 'cost' of this premium on to the client, perhaps resulting in a pop-up box that displays to the user a range of authentication mechanisms available to the client, from most to least onerous, and lists the 'premium' associated with each.

Our argument is that a pop-up box which offers to insure a user against a particular loss associated with a proposed online access in exchange for a specified and explicitly stated premium would be easier for a member of the public to interpret than the currently typical requests for confirmation, which are often couched in purely (and user-unfriendly) technical terms, and which leave the naïve user unable to assess the degree of residual risk to which they are exposing themselves [1,2].

The premium demanded need not be in the form of money: it may correspond to a loss of reputation (like a credit score) incurred in the event of a 'claim'[5].

---

[3] It seems, however, that in this case card issuers may be attempting to pass some of the cost of this risk on to the cardholder, as the latter is charged for these transactions until and unless they identify them on their statements and inform the issuer [6].

[4] Suitable mechanisms for this are provided, although not described in these terms, by Chuang and Wernick [3].

[5] A claim corresponds to a case where the access is subsequently determined to have been unauthorized.

A limitation of the original Chuang and Wernick [3] approach is that the mechanisms proposed to combine credibilities are still constrained by the need for a binary result – the final access decision can only be either "allow" or "deny". The risk-based approach we propose here can be extended to provide additional flexibility by adding conditions ('endorsements') to this binary aspect of current security mechanisms. A more flexible mechanism would be a ternary allow/allow-only-with-limitations/must-deny decision, based on what is learned during the authentication or authorisation process. This enables security policies to be combined in a more flexible manner than is currently possible[6]. In particular, it can allow a partial authentication to be accepted and acted upon, perhaps on the basis that it represents a higher level of risk commanding a larger premium, or by permitting only a restricted form of access or functionality such as a time-limited downloadable version of a text instead of a permanent copy.

A naïve risk-based security mechanism has some weaknesses. An attacker could game the system by making a series of low-risk (and therefore less likely to be detected) requests until they could estimate the level at which higher-level controls would be applied. They could then exploit this knowledge in order to gain regular unauthorised access with a low risk of being caught. This gaming could be countered by providing non-deterministically some chance of applying a higher level audit control on access attempts even at the lowest levels of risk.

Such a control can readily be applied post-access [5] in cases, such as the medical scenario mentioned above, where authorisation is in doubt, rather than authentication. The probability of being audited can be made to depend on specific circumstances such as the history of past access attempts from this user.

In the case where authentication is in doubt, access could be granted subject to an up-front payment, refunded subsequently if and when strong authentication is provided. As before, the payment need not be made in money. The point is that it should be set so as to make repeated fraudulent access attempts unworthwhile, by ensuring that the cost of multiple failures will outweigh the prospective benefits of eventual success.

To summarise, we propose a probabilistically-based security mechanism, with the final decision being based on non-deterministic algorithms which have the option to charge a monetary or other 'premium' each time an access request is made, with a probability depending on the level of access requested and the history of this actor. The access decision may be extended to allow the request, deny it, or to provide limited access subject to further restrictions or via a sandbox.

In addition to providing greater flexibility in security mechanisms, and making them easier and more intuitive for the naïve user to interface with, this risk-based approach can also raise the cost of a denial of service attack, and help to ensure that the owner of a machine incorporated in a botnet becomes rapidly aware that their system has been compromised.

---

[6] If two non-identical binary access control policies are jointly enforced then, for some query, conflicting outcomes ('allow' and 'deny') must be combined. Usually this combination is interpreted as 'deny' which, as indicated above, can be problematic.

The Price of Belief: Insuring Credible Trust?
(Transcript of Discussion)

Bruce Christianson[✉]

University of Hertfordshire, Hatfield, UK
b.christianson@herts.ac.uk

I'm going to endorse several of the things other people have already said. The basic thesis of this talk is that we are getting better and better at solving the access control problems we had in the 1970s, and it's probably time to stop doing that and start thinking about the problems we've actually got now.

We're currently in the position of these politicians saying, "Okay, perhaps we need to tweak our policies, but the real problem is that the electorate just aren't getting our message." The electorate are saying, "Actually the message is coming across loud and clear, and we don't like it. We want you to come up with some different policies that we might actually vote for."

We're trying to sell a vision of security to users that they simply won't have any part of. It's not that we need to work out a slightly better interface for presenting our current mechanisms to users. They are just not going to act the way our models require, and we need to adjust our world-view to take account of that.

One of the differences between our world-view and theirs, for example, is that we still see security as absolute. A system is secure or it's not. Somebody is authenticated or they aren't. They are either authorized to do something or they're not. In the real world, it isn't like that. People don't have binary beliefs. They have views, and they are happy to make decisions based on their views, but those views are then going to change depending on the outcomes of their decisions.

If Dr. X wants to do something on Ward 12 then okay, some things are clear-cut. No, she definitely *can't* authorize a payment of a million pounds; yes, she definitely *can* look at this particular patient record. But there's a lot of stuff that's in a grey area in the middle: sometimes it's not so much that she is not *authorized* to do something, it's more that I'm not *expecting* her to *want* to do that. *Why* does she want to do that?

In some cases I'm quite happy for her to do it, but I really want a much higher level of authentication than I would do for other things. However it's probably not helpful to to interrupt her, right at the moment that she's engaged in a crucially sensitive procedure, and say, "To proceed, you must now enter the authentication code showing on the device that you've left in your handbag which is in your office on the next floor." It's probably much better if the system pages a staff nurse and says, "Can you verify to me that Dr. X is in the ward right now, and also can you tell me what she appears to be doing, please?"

In the real world we're inclined to decide whether or not something's okay based on previous dealings that we've had. We're probably all right about saying,

© Springer International Publishing AG 2017
J. Anderson et al. (Eds.): Security Protocols XXIV, LNCS 10368, pp. 39–46, 2017.
DOI: 10.1007/978-3-319-62033-6_6

"Okay. So you forgot your identity card, can you get someone that we *can* authenticate to verify who you are to us please?" Yes, they might be lying, but we're primarily trying to reduce the *risk* of making a bad decision. This interacts with the problem touched on a little bit earlier, which is that we're outsourcing security. More and more access control decisions are being made by a third party which doesn't have an investment in the client, or in the data owner.

This kind of outsourced access control mechanism naturally desires to have very binary decision trees that lead to a very clear-cut audit trail. This means they can show that the patient died, the plane crashed, and the money was embezzled; but it wasn't their fault, because they can prove that they complied with the policy that they were given. The difficulty is we're outsourcing security, but we're not delegating the risks and opportunities in a way that aligns the incentives. So the incentives are not aligned: the "good guys" don't all want the same outcome anymore, no matter what the security model says.

For example, denying access is no longer the "safe" option. It's not true to say, "Nobody ever got fired for denying access in a medical scenario," for instance. Interestingly, in the medical scenario, we do now see new protocols emerging, such as the break-the-glass access control protocol. There's no actual glass involved, by the way, it's purely a noughts-and-ones protocol, that allows non-binary outcomes to access control decisions. It's not just deny or allow, there is the option to say "This is a special case that we didn't see coming. We need to allow this for now, and shall sort out afterwards whether we should have allowed it or not." Access control mechanisms need to allow explicitly for these tradeoffs.

The model I'm going to use to do this is the insurance model. I'm not actually suggesting that we need to quantify risks in the same way that insurance adjusters do. Although, I suppose you could do that if you want. Alice could charge Bob a cost for doing something that is based on what Alice expects it to cost her to let Bob do it. But actually it's enough if Alice picks the amount she charges Bob to be such that it aligns his incentives with hers. The cost is designed to promote wholesome behaviour over unwholesome behaviour on Bob's part, rather than to make Alice a "profit".

The idea is to look at who is risking what. We've got a server that's going to decide whether to allow access or deny it. At the moment, if the server allows access when it shouldn't, the server's going to suffer. But, consider the person with the rights on the data object: if nobody accesses that object, they're going to go out of business. So default-deny isn't acceptable either.

It's a little bit like the situation with shoplifting. If you own a shop then you have to put up with a certain amount of shoplifting. It's easy to eliminate shoplifting completely, but then no one will shop in your shop. If they're getting their crotch sniffed by a large dog every time they go in to buy a can of tomatoes, they'll probably shop somewhere else.

So, it's a matter of presenting users and data owners with the incentives and the disadvantages, the contextual clues that we use in real life, and allowing them to make, possibly in an automated way, rational decisions based on that information.

The first thing is to get straight about what are the risks, and what are the opportunity costs? This isn't new, David Wheeler was advocating a version of this approach in the fourth of these workshops 20 years ago. However I think David tended to underplay the fact that variance was important as well as expectation: very often you do want to give people a way to trade one off against the other. People buy insurance, but people also buy lottery tickets. In each case, they are willing to accept a less favourable expectation in exchange for either a higher or a lower variance.

The proposal that we're making is to apply this approach to security decisions. Let's think about the risks and opportunity costs, and then let's pass them along. The data owner might say to the server, "I'm happy for you to grant this access provided you obtain this stipulated amount for it." You can think of this amount as being like an insurance premium. And the server might choose to pass that cost along to the client, if that's the model you want to use. It might be that the system says to you, "We're not sure whether you are Dr. X or not, but I'll tell you what, if you put 1000 pounds into the machine in the corner then we'll give you access. And maybe you are really a journalist, but at least we got 1000 pounds for the data."

If Dr. X subsequently logs in, authenticates herself, and validates the transaction, then we'll give her your 1000 pounds back. Or maybe we want two people that are authenticated to each put 100 pounds in and say that you are Dr. X. If Dr. X subsequently authenticates herself "properly" and affirms the earlier transaction then the two guarantors get their money back. Or maybe clients are going to pay in terms of reputation. Perhaps there's a kind of a credit score, or loyalty points. Frequent flyer miles. Something like that, that you can spend in order to obtain these accesses. And maybe how *many* points you require for an access depends on how contentious that particular access is.

We might say, "Well, if it turns out that the access was bad and you shouldn't have had it, we'll charge you a million points. Alternatively, you can pay 100 points up front now, and we'll indemnify you against this going wrong." Just like an insurance policy. Or else we might have a system that's more like a bail bond, where you buy the bail bond; we let you into the system; but if it turns out that we shouldn't have, then we send the equivalent of bounty hunters after you.

The user interface for our new approach would be very different to the sort of pop-up box you typically get at present: "There is a security problem. The certificate from <some server that you have never heard of> is self-signed. Would you like to 1. Proceed? (In which case whatever goes wrong, it's your fault.) 2. Abort? (In which case there is no way for you to get what you want done.) or 3. View the certificate?"

I love that third alternative; I think this is an absolute brainwave on the behalf of whoever thought it up. It's a totally brilliant idea to have a non-expert user confronted with an endless string of ASCII or if they are lucky X.509 or something. They can look at that for a while and then they have to click on one of the other two buttons anyway.

Instead of all that, our approach would have a pop-up box that said, "What you are trying to do is an unsafe sort of transaction, and here are a number of options. You can risk a million Tiger points; or you can pay a hundred Tiger points now and indemnify yourself against it. Or you can take the time and trouble to authenticate yourself and various other parties more carefully, in which case the price will come down to about 8 points, depending on how much effort you are willing to put in." Or you can have various other options, which are based on how carefully you've authenticated yourself, what kind of protocol you're connected over, how many of your transactions have gone bad in the past. The key point is that we do not expect you to have a fetish about getting perfect security. The point is rather that you're on a limited budget. Your supply of these loyalty tokens, or whatever it is, is limited.

Ross Anderson: This is perhaps very apposite given all the discussion about exceptional access. If you want exceptional access as a civilian, either with an Anton Piller Order or Norwich Pharmacal Order, you have to give money up front to lawyers. For an Anton Piller Order you typically put twenty or thirty thousand pounds surety, in case the person whose house you search comes back and sues you for damages. If the UK police are looking to get information from a US service provider like Google or Yahoo, they typically have to go through MLAT, which involves time and expense. All of these things are good. The fact that it used to cost them 200 pounds to get a mobile phone location trace was good, because it meant they didn't do it all the time.

The problem is that governments try to legislate for zero marginal cost access. How can you prevent this systems failure with this insurance structure?

Reply: In other words, how can we prevent governments from requiring us to insure them for nothing? I don't have a good answer to that, we're primarily concerned here with the commercial world. It's really hard to throttle governments against their will, but we can try to persuade them that it would be in their own interest to limit the rate at which they are able to do things. Chelsea Manning is an example of somebody doing something that they were authorized to do. Do you want to allow a sysadmin to move a file from once place or another? Yes, you do. Do you want them to be allowed to do it four million times in quick succession? Probably not. Associating a very small cost with each time they did it, that counts against an allowance, would allow you to detect and respond to that quite rapidly. The government is perhaps missing a trick here by not applying this type of throttle to its own security policies, internal as well as external.

The key point is to give the user an interface where they feel they're in control. They're presented with some data. They're making a decision. We've rigged the game so that their incentives are aligned with ours as security people, and we're giving them a budget and more importantly we're expecting them to spend it. Instead of saying, our objective is perfect security, we're saying, our objective is security that's good enough against some metric.

Jonathan Anderson: There are some other currencies, which you haven't talked about, which involve functionality and performance. We might say, so, your certificate appears valid and it's signed by a CA who's in our list of trusted CAs; however, that's a very long list and our certificate transparency doesn't really like it so, tell you what, we'll let you view the webpage. We're not going to ask you whether you *really* want to view the page that you already said you wanted to view, answer yes, or no. But we won't run JavaScript. Or we won't display password prompts. Or there's some degradation of functionality. Or we'll have increased sandboxing that makes the thing run much more slowly, but ... [next slide] What a very nice slide you have there [laughter].

Reply: And what a very insightful comment. Okay. The other basic problem with access control is that currently outcomes are binary. It's allow or deny. There's nothing in the middle. But, just as Jon points out, we could allow the access but put you in some sort of sandbox, where you can't do anything terribly irrevocable. It's fine to explore the catalogue, but we're not actually going to let you buy anything. Or you're going to be subject to audit controls, perhaps definitely or perhaps you're just going to have a higher chance of being subjected to an audit control.

A very small proportion of transactions are routinely selected for a random in-depth audit. There's always a problem with people gaming to see where the threshold is for triggering an automatic audit, and then putting through transactions that are just below that level. One of the other difficulties with current access control mechanisms is that we expect them to be deterministic: to give us the same answer if we ask the same question. A good counter-measure may be to have non-deterministic mechanisms, so that whether you are audited or not is actually random, but what you're doing affects the probability.

In summary: non-deterministic algorithms; a premium depending on what access you're requesting, what authentication you're offering, and what your past history is; and choosing from a range of alternative premiums, depending on what precautions you are willing to take. You can decide how much security you are willing to apply and the system can respond accordingly. The access decisions include other alternatives besides allow or deny.

As well as delivering more flexible services and interfaces that users might actually be willing to use, this approach also allows you to do security auditing by simply following the money. For example, if your computer has been taken over and is being used as part of a bot-net, you're going to notice very rapidly that there's a flow of security points out of your system with no corresponding flow of goodness in, and you're going to say, "Why is that? Why am I spending all this stuff and not getting anything for it?"

Simon Foley: Would this work for Acceptable Use Policies? Currently, we're using servers with Acceptable Use pop-ups that you have to agree with in order to get the service. If the conditions are reasonable, you might agree, but if it's totally clueless you might still agree, because ...

Reply: The alternative is not getting the service at all, under any conditions.

Simon Foley: In principle I can say, "Well this is restrictive, or co-optive to my data", but the difficulty is there's no fairness, because once they have my data I have to take them to court to prosecute, and I can't afford to do that as an individual. Do you think a mechanism like the one you are proposing could help?

Reply: It depends to some extent on what market pressures produce. In principle, it would allow things to evolve that say, "All right, would you instead be prepared to agree to this less onerous agreement in exchange for more limited access?" This is what a lot of academic licenses already do. A lot of data repositories have a licence where they say, if you log on at a university that's one of our clients, then you get access that is restricted, in exchange for not agreeing to some of our commercial conditions.

Simon Foley: Again, there's an asymmetry to it. I might end up agreeing to the policy because I don't understand it, or I have some malicious reaction to the policy and I know I can't be enforced. It comes down to the consequences. The cost to me to demonstrate the uniqueness of that policy is too high.

Reply: I'm going to try and wriggle out of this, by saying I think now you're presenting a softer version of Ross' objection. Ross is the extreme end where you've already signed up involuntarily to a policy that's completely outrageous, and even going to court won't help you. You're putting forward a softer version of this, and asking how far can an approach like mine get you? I think the answer is, if people are doing this for money - if people have a data asset they're trying to make money from - then it's a marketing question. Can I make enough money from suspicious people like you to make it worth my while offering a softened variant of the product?

The answer to this question is not obvious: the reason there isn't a really secure iPhone is there's no market for it, right?

Hugo Jonker: Two comments. One is that you seem to be assuming cloud forums where everyone chooses the system. Like the nice example that you had, where they self-sign certificates.

Reply: No, no, I'm not necessarily assuming that.

Hugo Jonker: The second question is: take the self-signed certificate. How would you determine a good pricing strategy? Imagine I want to attack you. I set up a website and I can find everyone here a deal, bringing down costs. Making me seem very reliable. As soon as you go there . . .

Reply: Suddenly I get a much worse deal.

Hugo Jonker: You get a worse deal, with seemingly little risk to me, so it's a spear attack.

Reply: Attacks like that generally work where somebody builds up their reputation because they want to do one big scam. Like borrowing lots of small amounts of money from a bank to build up your credit record so that they'll lend you a big amount of money, and then running away.

Hugo Jonker: This system you propose seems particularly vulnerable to that sort of attack.

Reply: Yes, it is. But if I'm in the position of the bank, which is the position you're putting me in, then that's a risk that I, the bank, am willing to bet on because, in the long run, it works out for me. Okay, I got scammed by you, but by engaging in that type of transaction I come out ahead across the piste in the long run. I expect to lose occasionally, and I'll probably insure myself against that.

Hugo Jonker: Yes, but there are actually two parties here. In the case of the self-signed certificates, the server giving the self-signed certificate and the user accepting it should both somehow be involved in saying, "I accept this risk". Both should somehow put credits into a pot.

Reply: What happens in practice, in the model I'm advocating, is that the server incurs the risk and then may decide to pass it along to the user; either at face value, or with a discount, or with a premium, depending on their risk model.

Hugo Jonker: Then how does the user forward *their* risk to the server?

Reply: Okay, that's fair enough. When I say user and server, this is unsatisfactory if we are really in a peer-to-peer setting. In that case we are talking about arbitrage, we're talking about using pop-up boxes, or whatever, to negotiate a contract.

Ross Anderson: Perhaps there's a simpler approach to this. If one imposed a rule that personal information could not be sold at a marginal price of zero, that might fix many things, because where companies monetize something they won't give it away. If you get access to stuff as a researcher that's also being sold to commercial companies, it comes with an NDA even if it isn't sensitive.

Reply: For revenue protection purposes.

Ross Anderson: Much of the privacy failure is because the marginal price of information tends towards zero for the usual information economics reasons, in the absence of something stopping it. The price of software can be kept above zero by copyright licensing mechanisms. Perhaps what is needed here is a privacy licensing mechanism.

Reply: That would impose a similar lower bound.

Ross Anderson: Which effectively imposes a government tax. Suppose this is the way forward: the Chancellor of the Exchequer simply says that every record containing personal information attracts a tax of one penny, and then all privacy violators are tax evaders and go straight to jail.

Reply: Actually, Caspar Bowden and I once had this very conversation as part of a discussion with the Information Commissioner about how to protect against information breaches. We reckoned that having a flat charge for personal information would be a very effective mechanism[1].

Jonathan Anderson: I think one of the problems with implementing this model is that the people tasked with enforcing the security policies in most organizations come from a part of the organization that is absolutely risk intolerant. They share in none of the benefits of enabling things, but they get egg all over their face whenever something goes wrong. I think the same is true in accounting departments or typical security in a lot of organizations, but there's kind of a fundamental organizational behavioral problem. How do you fix that? How do you get them to *want* to do this?

Reply: So, how do we get people like us to buy into a model that says, if you're never making mistakes, then you're not taking enough risks; and that means the business is losing money relative to our competition, and that's why I'm firing you. How do we entice security to move into that model? That's a really good question on which to end, I think.

---

[1] In the scheme Caspar and I came up with, the tax took the form of a per-datum spot fine for being in possession of personal information that was not tagged with a valid ACL and a conforming audit trail.

Defending Against Evolving DDoS Attacks: A Case Study Using Link Flooding Incidents

Min Suk Kang, Virgil D. Gligor$^{(\boxtimes)}$, and Vyas Sekar

Carnegie Mellon University, Pittsburgh, PA, USA
{minsukkang,gligor}@cmu.edu, vsekar@andrew.cmu.edu

Abstract. Distributed denial-of-service (DDoS) attacks are constantly evolving. Over the last few years, we have observed increasing evidence of attack evolution in multiple dimensions (e.g., attack goals, capabilities, and strategies) and wide-ranging timescales; e.g., from seconds to months. In this paper, we discuss the recent evolution of DDoS attacks and challenges of countering them. In particular, we focus on the evolution one of the most insidious DDoS attacks, namely link-flooding attacks, as a case study. To address the challenges posed by these attacks, we propose a two-tier defense that can be effectively implemented using emerging network technologies. The first tier is based on a deterrence mechanism whereas the second requires inter-ISP collaboration.

1 Introduction

Distributed denial-of-service (DDoS) has been and is a growing threat to critical services on the Internet. We have observed a dramatic escalation in the number and scale of DDoS attacks during the past few years. For instance, the maximum reported volume of a single attack has been doubled from 300 Gbps [32] to 600 Gbps [23] over the past couple of years. Aside from increasing attack volume, the evolution of DDoS attacks in other dimensions (e.g., number of hosts affected) have not been particularly noticeable during the past few years. In general, a DDoS attack targeted a single system resource (e.g., computation, memory, access bandwidth) for the duration of an attack, utilizing a static set of attack capabilities; e.g., traffic amplification capabilities. Although use of multiple capabilities can diversify an attack, their static use enables detection and blocking by current defense tools [3,5,31].

Recently, however, we have seen evidence of attack evolution in reported DDoS incidents. This ranges from changes of attack goals and capabilities to real-time flexible changes of attack strategy. For example, in 2013, an attack against Spamhaus [9] demonstrated that an adversary can adaptively change the attack targets from end-point servers to routers in Internet exchange points (IXPs) in response to the defense mechanism changes. In 2015, during an attack against ProtonMail [16], we noticed that the adversary also changed the attack strategies in *real-time* to react to defense strategy changes, which creates an interactive game between attackers and defenders [29].

© Springer International Publishing AG 2017
J. Anderson et al. (Eds.): Security Protocols XXIV, LNCS 10368, pp. 47–57, 2017.
DOI: 10.1007/978-3-319-62033-6_7

The goal of this paper is to illustrate the evolution of DDoS attacks and discuss the challenges and opportunities in handling them. In particular, we observe the trend of attack evolution in three dimensions (i.e., goals, capabilities, and strategies) and on both coarse and fine timescales. For instance, attack capabilities evolve on a coarser timescale since they are typically a consequence of changes in technology and Internet economics; e.g., the widespread availability of inexpensive botnets enables the provision of DDoS capabilities as a service [6,22]. In contrast, on a more fine-grained timescale, we observe the evolution of the attack strategies employed using a given set of capabilities and goals; i.e., changing how the available capabilities are employed for a chosen attack goal [9,16,21,29].

In this paper, we focus on a particularly insidious type of DDoS attack, namely link-flooding attacks. Through this case study, we identify three major advantages of adversaries over defenders, which make the mitigation of link-flooding attacks especially challenging. However, we also also see opportunities to defend against these attacks and propose a two-tier defense approach using emerging network technologies.

In Sect. 2, we illustrate the evolution of DDoS attacks in multiple dimensions and timescales, using recent attack incidents. In Sect. 3, we present a new approach for countering these attacks. Section 4 concludes the paper.

2   Evolving DDoS Attacks

DDoS attacks have evoloved on multiple dimensions and timescales, as evidenced by recent incidents. If one defines an attack by the triple ⟨*goal, capabilities, strategies*⟩ [15], one can observe evolution on all three dimensions in the case of these attacks. Moreover, one can also observe evolution on a wide-ranging timescale: a coarse timescale of months or years, and another with a fine timescale of seconds, minutes, or hours. In the rest of this section, we review some of the patterns that we have observed in the case of DDoS attacks.

2.1   New Capabilities

Recent changes in Internet technologies (e.g., the adoption of new protocols) and economics (e.g., pay-per-install botnet markets) have enabled new attack capabilities. In particular, we summarize three noticeable patterns of attack-capability evolution.

Low cost of botnets. Botnets have become an essential commodity of DDoS attacks and the maturity of botnet markets has led to their rapid cost reduction and availability. For example, renting 1,000 bots costs anywhere from a few U.S. dollars to a little more than 100 U.S. dollars [10]. Furthermore, as DDoS attacks begin to marshall emerging Internet-connected devices (e.g., sensors, refrigerators, and dryers) [17,38] and already inexpensive cloud resources, botnets are likely be even more affordable to a wide range of adversaries in the near future.

Attack-traffic amplification. The use of traffic amplifiers to dramatically increase traffic volume (e.g., amplification factors of tens to thousand times) has become popular during the past few years. The ability to amplify attacks is widely available due to the lack of security-aware management of public Internet services (i.e., DNS, NTP) and universally deployed countermeasures against IP spoofing (e.g., ingress filtering [13]); e.g., 20–30% of the Internet ASes cannot detect and block IP spoofing [8].

Flooding core network links. Another new attack capability is provided by the *routing bottlenecks*, which are links in the "middle" of the Internet (i.e., Tier-1/2 networks) that lie on a significant fraction of the traffic to targeted hosts. Flooding these links can severely disrupt connectivity of the host targets [19, 21, 33]. Unlike the direct server-flooding attacks, these attacks are indirect as the flow of traffic may not even be destined for the server targets and thus can be stealthy [9, 16, 21].

2.2   New Strategies

Acquiring new attack capabilities typically occurs on a relatively long timescale. In contrast, changing attack strategies can occur on very short timescales. For example, the adversary observes the defensive posture that the victims adopt and responds by changing how the available attack capabilities are exploited to achieve the same goal; e.g., changing the locus of the attack while maintaining the same set of target hosts in a matter of minutes.

There is already plenty of reported evidence of attack-strategy evolution within real attack campaigns during the past couple of years. In 2013, we witnessed the first large-scale Internet attack where an adversary changed the locus of attack and adapted on a short timescale. That is, after the Spamhaus service was moved to the cloud service (i.e., CloudFlare) in response to a massive DDoS attack, end-host flooding became infeasible. In response, the adversary changed his attack strategy by flooding a few links of four major Internet exchange points (IXPs) in Europe and Asia to degrade the connectivity of the cloud service and implicitly of Spamhaus [9].

An adversary's rapid strategy change was recently observed in a large-scale DDoS attack against ProtonMail, an email provider in Switzerland. Here is a quote from an Internet Service Provider who helped mitigate the attack [29]:

> "First we moved the BGP IP prefix," said Gargula as he detailed the attack, "I tried to isolate legit human traffic from bot traffic and not to mix it up. We sacrificed one of their three BGP uplink layers as a 'canary' to test the sophistication of the attack. Then we changed the configuration for the IP uplink." The new attackers were incredibly advanced, Gargula explained, and became more sophisticated through the week. "Every time we made a change in tactics, they responded with a change," he said. "It was like Chess: you move a piece, they move a piece. At this point, it became clear that we had a very serious situation on our hands."

2.3   New Goals

The evolution of DDoS adversary goals is particularly visible in the selection of attack targets. Three new types of critical-infrastructure targets appear to be particularly vulnerable; i.e., emergency, cellular, and power-grid services.

Emergency Services. Increasingly, we see DDoS attacks targeting emergency services [28] by automatically initiating bogus calls. In particular, we see a trend where the emergency networks are utilizing the public Internet since the standardization of the Next Generation 911 (NG911) by National Emergency Number Association (NENA) in the US in 2011 [27]. Unfortunately, by embracing IP technologies and the public Internet, the emergency networks in the US inherit new vulnerabilities. Specifically, the gateways that interconnect the public Internet and the traditional 911 emergency networks can be targets of traditional flooding attacks. This kind of threat is real and significant; e.g., a recent 911 outage in April 2014 showed that even a single device failure (due to a software bug in this case) can cause a 911-service outage affecting about 7 million people in seven US states for six hours [12]. Considering that a single device failure caused a severe outage in emergency services, a well-crafted targeted attack can possibly endanger the public safety of an entire country.

Cellular Services. DDoS attacks against the cellular datacenters can impair cellular service over a large area. According to a recent study on national cellular infrastructure, major cellular carriers in the US in general have only a handful of datacenters throughout the nation [34]. A successful attack against one cellular datacenter (e.g., covering the east coast of the US) could disable the majority of cellular connectivity (both voice and data) of tens of millions of people. Similarly, an adversary could launch large-scale connection degradation (e.g., link-flooding) attacks against cellular-network gateways to the Internet and VoIP servers causing major communication disruption.

Power Grids. Increasing deployment of Internet-of-Things devices, where traditional embedded systems can be programmed and controlled via Internet connections (e.g., Google NEST or Samsung's Smart Home Automation System), can pose significant DDoS challenges for the power grid [25]. Such embedded systems are based on powerful compute platforms with non-trivial processing and network capabilities. Their increased sophistication and features also cause greater threat of compromise. For example, the operation of power grids could be broken by simple on/off cycling HVAC systems over the Internet [11]. On a smaller scale, power surges triggered by attack-induced, server-rack power demand could trip circuit breakers disrupting data center operations [35]. In the simplest case, the attacker overloads the grid by increasing energy consumption. More subtle attacks can lead to cascaded failures or induce persistent load oscillations. In an even more insidious attack, the adversary could use a combination of the grid-overloading attack together with one where access to the pricing server is denied to magnify the impact by preventing legitimate users from being able to scale back their consumption.

3 Evolving Defenses: A Case Study of Handling Link-Flooding Attacks

Evolving DDoS attacks create significant *advantage* for DDoS adversaries over defenders, which makes it challenging to handle the attacks. To understand the challenges using concrete examples and to illustrate specific opportunities for emerging network technologies as evolving defenses, we focus on a case study of handling link-flooding attacks, one of the most powerful DDoS attacks. First, we identify the three basic challenges of handling link-flooding attacks in Sect. 3.2. Then we present a particular defense strategy based on emerging network technologies that can effectively handle link-flooding attacks in Sect. 3.3.

3.1 Link-Flooding Attacks

A new class of *link-flooding attacks* appeared recently, which have several characteristics that make them hard to handle: (1) they make attack flows *indistinguishable* from legitimate flows[1], and hence become undetectable; (2) they can attack targets *indirectly* in the sense that the locus of attack is different from the actual targets, and hence they cannot be easily detected by the actual targets since they do not receive attack flows; and (3) they are *adaptive* in the sense that they adopt evolving and changing attack postures while achieving the same DDoS goals with the same capabilities; e.g., botnet hosts attack targets as soon as targets recover or deploy a specific mitigation mechanism.

To launch these attacks, an adversary carefully maps the network connectivity infrastructure of the target(s). Having constructed this network map, the adversary identifies routing bottleneck links in the Internet core (e.g., Tier-1/2 networks) that lie on a significant fraction of the traffic to targeted hosts [19,21].

The two real-world attacks mentioned in the previous sections (e.g., attacks against Spamhaus and ProtonMail) utilized different types of link-flooding attacks in different degrees. Moreover, several academic studies have shown the feasibility of link-flooding attacks [21,33].

3.2 Basic Challenges

An effective defense against the link-flooding attacks must address three fundamental challenges, namely *inability to distinguish* attack flows from legitimate ones, the *adversary's asymmetric advantage* over the defender in the Internet, and the *defender's dilemma*.

---

[1] A flow is defined by 5-tuple, which is a stream of packets having the same source and destination IP addresses, same source and destination port numbers, and same protocol number.

1. **Inability to Distinguish Flows.** The first challenge a defender faces is that an adversary can craft link-flooding flows that are *indistinguishable* from legitimate flows in the targeted routers. The main reason for this is that the immediate targets of the attacks are the router, *not* the end-point hosts. That is, routers are supposed to forward *all* Internet traffic while end-point servers usually are intended to receive *only* certain types of traffic; e.g., web servers expect to see mostly web traffic. Therefore, it is much harder for routers to define and filter out protocol *non-conforming* traffic than end-point servers. For example, the Crossfire attack generates low-rate, protocol-conforming flows and their flows can remain indistinguishable from legitimate traffic in routers [21].

   When attacks use flows that are indistinguishable from legitimate ones, handling link flooding at a target router reduces to a *resource-sharing problem*, where multiple indistinguishable resource requesters (i.e., both legitimate and malicious) contend for the same resource; i.e., the network link bandwidth. In this case, the operation of any requester becomes dependent upon the operation of other—often malicious and unknown—requesters of that resource. The existence of this type of *undesirable dependency* among requesters is the necessary condition for all denial of service in resource-sharing problems [14], and can be countered only by enforcing *agreements* among requesters (i.e., constraints placed on requester behavior) *outside* the shared-resource service [36].

2. **Adversary's Cost Advantage.** Whenever a countermeasure to link flooding reduces to finding a solution to a resource-sharing problem, the cost of the resource for both adversaries and defenders (i.e., the cost of targeted routers bandwidth) becomes a key factor in determining the effectiveness of both attacks and defenses. For example, if the cost of generating attack traffic (i.e., the cost of the shared resource requests) is extremely high, or if the cost of available bandwidth (i.e., resource provisioning) at the target network (i.e., resource manager) is negligible, attacks would become very unattractive.

   Unfortunately, in the current Internet, the opposite cost relation prevails, which makes link-flooding attacks very attractive. That is, the cost of bandwidth for generating attack traffic is *orders of magnitude* lower than that of provisioning backbone-link bandwidth.[2] In other words, a severe *cost asymmetry* exists that favors the adversary over the defender. Furthermore, removing this cost asymmetry is not only a matter of changing the Internet design. Instead, whether the asymmetry can be removed depends on two independent markets: the botnet markets and backbone bandwidth markets. The former is an underground online e-commerce market [10], where bot buyers can demand and sellers supply attack bots, whereas the latter is a legitimate

---

[2] For example, the adversary's cost of flooding a 10 Gbps with bots whose uplink bandwidth is only 1 Mbps averaged about $920 with a minimum of about $80 in the US in 2011 [10]. In contrast, the cost of 10 Gbps bandwidth in Internet transit was about $6,300 in 2015 [1]. This represents a cost advantage of 7–80 times of the adversary over the defender.

network-infrastructure market, where many entities compete by well-established rules that determine the market price of backbone bandwidth.[3]

We note that removing the cost asymmetry, and even reversing it to favor the defender, does *not* completely deter link-flooding attacks; e.g., cost-insensitive adversaries, such as those sponsored by a state, could still launch link-flooding attacks. However, it would change today's severely imbalanced cost structure and would certainly deter cost-sensitive (e.g., rational) adversaries. Hence, it would yield an effective first line of defense as argued in the later this section.

3. **Defender's Dilemma.** Many link-flooding attacks rely on the existence of *a few* link targets whose congestion would disrupt the majority of routes that pass the Internet core from a set of sources to a set of destination hosts. These links are called the *routing bottleneck* of a set of sources and destinations and shown that its existence is an *undesirable artifact* of Internet design [19]. Although in the attack-free mode of operation these bottlenecks are not an operational hazard, we seek to remove them since they can constitute an Internet vulnerability in the presence of a link-flooding adversary.

However, as shown in a recent measurement study [19], removing routing bottlenecks to prevent link flooding is impractical in the current Internet because they are the result of employing a *cost-minimizing* (or revenue-maximizing) policy of the Internet routing and topology designs. In other words, the source of many link-flooding vulnerabilities is, in fact, a very *desirable* feature of the Internet business model. Hence, a defender faces the following dilemma: *how can one remove a vulnerability of a system when it is caused by a very desirable feature of the system's design and operation?*

As long as the causality between a route-cost minimization policy and the existence of flooding targets holds, any attempt to remove the latter would necessarily affect the former. However, in the highly competitive Internet transit markets ISPs would naturally be very reluctant to adopt any countermeasure that would increase the operating cost.

3.3 Evolving Defense: Two-Tier Approach

We argue that new defense mechanisms become necessary to counter the basic challenges of handling link-flooding attacks. To that end, we present a *two-tier* defense approach. In the two-tier approach, a *first-line* defense uses low-cost, light-weight, and readily-deployable mechanisms to handle frequently-used attacks while a *second-line* defense is invoked to perform high-cost defense mechanisms only for infrequent attacks that have not been handled by the first-line defense. Considering the defender's dilemma, the use of first-line defenses is very desirable *even if they do not counter all possible attacks* because they render the use of complex high-cost mechanisms for handling uncommon adversaries necessary only infrequently.

---

[3] The market involves many layers of businesses, including equipment companies, optical cable companies, undersea cable companies, Internet exchange points (IXPs), etc.

First-Line Defense: Deterrence. In our first-line defense, we focus on the *attack deterrence*, particularly targeting *rational* adversaries *only*; i.e., *cost-sensitive* adversaries who wish to remain *undetected*. All other (e.g., irrational, cost-unbounded) adversaries would not be deterred by the first-line defense and need to be countered by a second line of defense.

We believe that the majority of link-flooding attackers are rational in the current DDoS attack landscape. According to a behavioral economics study [30], there is strong evidence that cyber criminals are economically motivated. Also, rational adversary behaviors in DDoS attacks are observed in a recent study that analyzed real DDoS attack incidents in 240 countries over 5 years [18]. Note that if the cost of bots drastically decreases to become almost negligible in the future, most adversaries could become cost-insensitive, making the invocation of a second-line of defense mechanism necessary. However, even when fewer cost-sensitive adversaries are deterred, a first-line defense mechanism would be useful since it has low-cost deployment and operation cost.

Cost-detectability tradeoff. To deter economically motivated (or cost-sensitive) adversaries, we focus on the aforementioned adversary's cost-asymmetry advantage with respect to defenders. Our approach is to reduce (or even reverse) the cost asymmetry to deter cost-sensitive adversaries. We create an *untenable tradeoff* between the cost and detectability. By definition, any countermeasure that can either substantially increase the attack cost relative to the defense cost or induce detectability will deter attacks by rational adversaries.

In recent work we showed that it is possible to force a link-flooding adversary into an untenable tradeoff by using only intra-domain network operations. The proposed system, which we called SPIFFY [20], implements a mechanism to *logically* increase the bandwidth of a targeted link by a large factor (e.g., 10 times) temporarily utilizing flexible intra-domain route control capability implemented by software-defined networking capabilities; e.g., OpenFlow [2], OpenSketch [37]. After the increase, SPIFFY attempts to distinguish attack traffic sources from legitimate ones by observing their response to the temporary bandwidth increase: legitimate sources running TCP-like flows will naturally see a corresponding increase in their throughputs as the bandwidth of their bottleneck link (i.e., the targeted link) has increased; however, attack sources will not observe this increase as a rational cost-sensitive attacker would have chosen to *fully utilize* the available bandwidth of the upstream links of the attack sources in the first stage. Alternatively, to avoid detection, the attacker could choose to keep each bot's attack traffic rate much lower than the available bandwidth of its upstream link. However, that this will increase the number of required bots and thus *increase attack cost* proportionally. In essence, adversaries are forced to either allow their attack sources to be detected or accept an increase in attack cost.

Note that adversaries *cannot* predict *when* a temporary bandwidth expansion will be executed since its operation is determined by defenders; e.g., network operators of link targets. The unpredictability of bandwidth expansion makes it difficult for the adversaries to temporarily purchase additional bots at a low cost to avoid the SPIFFY's cost-detectability tradeoff. This is because the botnet markets *cannot* provide low-cost temporary bot purchase since the markets are required to reserve large numbers of bots that are *always ready* for the temporary bot demands.

Second-Line Defense: Collaborative Defenses. Countering link-flooding attacks by cost-insensitive, irrational adversaries requires collaboration among multiple ISPs. For example, CoDef [24] requires coordination between the ISPs hosting the attack sources and targets to defend against link-flooding attacks. SENSS [4] requires coordination between ISPs hosting the attack target and the intermediate ISPs that control the incoming attack traffic. SIBRA [7] utilizes global coordination among ISPs to create entire end-to-end Internet paths to protect a user's traffic. Although ISP collaboration-based defenses are generally harder to orchestrate in a climate of competitive relationships between ISPs in the current Internet [26], when they are used as a second-tier defense they can be effective for the less frequent cases where the adversary is cost-insensitive or irrational.

4 Conclusions

Evolving DDoS attacks that target the critical-infrastructure services (e.g., emergency, power grids, and cellular communications services) require new countermeasures that are currently unavailable on the Internet. As a case study, we investigate link-flooding attacks and discuss the particular challenges and opportunities in handling them. We argue that defenses against link-flooding attacks should be multi-tiered. We provide an example of a two-tier defense scheme where the first line of defense deters cost-sensitive rational adversaries, who appear to be responsible for the vast majority of DDoS attacks. The second tier is a collaborative defense intended to counter attacks by cost-insensitive or irrational adversaries, which can be more costly since it is infrequent in practice.

References

1. Internet transit pricing: historical and projected. http://drpeering.net/white-papers/Internet-Transit-Pricing-Historical-And-Projected.php
2. Open flow. https://www.opennetworking.org
3. Akamai: The state of the internet 2nd quarter. Report (2012)
4. Alwabel, A., Yu, M., Zhang, Y., Mirkovic, J.: SENSS: observe and control your own traffic in the Internet. In: Proceeding of ACM SIGCOMM (2014)
5. Arbor Networks: Worldwide infrastructure security report, volume IX. Arbor Special Report (2014)
6. Barker, I.: 2016 will see the rise of DDoS-as-a-service. In: BetaNews (Dec 28 2015). http://betanews.com/2015/12/28/2016-will-see-the-rise-of-ddos-as-a-service/
7. Basescu, C., Reischuk, R.M., Szalachowski, P., Perrig, A., Zhang, Y., Hsiao, H.C., Kubota, A., Urakawa, J.: SIBRA: Scalable internet bandwidth reservation architecture. In: Proceeding of NDSS (2016)

8. Beverly, R., Koga, R., Claffy, K.: Initial longitudinal analysis of IP source spoofing capability on the Internet (2013)

9. Bright, P.: Can a DDoS break the Internet? Sure.. just not all of it. In: Ars Technica (2 April 2013). http://arstechnica.com/security/2013/04/can-a-ddos-break-the-internet-sure-just-not-all-of-it/

10. Caballero, J., Grier, C., Kreibich, C., Paxson, V.: Measuring pay-per-install: The commoditization of malware distribution. In: Proceeding of USENIX Security (2011)

11. Cerf, V.: The freedom to be who you want to be: strong authentication and pseudonymity on the internet. In: RSA Conference (2013)

12. FCC: April 2014 Multistate 911 Outage: Cause and Impact. Public Safety Docket No. 14–72, PSHSB Case File Nos. 14-CCR-0001-0007 (2014)

13. Ferguson, P.: Network ingress filtering: Defeating denial of service attacks which employ IP source address spoofing. IETF RFC2827 (2000)

14. Gligor, V.D.: A note on the denial-of-service problem. In: Proceeding of IEEE Security and Privacy (1983)

15. Gligor, V.: Dancing with the adversary: a tale of wimps and giants. In: Christianson, B., Malcolm, J., Matyáš, V., Švenda, P., Stajano, F., Anderson, J. (eds.) Security Protocols 2014. LNCS, vol. 8809, pp. 100–115. Springer, Cham (2014). doi:10.1007/978-3-319-12400-1_11

16. Goodin, D.: How extorted e-mail provider got back online after crippling DDoS attack. In: Ars Technica, (10 November 2015). http://arstechnica.com/security/2015/11/how-extorted-e-mail-provider-got-back-online-after-crippling-ddos-attack/

17. Greene, T.: Bot-herders can launch DDoS attacks from dryers, refrigerators, other Internet of things devices. In: NetworkWorld (24 September 2014)

18. Hui, K.-L., Kim, S.-H., Wang, Q.-H.: Marginal deterrence in the enforcement of law: evidence from distributed denial of service attack. In: Workshop on Analytics for Business, Consumer and Social Insights (BCSI). Singapore, August 2013

19. Kang, M.S., Gligor, V.D.: Routing bottlenecks in the internet: causes, exploits, and countermeasures. In: Proceeding of ACM CCS (2014)

20. Kang, M.S., Gligor, V.D., Sekar, V.: SPIFFY: Inducing Cost-Detectability Trade-offs for Persistent Link-Flooding Attacks. In: Proceedings of NDSS (2016)

21. Kang, M.S., Lee, S.B., Gligor, V.D.: The Crossfire Attack. In: Proceeding of IEEE S and P (2013)

22. Karami, M., McCoy, D.: Understanding the emerging threat of DDoS-as-a-service. In: Proceeding of USENIX Workshop on Large-Scale Exploits and Emergent Threats (LEET) (2013)

23. Khandelwal, S.: 602 Gbps! This may have been the largest DDoS attack in history. In: NetworkWorld (8 January 2016)

24. Lee, S.B., Kang, M.S., Gligor, V.D.: CoDef: collaborative defense against large-scale link-flooding attacks. In: Proceedinf of ACM CoNEXT (2013)

25. Mo, Y., Kim, T.H.J., Brancik, K., Dickinson, D., Lee, H., Perrig, A., Sinopoli, B.: Cyber-physical security of a smart grid infrastructure. Proc. IEEE **100**(1), 195–209 (2012)

26. Mortensen, A.: DDoS Open Threat Signaling Requirements. IETF draft-mortensen-threat-signaling-requirements-00 (2015)

27. NENA: NENA i3 Technical Requirements Document. NENA VoIP/Packet Technical Committee Long Term Definition Working Group (2006)

28. Nussman, C.: DHS Bulletin on Telephony Denial of Service (TDOS) attacks on PSAPs. In: National Emergency Number Association (NENA), (17 March 2013). https://www.nena.org/news/119592/DHS-Bulletin-on-Denial-of-Service-TDoS-Attacks-on-PSAPs.htm

29. Patterson, D.: Exclusive: inside the ProtonMail siege: how two small companies fought off one of Europe's largest DDoS attacks. In: TechRepublic, (13 November 2015). http://www.techrepublic.com/article/exclusive-inside-the-pro tonmail-siege-how-two-small-companies-fought-off-one-of-europes-largest-ddos/

30. Png, I.P., Wang, C.Y., Wang, Q.H.: The deterrent and displacement effects of information security enforcement: International evidence. J. Manag. Inf. Syst. **25**, 125–144 (2008)

31. Rossow, C.: Amplification hell: revisiting network protocols for DDoS abuse. In: Proceeding of NDSS (2014)

32. Storm, D.: Biggest DDoS attack in history slows Internet, breaks record at 300 Gbps. In: ComputerWorld (27 March 2013)

33. Studer, A., Perrig, A.: The coremelt attack. In: Backes, M., Ning, P. (eds.) ESORICS 2009. LNCS, vol. 5789, pp. 37–52. Springer, Heidelberg (2009). doi:10. 1007/978-3-642-04444-1_3

34. Xu, Q., Huang, J., Wang, Z., Qian, F., Gerber, A., Mao, Z.M.: Cellular data network infrastructure characterization and implication on mobile content placement. In: Proceeding of ACM SIGMETRICS (2011)

35. Xu, Z., Wang, H., Xu, Z., Wang, X.: Power attack: An increasing threat to data centers. In: Proceeding of NDSS (2014)

36. Yu, C.F., Gligor, V.D.: A formal specification and verification method for the prevention of denial of service. In: Proceeding of IEEE Security and Privacy (1988)

37. Yu, M., Jose, L., Miao, R.: Software defined traffic measurement with opensketch. In: Proceeding of USENIX NSDI (2013)

38. Yu, T., Sekar, V., Seshan, S., Agarwal, Y., Xu, C.: Handling a trillion (unfixable) flaws on a billion devices: Rethinking network security for the Internet-of-Things. In: Proceeding of HotNets (2015)

Defending Against Evolving DDoS Attacks: A Case Study Using Link Flooding Incidents (Transcript of Discussion)

Virgil D. Gligor[✉]

Carnegie Mellon University, Pittsburgh, USA
gligor@cmu.edu

In this presentation I'll talk about the evolution of distributed denial of service (DDoS) attacks and, of course, the evolution of the adversary who launches them, and finally how to defend against them. This is based on joint work with my graduate student Min Suk Kang and my colleague Vyas Sekar at Carnegie Mellon University.

The first experimental DDoS attacks appeared in the late 1990 s and the first real-life attacks in the early 2000. To launch them an adversary gathers a substantial amount of traffic from a variety of sources, such as DNS recursors and NTP services, and channels it towards a particular target host or network. In the last five or six years, the intensity of the attack traffic that could be gathered exceeded 100 Gbps and now reaches 600 Gbps. Attacks of this intensity cause legitimate users to be denied access to most targeted services. We call this type of attacks the *traditional* DDoS attacks.

Recent statistics show that we now experience roughly about 20,000 such attacks per day in the Internet worldwide at a cost of about $100,000 per hour of denied service, or roughly of $1,000,000 worth of losses. These are statistics published by Arbor Networks and American Bankers Association and others. The reason I mention them is that, about 10 years ago, DDoS was not one of the major problems in the Internet. However, over the past decade the adversary has evolved and so has the sophistication of these attacks. Today one would consider DDoS a problem worth worrying about.

The class of attacks that I'm going to focus on in this talk are what I call the *non-traditional* DDoS attacks. Unlike the traditional attacks where the targets are the end-point hosts, in non-traditional attacks, the targets are links of the Internet. Nevertheless, adversary-selected end-point hosts are still the victims of an attack. The targets could be inter-AS links, such as inter-ISP links, or it could be internal AS links. Essentially the attack idea is the same as before: focus traffic on a particular link, or in a particular set of links and, of course, communication to the victim hosts is going to be degraded, possibly even cut off.

The classic example of a non-traditional attack was the Coremelt Attack[1]. This attack could be launched by a bunch of bots merely by exchanging messages with each other. Clearly, all the traffic created is wanted by the end-point hosts

---

[1] Ahren Studer and Adrian Perrig. The Coremelt Attack. In Proceedings of ESORICS, LNCS 5789, Springer, 2009.

© Springer International Publishing AG 2017
J. Anderson et al. (Eds.): Security Protocols XXIV, LNCS 10368, pp. 58–66, 2017.
DOI: 10.1007/978-3-319-62033-6_8

(i.e., by the bots), and hence none is going to complain. However, if all of these messages could meet in the core routers of an AS, the routers would obviously become flooded and go of business for a while. If a router's bandwidth is degraded by flooding, the degradation can cause connectivity degradation. Packets will be repeatedly dropped and connection setup protocols, such as the three-way handshake of TCP, will fail. Coremelt was one of the first examples of non-traditional DDoS attacks.

One of the first examples of a major non-traditional attack in the Internet was the Spamhaus attack of 2013. The second major attack, which was more interesting than Spamhaus, was the Proton Mail attack launched against a Swiss mail service in November 2015. What made this attack particularly interesting was the fact that this was the first instance when the adversary adapted to the defense countermeasures in real-time.

In the Spamhaus case, the attacker also adapted, but *not* in real time. First, he launched a traditional DDoS attack: he generated a large volume of attack traffic by using DNS recursors, focused it on the Spamhaus server, and blocked the server for two and a half days. Then, the Spamhaus administrators moved their service to Cloudflare, which is a cloud operator, which distributed the Spamhaus service across across multiple servers. The attacker couldn't scale up the traffic volume sufficiently to block all the Cloudflare servers, and the first attack ended. However, the adversary adapted to the defense countermeasures and began attacking the IXPs servicing Cloudflare. In effect he adapted to the defense countermeasure by targeting the Internet infrastructure, after observing the defense countermeasures. However, his IXP attack was non-persistent; it was countered in less than two hours.

In contrast, in the ProtonMail case the adversary launched a non-traditional link-flooding attack and adapted *in real time*. That is, he flooded selected links around Europe such that traffic to the Proton Mail servers was severely degraded. It turns out that the attack caused collateral damage: Internet traffic was disrupted in widely different regions of Europe, from St. Petersburg and Moscow to Kiev and Stockholm. The reason for this damage was that the flooded links were located in tier 1 and tier 2 networks that were not that close to Proton Mail servers. Instead, they were several hops away.

This attack has two important characteristics. The first is that the attack was difficult to detect, since the victim servers were not flooded, but instead their connectivity was degraded. The second is that the attack targeted Internet links located in different ISPs and changed the set of targeted links in real time. Thus, recovery required inter-ISP collaboration and manual operation, and hence was very slow; i.e., the attack persisted for about a week. The adversary changed the locus of the attack (i.e., the targeted links) and still blocked communication to the initially chosen end-point victim servers. In a 2013 paper[2], Min Suk Kang, Soo Bum Lee and I called this the *moving-target attack*, which is a new form of real-time adaptive attack.

---

[2] Min Suk Kang, Soo Bum Lee and Virgil D. Gligor. The Crossfire Attack. In Proc. of IEEE Symp. on Security and Privacy, San Jose, CA, May 2013.

How has the DDoS adversary evolved over time? To describe how the adversary has evolved, we have to have a definition of the adversary, and in particular a definition of an adversary attack. The adversary can always be characterized by the set of possible attacks s/he can launch. As some of you may remember from *SPW 2014*, my way of characterizing an attack via the triple < goal, capabilities, strategy >. In this context, the goal consists of the target selection, scalability of the attack and its persistence. The capabilities are the necessary means the adversary must employ to achieve the goal and the strategies are different ways in which the adversary uses the available capabilities. Sometimes people cannot readily distinguish between strategies and capabilities, but as you'll see shortly, they are quite different.

The attack goals of the recent adversaries have evolved in three different ways. First, they seek new targets, and critical infrastructure services are obvious choices. For example, in the US, the 911 emergency services are actually moving to the Internet, and these services will likely become subject to denial-of-service attacks. Similarly, a lot of cellular phone traffic currently spills over to the Internet from the cellular network via a set of gateways. If one attacks those gateways, obviously some of the cellular services will be degraded. The power grid will likely face DDoS attacks when its management and control are performed via the Internet. Second, the adversary seeks attack scalability; i.e., the adversary seeks to bring down lots of servers with fairly little effort. Third, the adversary also seeks to launch attacks that persist; i.e., attacks that will last for many days, not merely hours. As we've witnessed in the ProtonMail case, the attack lasted roughly seven days. Most previous DDoS attacks lasted for at most two and a half days, and the average was about half a day. An attack that lasts longer exhibits serious persistence.

The new adversary began employing new capabilities. Starting with 2009, many attacks began targeting Internet links, not end-servers. More recently, attack traffic directed to a link have the characteristics of legitimate traffic (e.g., protocol conforming, low intensity messages) and becomes *indistinguishable from legitimate* traffic by link routers; i.e., they cannot tell that a particular packet comes from an adversary or comes from a legitimate source. Furthermore, attack traffic that floods a link can avoid triggering congestion alarms.

How is it possible to avoid congestion alarms? By attack adaptation. The new adversary observes the target's defense, and uses the same capabilities to deny access to the same victim service by changing the target of the attack, possibly in real time. Before I give an example of adaptation, I would like to point out that the evolution of attack capabilities has been on a fairly large timescale and reflects an evolution in technology and Internet economics.

Frank Stajano: This may be a naive question, but it sounds to me like the attack where the malicious players cooperated, sending message to each other, and melt down the core of an AS is a failure of properly charging for the traffic because they do something that looks like a legitimate operation. Then, by that argument servers should be paying for the successive traffic to an extent that, first of all, makes the servers spend a lot of money and, second, prevents them from doing it at scale.

Reply: Frank is referring to the Coremelt attack. This attack had two characteristics. First, it did not have any specific end-point server victims. What end-point server was affected was uninteresting. The end-server bots were sending legitimate traffic to each other and targeted a core AS. Unfortunately for the adversary, the attack does not scale quadratically in the number of bots since the uplink bandwidth of each bot is usually limited, so a bot may be unable to send messages to *all other bots* during an attack. To answer the part of your question regarding failure of attack prevention, the messages bots exchanged were legitimate. No end-point server would complain about unwanted messages.

Frank Stajano: Maybe I didn't make my question very clear. I meant to say: is this not a failure of charging people properly for their traffic? If I imagine a parallel of making the attack on the city of Brno traffic system by having each of us take lots of taxis and go from to one place to another. If we take enough taxis, then traffic downtown Brno will get to a stand still, but we'll have to each pay a taxi fare. Did these guys not have to pay?

Reply: The point is if a bot is on one's computer, one has already paid for the bandwidth available to the bot. The attack scales up to the available uplink bandwidth of each computer, but it would not necessarily persist in time. Indeed, as you point out, an operator would notice that the core is melting and start pushing back messages. Although, the Coremelt Attack could be tweaked so that the messages would come at a slower rate, and use less bandwidth, the attack could certainly concentrate messages in the core itself. I don't know if I answered your question, but if I didn't ...

Frank Stajano: Maybe I'll take it up later.

Reply: Okay.

In more recent attacks, the strategies employed by the adversary use the same capabilities for the same targets, but they adapt on a short time scale. Let me give you an example of the Crossfire Attack. This is the simple version of the single-link attack. Then I will make the case for the multi-link attack.

Assume that the adversary has a bunch of bots that send messages to decoy servers. These are legitimate servers and are not the subject of connectivity degradation. The servers being attacked are somewhere else. The bots send traffic to decoy servers without having to spoof any IP address. All attack traffic sent is authentic. Say 10,000 bots send 4 Kbps traffic to 1,000 decoy servers, which are public servers. This generates 40 Gbps of traffic in a single link and clog it up.

One may wonder why would the routers of that link not signal congestion. The reason for that is the attack adapts to the congestion controls: it suspends the flows and restarts them on and off for a while. It turns out that it takes over 200 seconds for a router to trigger congestion-control alarms. If the attack traffic lasts between one and two minutes before it is temporarily stopped, congestion alarms are not going to be raised, and yet the link is clogged up.

In the multi-link Crossfire attack the adversary selects several links to flood so that the legitimate traffic to chosen end-point servers is cut off or degraded. The reason why this attack works globally is that the Internet has what we call *routing bottlenecks*. A routing bottleneck comprises a small set of links such that if these links are clogged up by an attack the traffic to a set of end-point servers is degraded or even cut off. Note that all routes between a set of senders and receivers typically have multiple bottlenecks, not all having the same small number of links. This enables an adversary to launch what's called a *moving-target attack*; i.e., the adversary sends attack traffic to the links of the first bottleneck, pauses the attack before congestion control is triggered, and resumes the attack by sending traffic to the second bottleneck. Then, before congestion alarms are triggered, the adversary stops and resumes the attack traffic to the first bottleneck. This can go on forever. Why? Because no router is going to raise an alarm.

Why do routing bottlenecks appear in the Internet? Wasn't the Internet designed to have plenty of path diversity between senders and receivers? If one computes the min-cut between a set of sources and a set of destinations on the Internet, one would find that a very large number of links would have to be cut (e.g., between 200 and 1000 in many cases) to block sender-receiver communication in most geographical areas. An adversary would have zero chance to clog all these links. However, one does not have to clog all the links of a min-cut to degrade sender-receiver communication. Instead, one could find bottleneck links among the links of a min-cut, which allow substantial connectivity degradation by an attack. Routing bottlenecks are no problem at all in normal mode of operation, as their links are all well provisioned. Hence routing bottlenecks are not bandwidth bottlenecks, and it turns out that routing bottlenecks are a consequence of a very good feature.

We conjectured that routing bottlenecks arise because of the *minimum cost routing* policies in the Internet, and then tested that conjecture by measurements in 15 countries and 15 large cities around the world. Our conjecture started with an analogy with an observation made in linguistics, first by George Kingsley Zipf and later by Benoit Mandelbrot. In English language communication very few words are used very frequently and lots of words are used very infrequently. This yields a power law in the frequency of word usage. Zipf[3] and Mandelbrot[4] showed that this phenomenon is attributable to the minimization of effort in human communication. By analogy, our conjecture was that routing bottlenecks could be caused by minimum-cost routing.

---

[3] George K. Zipf. Human Behavior and the Principle of Least Effort: An Introduction to Human ecology. Addison-Wesley Press, 1949.

[4] Benoit Mandelbrot. An Information Theory of the Statistical Structure of Language. In Proceedings of the Symposium on Applications of Communication Theory. Butterworths, London, 1953.

Ross Anderson: It's much more complex than that. We wrote a book on the resilience of the Internet inter-connection ecosystem a couple of years ago[5]. There are all sorts of things going on as ISPs and ASes connect with each other via peering and transit agreements. We've got a lot of stuff in there that might be worth digging around here.

Reply: Could very well be, but those are set up by peering arrangements.

Ross Anderson: Our colleague Chris Hall knows this inside out since he was actually involved in negotiating peering arrangements for a number of big ASes.

Reply: Right. There's a difference between the peering arrangements between ISPs/ASes and intra-domain minimum cost routing. However, while peering arrangements between ISPs are policy based, they don't violate minimum-cost routing. We tested this fact in prior work[6].

Again, routing bottlenecks are not a problem in normal mode of operation. They're a problem only when an adversary targets them in a flooding attack. The dilemma we face here is a classic *defender's dilemma*: how can a defender remove the vulnerability of the routing bottlenecks to flooding attacks, when, in fact, the vulnerability is caused by minimum-cost routing, which is a very useful feature? This is the type of dilemma we faced in security from day one. Remember the old observation: among the three design requirements, namely security, cost-performance, and object-code compatibility, any two out of the three are easy to satisfy, but all three of them is nearly impossible.

How does one diversify routing to avoid a link-flooding attack? One could certainly attempt to do it via ISP collaboration. If ISPs don't care about costs that much, and if they are willing to make lots of peering agreements, one could diversify routing. That, of course, would be expensive, so we started looking at defense without ISP collaboration.

The first line of defense we explored was that of *deterring rational adversaries* from exploiting routing bottlenecks. We define a rational adversary as one who is cost-sensitive and avoids detection and punishment. In this sense, most adversaries are rational[7,8]. Two attack characteristics makes deterrence challenging. The first is the fact that the adversary uses legitimate-looking attack flows and the attack does not trigger any congestion alarms. The second is the adversary

---

[5] Chris Hall, Richard Clayton, Ross Anderson, and Evangelos Ouzounis. InterX: Resilience of the Internet Interconnection Ecosystem. ENISA Technical Report, April 2011. (available at http://www.lightbluetouchpaper.org/2011/04/12/resilience-of-the-internet-interconnection-ecosystem) .

[6] Min Suk Kang and Virgil Gligor. Routing Bottlenecks in the Internet: Causes, Exploits, and Countermeasures. In Proceedings of the ACM CCS, 2014.

[7] Ivan PL Png, Chen-Yu Wang and Qiu-Hong Wang. The deterrent and displacement effects of information security enforcement: International evidence. In *Journal of Management Information Systems,* 2008.

[8] Hui, Kai-Lung; Lim, Seung-Hyun; and Qiu-Hong Wang. Marginal deterrence in the enforcement of law: Evidence from distributed denial of service attack. Workshop on Analytics for Business, Consumer and Social Insights (BCSI). Singapore, August 2013.

has an asymmetric cost advantage vis-a-vis the defender. For example, 10 Gbps of defender bandwidth costs a lot more than 10 Gbps of attack-traffic bandwidth. How much more? Between 70 and 80 times more. The adversary's botnet cost is low whereas the defender's link bandwidth provisioning is high.

Facing these technical deterrence challenges, we thought that an adversary might be deterred by law. For example, the Council of Europe has a Convention on Cybercrime which prescribes all sorts of measures countries should take to protect their cyber infrastructure, what punishments they should administer to miscreants, and so on. By 2013, 47 countries signed it including the US and most European countries and about 30 ratified and enforced it. However, recent results by Hui *et al.* – referred to above – show that, while the rational-adversary hypothesis holds, the International Convention on Cybercrime has failed to deter *traditional* DDoS attacks. The reason for failure is lack of *marginal deterrence*. Marginal deterrence is a very basic principle in law which says that one should punish gradually. In other words, for small offenses, small punishment, and for big offenses, large punishment. That's not what the Convention on Cybercrime prescribes.

Given that law does not always deter, we thought of forcing a trade-off between attack detection and cost. In other words, if the adversary wants to remain undetected, the cost of the attack should skyrocket. In effect, we put the adversary in a conflict of interest to remove part of the cost asymmetry the adversary enjoys in DDoS attacks. That's essentially the gist of our proposal. For details, please see our the recently published paper at the NDSS 2016[9].

Here I'll give you an example of one possibility out of the many that exist in designing such trade-offs. Suppose that a given link is flooded by an attack and legitimate senders end up sending their traffic at a degraded rate, which is much lower than the adversary's attack traffic rate. The rate difference follows from flow fairness. If one sends lots of traffic, fairness says that one gets more bandwidth, and that's what the adversary exploits. Despite the differences between the two traffic rates, individual attack flows are indistinguishable from legitimate ones.

Now, suppose that all of a sudden the defender can expand the link bandwidth *temporarily*. By how much? By a factor of seven to ten times the normal rate. Our research shows that this is possible, in principle, with some SDNs by taking advantage of their re-routing capabilities which spread traffic and include underutilized links. What are the consequences of the temporary bandwidth expansion (TBE)? The legitimate sources using TCP-like flows will experience a corresponding increase in their throughputs. In contrast, attack sources will not observe this increase in bandwidth because cost-sensitive adversary would have already chosen to fully utilize the available bandwidth of the upstream links of his attack sources in the initial stage of the attack. Hence, attack flows become distinguishable from legitimate ones.

---

[9] Min Suk Kang, Virgil Gligor, and Vyas Sekar. SPIFFY: Inducing Cost-Detectability Tradeoffs in Persistent Link-Flooding Attacks. In Proceedings of the 2016 Symposium on Network and Distributed Systems Security, February 2016.

Alternatively, the adversary may elect to keep the traffic rate of each of its bots far below the available bandwidth of their upstream links and increase the rate during TBE to remain undetected. However, this strategy under-utilizes the adversary's bandwidth and the adversary will have to increase the number of required bots for the initial stage of the attack. This will increase the attacks' cost proportionally with the number of additional bots needed. This is what our modeling and simulation experiments show. I will skip the rest of the details. For the rest of the attack analysis, please see the companion paper.

In short, our deterrence mechanism aims to temporarily create an unpleasant trade off for rational adversaries: either the adversary's flows get detected and dropped or the adversary has to pay a lot more for a successful attack. This removes at least some of the adversary's cost advantage in a link-flooding attack.

We argued that our first line of defense should be deterrence, and if law doesn't deter, we have to employ technical means for deterrence, at least for rational adversaries. However, how can one deter *irrational adversaries*; i.e., state-sponsored, cost-insensitive, who do not care about by the possibility of getting detected? Since these adversaries are irrational, we have to fall back on the second line of defense, which requires ISPs to collaborate. Currently, this is a costly proposition and the Internet does not have the proper infrastructure for ISP collaboration. However, we note that the IETF put together a group tasked to define a *signaling protocol* between the ISPs so they could inform each other when there is a link-flooding attack.

I suspect that ultimately we will have to employ both deterrence of rational adversaries, either by mechanism or by new laws, and of irrational adversaries by ISP collaboration; e.g., the CoDef protocol for a possible deterrence mechanism based on ISP collaboration[10]. That's basically my message.

David Llewellyn-Jones: If you go with a temporary bandwidth expansion for attack-flow detection, which is very clever, isn't there a danger the bot suppliers go to a surge pricing model to compensate?

Reply: We looked at the price of bots and how they evolved in time. It turns out that they won't be able to decrease the cost as fast as we can do the temporary bandwidth expansion (TBE). In other words, if one gets a factor of seven to ten in TBE, the decrease in bot costs may not be able to offset that, since they decrease at a much slower rate.

David Llewellyn-Jones: Because the bots don't exist or because people don't need to buy them?

Reply: Bot networks do exist... One can buy them over the Internet.

David Llewellyn-Jones: Is the problem that people aren't willing to pay for the extra bandwidth?

Reply: That's right. That's why TBE works. If all of the sudden this extra bandwidth becomes necessary for the attack to succeed, the adversary is stuck.

---

[10] Soo Bum Lee, Min Suk Kang and Virgil Gligor. CoDef: Collaborative Defense Against Large-Scale Link-Flooding Attacks. In Proc. of ACM CoNEXT 2013, 2013.

The Evolution of a Security Control

Olgierd Pieczul[1,2(✉)] and Simon N. Foley[2]

[1] Ireland Lab, IBM, Dublin, Ireland
olgierdp@ie.ibm.com
[2] Department of Computer Science, University College Cork, Cork, Ireland
simon.foley@imt-atlantique.fr

Abstract. The evolution of security defenses in a contemporary open-source software package is considered over a twelve year period. A qualitative analysis style study is conducted that systematically analyzes security advisories, codebase revisions and related discussions. A number of phenomena emerge from this analysis that provide insights into the process of managing code-level security defenses.

1 Introduction

During an application's lifecycle, the ideal is that there is a continuing process for vulnerability discovery and repair. A more pragmatic viewpoint of the process is that vulnerabilities are unknowingly introduced (or re-introduced) during code maintenance, existing vulnerabilities are missed, misreported and misinterpreted and repairs to defenses are incomplete. Even when a threat is clearly identified it can be a struggle to provide an adequate security defense. PHP's "safe mode" as a means to provide security for multi-hosting is a case in point; ever since its introduction, new ways of bypassing its latest defense/repair have been repeatedly discovered, eventually leading to the decision to remove it from PHP. One might argue that the difficulty in providing an adequate mechanism in this case is attributed to a flawed design and the relatively large scale of the software. However, this kind of problem can also be observed at a smaller scale and in simpler code that implements routine tasks. The Shellshock vulnerability in the Bash shell allowed custom code execution due to a bug in code parsing the environment variables. The fix was released quickly in 2014, however, it took five further vulnerabilities and remediations before the issue was believed fixed.

Research aimed at gaining insights into these kinds of issues has tended towards quantitative studies. Metrics such as number of bugs over time, rate of appearance, type and severity, can be gathered and statistically analyzed [1,2]. Such measurements can point to interesting trends, however, they rely on their hypothesis and the efficacy of the underlying data which, for example, may include attributes such as CVSS scores and lines of code. Furthermore, it cannot help one understand why a particular security weaknesses persists over time and cannot be properly addressed, nor what causes the implementation of a weak security mechanism. While a quantitative study can provide a basis

© Springer International Publishing AG 2017
J. Anderson et al. (Eds.): Security Protocols XXIV, LNCS 10368, pp. 67–84, 2017.
DOI: 10.1007/978-3-319-62033-6_9

for supporting a hypothesis, where a hypothesis does not form the basis of the research question an exploratory approach is informative.

In this paper we take an exploratory approach to gaining insights into these issues. Informed by qualitative research techniques, we carried out a systematic study of the evolution of a security control over a long period of time with a view to discovering security-relevant phenomena that emerge. The paper is organized as follows. Section 2 outlines the methodology that was followed during the study. The study is based on a security control in Apache Struts and Sect. 3 provides the background necessary to understand the technical account given on the evolution of this control in Sect. 4. Section 5 discusses a number of phenomena that emerge during the analysis of this control.

2   Methodology

We based our study on Apache Struts, a popular web application framework for Java, developed under the auspices of the Apache Software Foundation. Our rationale for selecting Struts as a good representative of contemporary software, is as follows. Struts is a mature and widely used package that has been developed according to best practices, both in terms of code implementation as well as development life cycle, with a documented policy and change management process. The security processes surrounding Struts are transparent and include documented processes for reporting vulnerabilities and publishing security advisories. We focussed our attention on the functionality of one particular Struts security control that has had a series of reported security vulnerabilities and has evolved over time. The chosen control is sufficiently critical to ensure both internal and public interest in identifying security problems, and that reported issues are treated seriously by the development team.

We performed a systematic analysis of the Struts source code published over twelve years from 2004 to 2015. This was done in a qualitative style, whereby the objective was to identify security-related phenomena, or patterns, that emerge from the activity of making code revisions. The analysis focused on the code revisions that arose as a consequence of, and/or were the cause of, the security advisories over that period. In particular, these were related to a security-control that is responsible for preventing the injection of malicious code into the framework via the parameters of web page requests. This security-control checks parameter values passed to the Struts `ParametersInterceptor` and `CookieInterceptor`, preventing their misuse. Note, that the `ParametersInterceptor` functionality originated in the XWork project and was later merged into Struts; during this initial period, the XWork source was the subject of the analysis.

We reviewed: the security advisories/vulnerability publications; code-updates (security-related or otherwise); related discussions on the development mailing list, and other publications often contributed by the vulnerability reporters who sometimes provided additional technical details. Often, only partial details of an attack were published, and in all cases it was possible to re-construct/implement the attacking code by reverse-engineering the code changes and published information. This led to the analysis of an estimated 300+ security-relevant code changes over the evolution of Struts.

In carrying out this analysis we identified the code changes that had an impact on security, either fixing a known vulnerability or introducing a security issue. For ease of exposition, the analysis is summarized in terms of aggregate changes over releases that culminate in a published security-related release, with one exception. In this way we believe that our inferences about the developer's intentions are more reliable than those based on (possibly incomplete) changes made in between security releases. While the observation of changes in-between the releases may provide an insight into security mechanism evolution, it was not clear whether the changes at these stages could be considered complete. As a result we discovered 20 key security related changes, presented by row in Table 1.

During our investigation we identified elements of the security mechanism and mapped the changes into the corresponding categories, give by the right-hand columns in the table. The identified changes often take a simplified form, of a regular expression or an acronym, representing the essence of the change. For simplicity, the significant element of the change is highlighted using **bold** text. Note that the categories discovered during analysis are not related to the actual structure of the code, as the corresponding security mechanisms were routinely moved/refactored within the source code, given different names, and so forth.

Throughout this process we strove to make observations about vulnerabilities, repairs and coding activities, based solely on the evidence in this corpus.

3   Struts Operation

This section provides an overview of those parts of Struts that are required to understand our analysis of the security control used in the study. Struts is a mature and popular web Model-View-Controller framework for Java. One of the features of Struts is the ability to easily separate the business logic from the operational details related to processing HTTP requests. For example, consider a sample piece of code of a web application responsible for handling a request to add an application user by an administrator, presented at Fig. 1. The listing shows three parts of the application: class `User` encapsulates the details of an application user; class `AddUser`, implemented as Struts *action*, provides the logic adding user to the system, and the JSP provides the fragment of the view *view* (a page is presented when the action is complete).

Note that `AddUser` does not contain any web-specific logic, which is handled by Struts. It defines getter and setter methods (`getNewUser` and `setNewUser`, respectively) for retrieving and setting the user object, and a `setSession` method (required by `SessionAware`) interface for Struts to set the Session object. For example, client may send a request such as: `http://application/user/add?newUser.name=john&newUser.role=support` in order to add a new support user. The request is received by Struts which, based on its configuration, decides whether it should be processed by an `AddUser` action.

```
public class User {
    private String name;
    private String role;
    ... // getters and setters for fields

    public boolean isAdmin() {
        return (role.equals("admin"));
    }
}

public class AddUser extends ActionSupport implements SessionAware {
    private User newUser;

    public User getNewUser() {
        return newUser;
    }

    public void setNewUser(User user) {
        this.newUser = user;
    }

    public void setSession(Map session) { // for SessionAware
        this.session = session;
    }

    public String execute() throws Exception {
        if (session.get("user").isAdmin()) {
            DAO.add(newUser);
            return SUCCESS;
        }
    }
}

<s:property value="#session['user'].name"/> added user <s:property
value="newUser.name"/> with role <s:property value="newUser.role"/>
```

Fig. 1. Sample MVC struts application

It instantiates the class and then (as it implements `SessionAware` interface) calls
`setSession` method with a session map for current user. Struts then parses the
parameters, creates a new User object using the values from the request, and
provides it to the action using the `setNewUser` method. Subsequently the `execute`
method executes, on the basis of all the properties that have been set. After the
user is added, the JSP page is rendered which in turn refers to action properties
such as newly added user and session.

3.1 Object-Graph Navigation Language

Struts uses Object-Graph Navigation Language (OGNL) [3], an expression language used to get and set properties of Java objects. OGNL expressions are evaluated against a collection of objects called *context*. One of the objects, called
root, is distinguished as the default root of the object graph. When processing a
request, Struts sets the current action object (for example `AddUser`) as the root.
In the example in Sect. 3 the expression `newUser.name` is used both in request
parameters and also in the JSP file. The values are being accessed through public getters and setters. For example, the OGNL `newUser.name` to get the name of
an object is equivalent to Java code `action.getNewUser().getName()`. Similarly,
using OGNL to set a value expressed as `newUser.name` to alice is equivalent to
Java code `action.getNewUser().setName("alice")`.

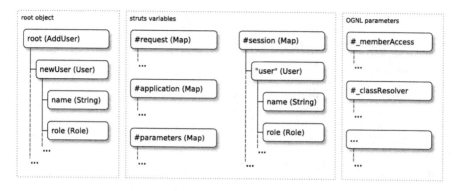

Fig. 2. OGNL context in example application

Other Struts-specific objects such as session, request and application configuration are also included in the OGNL context. For example `#session['user'].name`, expression can be used to access a `name` property of an object that exists in session map under index `'user'`. Finally, context contains number of variables that control OGNL behavior, such as rules for accessing classes depending on type, access restrictions, caching and so forth. Figure 2 provides an overview of context structure at the time of execution of `AddUser` action.

3.2 Struts Interceptors

Struts *interceptors*, upon which our study is based, parse request parameters and set corresponding values in action objects. Interceptors in Struts are responsible for handling common tasks before/after the action is executed. Typical tasks performed by interceptors is handling HTTP requests (such as request parameters or cookies), input validation, access control, caching and so forth.

Processing request parameters is performed by `ParametersInterceptor`. Our study started on the codebase published at the beginning of 2004, with the release of the XWork 1.0 library in which the interceptor was first implemented and the later merged into Struts. Since then, the functional requirements of the parameter interceptor have not changed. It iterates over each parameter and sets the action values using parameter name as OGNL expression to identify the object and parameter value as the value to set. Starting from June 2007 `CookieInterceptor` sets action properties based on HTTP cookies.

4 Tracing the Evolution of a Security Control

The parameters and cookie interceptors allow clients to provide a custom OGNL expressions that are evaluated by Struts. OGNL expressions can result in the execution of custom code which accesses program variables. From its first release,

Table 1. Security mechanism evolution: 2004–2015

date	accepted parameters	accepted cookies	excluded patterns	OGNL
Jan 2004	[empty]	n/a	n/a	**ME**
Dec 2004	excluded: {'=', ',' ,'#'}	n/a	n/a	ME
Feb 2007	excluded: {'=', ',' ,'#', ':'}	n/a	**dojo\..***	ME
Jun 2007	excluded: {'=', ',' ,'#', ':'}	[empty]	dojo\..*	ME
Jul 2008	excluded: {'=', ',' ,'#', ':'}	[empty]	dojo\..*	ME, **SM**
Jul 2008	ex: {'=', ',' ,'#', ':', \u0023}	[empty]	dojo\..*	ME, SM
Oct 2008	[\p{Graph}&&[^,#:=]]*	[empty]	dojo\..*	ME, SM, **25**
Aug 2010	**[a-zA-Z0-9\.\]\[\(\)_'\s]+**	[empty]	dojo\..*,^struts\..*	ME, SM, **SC**
Dec 2011	[a-zA-Z0-9\.\]\[\(\)_'\s]+	**[a-zA-Z0-9\.\]\[_'\s]+**	dojo\..*,^struts\..*	ME, SM, SC
Dec 2011	**[a-zA-Z0-9\.\]\[\(\)_']+**	[a-zA-Z0-9\.\]\[_'\s]+	dojo\..*,^struts\..*	ME, SM, SC
Jan 2012	\w+((\.\w+)|(\[\d+\])|(\(\\d+\))| (\[\w+'\])|(\('\w+'\)))*	[a-zA-Z0-9\.\]\[_'\s]+	dojo\..*,^struts\..*	ME, SM, SC, **EE**
Apr 2012	\w+((\.\w+)|(\[\d+\])|(\(\\d+\))| (\[\w+'\])|(\('\w+'\)))*	[a-zA-Z0-9\.\]\[_'\s]+	dojo\..*,^struts\..*,**^session\..*,^request\..*,^application\..*,** **^servlet(Request|Response)\..*,parameters\...***	ME, SM, SC, EE
Aug 2012	\w+((\.\w+)|(\[\d+\])|(\(\\d+\))| (\[\w+'\])|(\('\w+'\)))* **[100]**	[a-zA-Z0-9\.\]\[_'\s]+	dojo\..*,^struts\..*,^session\..*,^request\..*,^application\..*, ^servlet(Request|Response)\..*,parameters\...*	ME, SM, SC, EE
Mar 2014	\w+((\.\w+)|(\[\d+\])|(\(\\d+\))| (\[\w+'\])|(\('\w+'\)))* [100]	[a-zA-Z0-9\.\]\[_'\s]+	**^class\..*,^dojo\..*,^struts\..*,^session\..*,** ^request\..*,^application\..*,^servlet(Rrequest| Response)\..*,^parameters\..*,^action:.*,^method:.*	ME, SM, SC, EE
Apr 2014	\w+((\.\w+)|(\[\d+\])|(\(\\d+\))| (\[\w+'\])|(\('\w+'\)))* [100]	[a-zA-Z0-9\.\]\[_'\s]+	**(.*\.|^.*\N[('|")])(c|C)lass(\.|('|")]|\[).*,^dojo\..*,** ^struts\..*,^session\..*,^request\..*,^application\..*, ^servlet(Request|Response)\..*,^parameters\..*	ME, SM, SC, EE
Apr 2014	\w+((\.\w+)|(\[\d+\])|(\(\\d+\))| (\[\w+'\])|(\('\w+'\)))* [100]	[a-zA-Z0-9\.\]\[_'\s]+	**default:** (.*\.|^.*\N[('|")])class(\.|('|")]|\[).*; **params:** ^dojo\..*, ^struts\..*,^session\..*,^request\..*,^application\..*, ^servlet(Request|Response)\..*,^parameters\..*	ME, SM, SC, EE
May 2014	\w+((\.\w+)|(\[\d+\])|(\(\\d+\))| (\[\w+'\])|(\('\w+'\)))* [100]	[a-zA-Z0-9\.\]\[_'\s]+	(.*\.|^.*\N[('|")])class(\.|('|")]|\[).*,^dojo\..*,^struts\..*, ^session\..*,^request\..*,^application\..*, ^servlet(Request|Response)\..*,^parameters\..*	ME, SM, SC, EE
Dec 2014	\w+((\.\w+)|(\[\d+\])|(\(\\d+\))| (\['(\w|[\u4e00-\u9fa5])+'\])| (\('(\w|[\u4e00-\u9fa5])+'\)))*	[a-zA-Z0-9\.\]\[_'\s]+	**config/params:** ^action:.*,^method:.* (priority) **default:** (.*\.|^.*\N[('|")])\bclass(\.|('|")]|\[).*,(^|.*\.#),dojo(\.|\[).*, (^|.*\.#)struts(\.|\[).*,(^|.*\.#)session(\.|\[).*,(^|.*\.#)request(\.|\[).* (^|.*\.#)application(\.|\[).*,(^|.*\.#)servlet(Request|Response) (\.|\[).*,(^|.*\.#)parameters(\.|\[).*,(^|.*\.#)context(\.|\[).*, (^|.*\.#)_memberAccess(\.|\[).*	ME, SM, SC, EE, **EC**
May 2015	\w+((\.\w+)|(\[\d+\])|(\(\\d+\))| (\['(\w|[\u4e00-\u9fa5])+'\])| (\('(\w|[\u4e00-\u9fa5])+'\)))*	[a-zA-Z0-9\.\]\[_'\s]+	(^|.*\.#)(dojo|struts|session|request|application| servlet(Request|Response)|parameters|context| _memberAccess)(\.|\[).*", ^(action|method):.*	ME, SM, SC, EE, EC
Sep 2015	\w+((\.\w+)|(\[\d+\])|(\(\\d+\))| (\['(\w|[\u4e00-\u9fa5])+'\])|(\(('(\w|[\u4e00-\u9fa5])+'\)))*	[a-zA-Z0-9\.\]\[_'\s]+	(^|\\%\(|((#?)(top(\.|\['|\["|]\[\d|\].)?)(dojo|struts|session| request|response|application|servlet(Request|Response| Context)|parameters|context|_memberAccess)(\.|\[).*, ^(action|method):.*	ME, SM, SC, EE, EC

this functionality has been considered a security threat and, a mitigating security control has always formed a part of its implementation. In this section we systematically trace the evolution of this control over a 12 year period: 2004–2015. The results are summarized in the Table 1 and described in detail in the reminder of the section.

In January 2004 the interceptor included just one security measure: disabling Java method execution (ME) through OGNL. By default, OGNL allows Java methods to be called in a manner similar to field access. For example, attempting to set a value to map[method()] results in the invocation of method against the root object in order to get the value to be used as map key. Disabling the method execution is implemented using a custom OGNL method accessor and controlled using context variable #context['xwork.MethodAccessor.denyMethodExecution'].

4.1 Tampering with OGNL

The first vulnerability identified since the initial release relates to overwriting context variables via parameters. For example, a parameter/OGNL expression `#session['user'].role` may be used to set the role of the current user stored in the session. A more advanced expression may set a number of properties at once while still retaining the original behavior, that is, setting the `newUser` parameter: `#session['user'].role=admin,#testMode=true,newUser.name'`.

In December 2004 the problem was fixed by modifying the interceptor to check if the name is acceptable, by verifying it against a blacklist of characters, using a condition:

```
name.indexOf('=') != -1 || name.indexOf(',') != -1 || name.
    indexOf('#') != -1
```

In July 2008 it was reported that the fix was incomplete, because the `#` character can be encoded using its unicode `\u0023` replacement, for example, by using a parameter `\u0023session['user'].role=admin`. This problem was fixed by adding string `\u0023` to the blacklist. Note that the other two already blacklisted characters, which could also be represented using the unicode string, were not included in the unicode form. Shortly after, the fix was further modified in a twofold way. First, the code was modified and the check routine replaced with regular expression: `[\p{Graph}&&[^,#:=]]*`. Note that the unicode replacements for the characters were no longer not excluded. In addition, the interceptor was modified to run OGNL operations against a separate temporary instance of context object (SC), without Struts-specific variables such as `session` preventing their manipulation.

At the same time, a new problem was discovered. OGNL allows accessing static fields in Java objects using the `@class@field` notation. For example, expression `@java.lang.System@exit(0).foo` can be used to call static `exit()` method, causing the JVM to exit. Static methods provided by the Java standard library can be used to perform a number of operations, including executing custom commands. This problem was fixed by adding an option to disable static method access (SM) in OGNL, and disabling it by default.

A vulnerability in this security mechanism was found in July 2010. It took advantage of the fact that context variables were still accessible through the unicode "trick" *and* that the OGNL-specific context variables controlling access to method execution, were available without restriction on the the temporary context. This allows a modification of the OGNL runtime configuration, allowing method execution and eventually custom method execution. An example sequence of OGNL expressions to perform the attack are [4]:

```
#_memberAccess['allowStaticMethodAccess'] = true
#foo = new java.lang.Boolean("false")
#context['xwork.MethodAccessor.denyMethodExecution'] = #foo
#rt = @java.lang.Runtime@getRuntime()
#rt.exec('mkdir /tmp/PWNED')
```

Such a sequence could be encoded in a parameter, bypassing the blacklist, by using unicode replacements for the `#=`, characters. This vulnerability resulted in a change in the regular expression to a stricter white list of characters: `[a-zA-Z0-9\.\]\[\(\)_-'\s]+`, effectively disallowing usage of the unicode replacements.

A year after this change, there was a report that while the restriction worked for regular methods it did not apply to public constructors. While execution of methods by OGNL was disabled through custom accessors, the logic did not cover constructor invocation. Some constructors may be useful to an attacker, such as `FileWriter` constructor creating or overwriting a file (`new java.io.FileWriter('filename')`). Rather than disabling constructor invocation in the existing custom accessor, the issue was fixed by disallowing a white space character, essential for constructor syntax, in the parameter name. As a result, the regular expression was modified to `[a-zA-Z0-9\.\]\[\(\)_-']+`.

A few weeks later, in December 2011 a new way of bypassing the restriction was discovered [5]. It took advantage of OGNL's ability to evaluate the content of variables that already exist in the context. The attack requires setting two parameters. The first parameter uses an acceptable name but has a value containing the OGNL expression, and the second refers to the first, for instance, as array key. For example, an attacker may first set the value of existing parameter to an expression, `newUser.name=OGNL code` and then evaluate the parameter value by referencing its name, `z[(newUser.name)(0)]=0`. When the second parameter is evaluated, OGNL will attempt to establish an index of `z` property, and evaluate the expression stored in `newUser.name`. In effect, the vulnerability allows character-based restrictions on parameter names to be bypassed. This, in turn, enables access to context variables that control method execution restrictions and lead to executing custom code. The vulnerability was fixed by modifying the regular expression, yet again. This time, it matched characters such as `[]` or `()` only in specific contexts so as to disallow expressions that may evaluate other variables. An additional logic to control the expression evaluation (EE) was added to OGNL customization code.

The last vulnerability related to tampering with OGNL using parameter names was reported and fixed in August 2012. As parsing OGNL parameters requires significant processing effort it is attractive as a target for denial of service attacks. Requests with particularly long/complex OGNL expressions can be used to exhaust system resources. The problem was fixed by limiting the size of parameter names to 100 characters.

4.2   Accessing Properties

Another set of security problems with processing request parameters relate to the ability to access properties of the root (action) object. In OGNL, access to the properties is controlled by the method or field access modifier in Java. For example, the `newUser` property is accessible because of the public getter `getNewUser`. If the method was defined as private or protected then the access would not be possible. The relationship between the ability to access, and actual method access, may not be clear or always intended. It may happen that the developer's code already has an object that would perfectly suit use within an action, but it includes a public method that should not be exposed. For example, a different implementation of the example application in Sect. 3 may use the `User` object but does not intend to allow the user to set the `role` parameter. In February 2007 a configuration parameter named `excludeParams` was provided in order to allow developers to prevent access to some properties. The parameter can be set to set of regular expressions defining patterns for parameters that should be ignored by the interceptor. Initially, the parameter was set by default to `^dojo\..*` and shortly after also to `^struts\..*`.

Struts uses a dependency injection software pattern. In particular, it allows action classes to acquire certain common runtime information by implementing specific interfaces such as `SessionAware` or `RequestAware`. The example application in Sect. 3 implements a `SessionAware` interface and corresponding `setSession` method. This instructs Struts to call it with the current server's session before action execution. Note that implementing a corresponding public getter (not required by the interface) could open up a session for manipulation using request parameter, such as `session['user'].role`. If the application implements such getter, it is expected to restrict access to the parameter in the configuration.

Between 2007 and 2011 various reporters pointed out that implementing a setter, as required by Struts interfaces may also allow for manipulation. While the user may not directly access session attributes due to the lack of a getter, it may override a session object provided to the action. For example, a parameter `session.user=a` results in creation of a new Map with a `user` key. The use of this vulnerability is rather limited [6], but in certain cases it may allow unintended manipulation of application internals. In April 2012 a fix was eventually implemented by including a number of common parameter names such as `session` to the `excludeParams` list. The problem was not completely solved as it only protects a few commonly used properties and the override mechanism is still available.

A more significant problem was discovered in March 2014. Every Java object contains a `getClass` method that returns a Java class for that object. The returned `Class` object contains a number of getters and setters, in particular `getClassLoader` which returns an instance of the current class loader. Access to this object allows manipulation of the application server's internal state and allows for custom code execution [7]. The first attempt to fix the vulnerability was to add the `^class\..` pattern to `excludeParams`. Within a few days a number of vulnerabilities related to an incomplete fix were reported. One, was the pattern matches `class` string at the beginning of the parameter name (`^`), but the `class` property does not necessarily has to be accessed through the root. As all Java objects contain `getClass` method, the class loader manipulation can be done through any of them, for example `newUser.class.classLoader`. Another reported vulnerability related to the fact that OGNL allows the specification of parameters in upper-case form, such as `Class`, which are not matched by the regular expression. An improvement was published on the Struts web page as a hot fix, including `(.*\.|^|.*|\[('|"))(c|C)lass(\.|('|")]|\[).*`. It must be noted however, that an upper-case version was considered only for `class`, but not for `session`, `request`, and others, that were previously excluded. Eventually, the code performing the regular expression matching was modified to ignore case, and the expression was also simplified.

The series of fixes related to the class attribute, resulted in number of rather ad-hoc code changes that were rationalized in December 2014. The default set of excluded patterns was moved from the configuration file directly to the utility class used for pattern matching. Two, security unrelated, patterns were kept in the configuration file. However, the code was implemented in a way that configuration parameters overwritten the default set, effectively removing all security related excluded patterns. This problem was fixed by moving the two patterns to the code and leaving the configuration empty.

The last vulnerability relates to a special variable called `top`, implemented for Struts-specific handling of OGNL, allowing access to the root object. Effectively, this variable allowed excluded patterns of parameters to be bypassed by allowing variables to be addressed in a way that does not match the regular expressions. As a result, the `top` parameter was added to the list of excluded patterns.

Finally, a more comprehensive fix was implemented. In addition to a regular expression specifying parameter names, a custom OGNL property accessor provided by Struts was modified to exclude classes (EC) by their types and package names. For example, any attempt to access an object of a type `java.lang.Class`, or any class in `javax` package (specific to J2EE objects such as session), will be rejected. This mechanism does not have the weaknesses of the string matching approach that was repeatedly bypassed, as the verification of the object type is done at OGNL accessor level, regardless of how the expression was constructed. However, the list of excluded classes and package names is rather arbitrary.

4.3 CookieInterceptor

Since June 2007, Struts includes the `CookieInterceptor` with functionality similar to `ParametersInterceptor` but applicable to HTTP cookies. The interceptor iterates over the cookies sent with the request and sets the value indicated by the OGNL expression provided by cookie name. The developer may configure the parameters/names to be processed in the interceptor configuration.

Our analysis revealed that in several instances, problems that were applicable to both interceptors were fixed only for the parameters. At the time of its first release, developers were aware of OGNL tampering issues and rudimentary protection was already implemented for parameters, as presented in Table 1. However, it took over four years and an external reporter to implement the white list of accepted characters, which was similar to that for parameters.

Additionally, issues related to accessing parameters, described in Sect. 4.2 were not considered for cookies for quite some time. Until April 2014 there was no restriction as to what properties can be accessed with cookies and the `excludeParams` configuration was applicable only to parameters. In particular, the initial fix for the critical class loader manipulation issue was also only applied to parameters. Only after the problem was explicitly reported was it fixed, though only for the `class` property and not for the `session`, `request`, and so forth.

5 Analysis of Security Control Evolution

As we traced the evolution of the security control, as outlined in the previous section, we observed a number of repeating phenomena related to introduction and prevalence of vulnerabilities, and inhibitors to the proper implementation of the security control.

5.1 The Dark Side of the Code

One challenge is the difficulty of properly understanding every aspect of an application's operation. Modern software development is built layer upon layer of components, each encapsulating lower level detail. However, security issues often relate to low level details that are not always accessible to the developer. As a result, programmers rarely understand all the operational details of the entire stack. This problem, referred to as the "dark side of the code" in [8], can be viewed as a gap between the possible operation of the application as perceived by developer and the actual operation of which the software is capable. While [8] argues, in principle, for the existence of the dark side of the code, our study of Struts observed this phenomenon occurring in a number of vulnerabilities and confirms its existence 'in the wild'.

When the Struts interceptor developers designed the initial set of forbidden characters, they did not consider their unicode alternatives that were later used to bypass the blacklist based security control. The OGNL library allows the use of such replacements, however there is inadequate information concerning the scope in which the characters can be used. In its coverage of String literals, the official OGNL documentation makes vague mention of escape characters. In addition, the information provided about escaping characters is done in the context of string delimiters such as " and ' and could be easily interpreted as applying only to them. The same issue applies to OGNL's ability to address properties using upper case.

Similarly, that the `getClass` method, implemented by the JVM and existing in every Java object, may be used to perform an attack might have not been expected by the Struts developer. The complexity of this attack confirms that an in-depth understanding of the Java internals, as well as the class loader specific to the application server is required in order to develop an attack vector. Additionally, the developers might have not expected that access to public constructors, exploited using file overwrite attack, could be harmful. As it is a best practice in object oriented programming to not implement constructors that cause any side effects, it may be difficult to appreciate that Java standard library includes one that allows writing a file.

Report Bias. A dark side can also exist when it comes to both documenting and/or interpreting vulnerability reports; the extent of the security problem may not be fully appreciated in its reporting. Security vulnerabilities are often identified by security researchers who are external to the development team. Usually the issue is reported with a detailed description of the problem, example attack vector, and so forth. Upon receiving the information about the problem, the developers may follow a detailed report in isolation, as the prescription for the vulnerability's remedy. However, often the reporter may not have a complete understanding of the application and their report may be incomplete; or they may limit their focus to a representative example. The vulnerability however, may have broader scope than that identified by the report or there may be further attack vectors related to the same root cause of the issue.

In Struts, the sequence of fixes related to `class` property exemplifies this phenomenon. Each time, the remediation was shaped by the way the issue was reported. This is exemplified by usage of the class parameter at the beginning of expression (while it can be used for any object) and failing to provide protection for `CookieInterceptor`.

Similarly, an issue related to the exposure of constructors when using OGNL was reported as a problem that led to the overwriting custom files. Although this was only one example of the attack vector, this is how the vulnerability was described in Struts official advisory, despite the problem having a broader scope. In reality, a number of other actions are possible, provided the availablity of a suitable public constructor in the class path [9].

Security Metric Bias. During analysis the vulnerabilities were compared to the published official security advisories. We noticed that in many cases, the CVSS score did not properly represent the problem. This can be attributed to incomplete understanding of the problem when the report was published. The CVSS documentation acknowledges that the characteristics of a vulnerability can change over time; the *temporal* metrics, used to calculate the temporal score include properties such as exploitability or remediation level. However, it is the base metrics, such as confidentiality/integrity impact that often change as the problem is better understood.

For example, CVE-2008-6504 describing the "unicode trick" to bypass the blacklist of characters has a CVSS score of 5.0. The impact metrics for confidentiality and integrity are, None and Partial, respectively. Another occurrence of the same problem, that resulted from an incomplete fix due to adding a temporary context object, published in CVE-2010-1870 has the same score. This is, however, not consistent with the actual impact of the vulnerability. Access to context variables effectively allows execution of custom Java code, system commands, and more. It is likely that the team was not aware of the impact when the first advisory was published; in the second case, however, the official advisory points out the variables used to control method execution. The last vulnerability reported for this problem, relating to evaluating OGNL expressions using two parameters, reported as CVE-2012-0392, has correct confidentiality/integrity impact metrics of Complete and an overall score of 9.3. While, in hindsight, it is clear that the impact of all three issues were the same, the published information is still incorrect: something that can only be revealed by detailed analysis.

Thus, CVSS values can be biased by the understanding of the problem at the time of advisory publication. Therefore, and irrespective of the objectivity of the measure, it may not be appropriate to use CVSS in a temporal context: using it to compare (in)security of an application may lead to incorrect conclusions. The extent to which this may influence the results of past studies is a subject for further investigation.

5.2   Developer's Blind Spots

Anticipating security problems requires a cognitive effort and often is distraction from the main objective of the developer. The research [10] shows that developers often fail to correlate security problems to their workload even if they are aware of the problem in general. Oliveira's experimental hypothesis was that vulnerabilities can be blind spots in developer's heuristic-based decision-making processes: while a programmer focuses on implementing code to meet functional demands, which is cognitively demanding, they tend to assume common, but not edge, cases. Supporting the hypothesis, the study [10] found that 53% of its participants knew about a particular coding vulnerability, however they did not correlate it with an experimental programming activity assigned to them unless it was explicitly highlighted.

Our analysis confirms the existence of this phenomenon in a mature product and experienced team. Even where developers are expected to be aware of the security problems (as they considered them in the past), they may fail to consider them. When the cookie interceptor was implemented, the developers were aware of possible issues related to evaluating OGNL expressions without restrictions. Some of the restrictions were already implemented for the parameters interceptor. Yet, for three years the corresponding protection was not considered for cookies. Similarly, the access to Struts-specific `top` object, that allowed bypassing the excluded parameters list was well understood by the team. The top object facilitates the extensions to OGNL provided in Struts and, as such, it is described in the documentation. However, for almost four years when various parameters were excluded for security reasons, it was not considered in the regular expressions.

Overlooking access to public constructors could also be partially attributed the problem of developers blind spots. While, at first, the developers might have not been aware of the potential security exposure it introduces, it was no longer the case after July 2010, when usage of the constructor was highlighted to the team in the context of another reported vulnerability. Also, the example exploit, included in the advisory published on the Struts website, took advantage of a `Boolean` class constructor. While invoking the constructor was not a primary objective of the attack, it was used to facilitate it. The usage of constructor was not considered when preparing the fix for the previous issue, even though it could have been easily included.

5.3 Opportunistic Fix

When developing the fix for a security problem, developers may prefer an implementation that fits their existing code. While the fix related to the root cause of the problem may be more suitable and more comprehensive, developers tend to develop fixes that are more convenient to implement and that do not cause disruption to the existing code structure.

Preventing modification of context variables or executing custom code was first implemented through simple pattern matching of OGNL expression strings, rather than limiting OGNL's capability to perform these operations, which followed later. As the the reasons for the fix are unknown, our analysis of the source code from 2004 shows that, in the code structure of the time, a more comprehensive solution required major changes in a number of helper classes and, perhaps, in the OGNL itself. Over time, and in response to numerous issues a more comprehensive solution at a lower level was implemented.

Similarly, preventing class loader manipulation was first implemented by adding a pattern to the list of excluded parameters that was already in place. Only after several problems with this approach, and a number incomplete regular expressions, was a more comprehensive fix implemented which involved specification of excluded classes and packages. At the time of writing, the defense against constructor execution, relies solely on the regular expression matching, specifically the lack of the white space among allowed characters. As the regular expressions were by-passed through various tricks, it may be more suitable to include protection against constructor execution at the OGNL level.

Compatibility Problems. Sometimes, implemented fixes are sub-optimal, as a result of issues such as compatibility with older versions and existing consumer workloads. Software consumers may rely on a particular functionality that was subsequently identified as a source of the security problems. Thus there must be a trade-off between a comprehensive fix that breaks consumer's code, and a less comprehensive fix that may be problematic.

In Struts, many of the past attacks were related to execution of static methods. This functionality is not critical, many applications take advantage of it, and this prevented the Struts team disabling it completely as the preferred fix. Instead, static method execution can be enabled through configuration. As a result, the property controlling method execution disablement became a frequent target for other vulnerabilities and allowed escalating any context manipulation issue to remote code execution. Complety turning off this functionality has been planned since 2014 and developers using struts have been warned that it should be considered obsolete. Similarly, the plan to remove the top object, rather then controlling access to it though excluded patterns, was recently announced.

5.4   Counterintuitive Mechanism

Some fixes can mean that security controls in the application can become difficult to understand or counterintuitive. While an application may not, strictly speaking, contain a vulnerability, systems using the application may introduce their own vulnerabilities, due to incorrect usage of the security controls.

The problems of developers not properly understanding the relationship between method access and property exposure was discussed in Sect. 4.2. Anecdotally, many application developers are not aware of the problems arising from implementing public getters/setters for sensitive objects, or are unaware of exposing them through inheriting a class that contains such methods. The Struts team also fall victim to this problem with the `class` property, which has not been considered for over 10 years.

Initially, the `excludeParams` configuration property was not implemented as a security mechanism. It was intended to make the interceptor ignore some of the URL parameters that other layers of the application, such as JavaScript framework dojo, may use for its own purposes (for example `dojo.preventCache`). Such parameters will not have the matching properties in the action classes, and attempting to set them results in errors/exceptions, hence they are easy to spot and include in the configuration. Some patterns (such as `^dojo\..`) were set in the default struts configuration file shipped within Struts JAR file. At that time, it was expected that developers would extend this configuration in their application configuration to add any application-specific parameters. The fact that by setting their set of specific patterns, the developer would overwrite the default pattern was not a concern, as developers were aware of what non-action parameters their application uses and will include a full list.

Then, gradually, security related parameters were added to the list in order to remediate reported vulnerabilities. In order to maintain security, the developer has to find the current set of security related patterns from the default configuration file and include it when specifying, application-specific patterns. In addition, each time the application upgrades to new version of Struts, the process has to be repeated as the new version may contain new patterns. At one point the Struts team itself accidentally became a victim of this process. In version 2.3.20, released in December 2014, the code responsible for applying the patterns has been modified. Most of the patterns had been moved to a separate class that handles pattern matching for both interceptors. The two remaining patterns were kept in the default configuration file. This change overwrote the patterns for security-related properties, such as `class`, by those in the configuration file. As a result, the release 2.3.20 shipped with (effectively) no security related excluded patterns and re-enabling all previously fixed attack vectors. The eventual fix to the problem was moving the two patterns from the configuration to the class itself. The configuration, empty by default, can still override the patterns if set by the application. Now, in order to include their own excluded patterns, the developer has to obtain current version of the default patterns from the Struts Java code and append their own patterns.

Assumptions About Consumers. A factor that contributes to the implementation of a counter-intuitive security mechanism is incorrect assumptions about the consumers' understanding of security mechanisms. The developers may not be aware that a typical consumer does not understand all subtleties of the security framework. In analyzing the discussion on the Struts issue tracking system, we noticed that some of the initial reports on security problems were dismissed, due to a technical ability to counter default insecure behavior by specific configuration or customization. Some of these issues were eventually admitted as vulnerabilities and the default behavior was changed.

Struts developers might have not realized how counterintuitive the management of the `excludeParams` property was until it impacted on themselves. In fact, at the time of publishing the fix for the accidental overwriting (described in the previous section), one of developers opened an issue in the Struts tracking system to change the behavior and make the patterns additive.

Another example of this problem is the exposure of J2EE objects such as session objects or requests through public getters and setters required by dependency injection mechanism, as described in Sect. 4.2. It was assumed that application developers would implement their own protection, such as custom parameter checks. However, it is unlikely that a casual Struts consumer will be aware of such an option or the need to use it. Many application developers are not even aware that implementing a getter to match a setter is required by the interface; this is common Java practice (but clearly poor Struts practice) which can expose sensitive properties such as `session`. At the time of writing, a query [7] to a popular github repository shows 5,237 instances where a class implementing `SessionAware` interface also implements a public `getSession` method. Eventually, access to these objects was recently disabled at OGNL level, regardless of getter/setter access modifiers or their inclusion in the excluded patterns.

5.5   Evolution of Phenonema

During our analysis we noticed that the above-mentioned phenonema tend to appear in the order given in Fig. 3: they evolve as the developer's knowledge about the security problem and understanding of the issue and the consequences of fix increases. At first, the developer may not be aware, or only partially aware, of a potential security problem. This may be caused by incomplete understanding of the full operation of the application or relying on incomplete advisory by the third-party. As they become more aware, they may fail to remediate the problem fully due to blind spots. The fix may be applied only for some scenarios or in some parts of the system. Later, the developer fix may not be sufficiently comprehensive, or fix the root cause of the problem. This may be a result of the the attempt to implement a fix with the least possible effort or due to the technical constraints such as compatibility with previous versions. Finally, the resulting security mechanism may be counter-intuitive resulting in incorrect use by the consumers. Note that the end of the sequence at one level of abstraction may become a starting point for the security problem at higher level, and the counterintuitive mechanism of a framework or the library contributes to the problem with comprehending system's low level details (dark side of the code) of the consuming application.

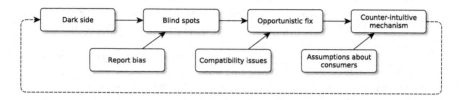

Fig. 3. Phenomena lifecycle

6   Conclusion

A systematic analysis of the Struts interceptor controls was carried out over a 12 year period. A number of phenomena emerged in the evolution of the control, and these provide insights into why insufficient controls were implemented. In addition we observed that the phenomena have their own lifecycle as developers' understanding of security issues increase. Whether this can be useful in improving security processes is a topic of future research.

Acknowledgments. This work was supported, in part, by Science Foundation Ireland under grant SFI/12/RC/2289 and Irish Research Council/Chist-ERA.

References

1. Massacci, F., Neuhaus, S., Nguyen, V.H.: After-life vulnerabilities: a study on firefox evolution, its vulnerabilities, and fixes. In: Erlingsson, Ú., Wieringa, R., Zannone, N. (eds.) ESSoS 2011. LNCS, vol. 6542, pp. 195–208. Springer, Heidelberg (2011). doi:10.1007/978-3-642-19125-1_15
2. Mitropoulos, D., Karakoidas, V., Louridas, P., Gousios, G., Spinellis, D.: Dismal code: Studying the evolution of security bugs. In: Proceedings of the LASER 2013 (LASER 2013), Arlington, VA, pp. 37–48. USENIX (2013)
3. Davidson, D.: Ognl language guide (2004)
4. Kydyraliev, M.: CVE-2010-1870: Struts2/XWork remote command execution. o0o Security Team blog (2010). http://blog.o0o.nu/2010/07/cve-2010-1870-struts2xwork-remote.html . Accessed 21 Jan 2016
5. Kydyraliev, M.: CVE-2011-3923: Yet another Struts2 Remote Code Execution. o0o Security Team blog (2011). http://blog.o0o.nu/2012/01/cve-2011-3923-yet-another-struts2.html. Accessed 21 Jan 2016
6. Long, J.: Struts 2 Session Tampering via SessionAware/RequestAware WW-3631. Code Secure blog (2011). http://codesecure.blogspot.ca/2011/12/struts-2-session-tampering-via.html. Accessed 21 Jan 2016

7. Ashraf, Z.: Analysis of recent struts vulnerabilities in parameters and cookie interceptors, their impact and exploitation. IBM Security Intelligence portal (2014). Accessed 21 Jan 2016
8. Pieczul, O., Foley, S.N.: The dark side of the code. In: Christianson, B., Švenda, P., Matyáš, V., Malcolm, J., Stajano, F., Anderson, J. (eds.) Security Protocols 2015. LNCS, vol. 9379, pp. 1–11. Springer, Cham (2015). doi:10.1007/978-3-319-26096-9_1
9. Dahse, J.: Multiple vulnerabilities in Apache Struts2 and property oriented programming with Java (2011). Accessed 21 Jan 2016
10. Oliveira, D., et al.: It's the psychology stupid: How heuristics explain software vulnerabilities and how priming can illuminate developer's blind spots. In: Proceedings of the Annual Computer Security Applications Conference (2014)

The Evolution of a Security Control

or

Why Do We Need More Qualitative Research of Software Vulnerabilties? (Transcript of Discussion)

Olgierd Pieczul[1,2(✉)] and Simon N. Foley[2]

[1] Ireland Lab, IBM, Dublin, Ireland
olgierdp@ie.ibm.com
[2] Department of Computer Science, University College Cork, Cork, Ireland
simon.foley@imt-atlantique.fr

Hi, my name is Olgierd Pieczul and this is a joint work with Simon Foley. Inspired by the theme of today's workshop we decided to look at evolution of security controls and vulnerabilities.

Today, evolution of software vulnerabilities tends to be researched mostly by using various types of quantitative analysis. These studies often take large numbers of software components, or security advisory records, and process them automatically. Based on that they make broad claims about the health of software security, identify trends, and so forth. These results are, however, somewhat expected, if not entirely, obvious findings. Although quantitative analysis provides some insight into general trends of vulnerability evolution, it does not really help to understand how and why software vulnerabilities and protection mechanims evolve. This is due to the fact that the studies are often based on data that is easy to acquire and process, for example, synthetic metrics such as CVSS. They are straightforward to analyze at a large scale and draw conclusions.

However, if you look at vulnerabilities in more detail, you fill find plenty of valuable information that is much harder to process. Unstructured, data such as bug reports, mailing list discussions or blog posts, that may give some insight into what is really going on and may help you with "why" and "how".

The problem is, how do we process this kind of data? Inspired by qualitative research we attempted to apply qualitative-style techniques to software vulnerabilities analysis. Typically, these techniques take raw, unprocessed data, such as interview transcripts and systematically analyze it in search for emerging themes. An example of that process has been presented at this workshop in 2009, where common expectations related to privacy of sharing photographs were established through a qualitative analysis of interviews.

Of course performing qualitative analysis at the scale seen in quantitative studies is not practical. We decided to perform a small scale experiment. Unlike in quantitative research, where simple metrics are analyzed for a large number

J. Anderson et al. (Eds.): Security Protocols XXIV, LNCS 10368, pp. 85–89, 2017.
DOI: 10.1007/978-3-319-62033-6_10

of security problems, we focused on a single component and looked much deeper into the available information.

The subject of our analysis was Apache Struts, a very popular MVC web framework that is used by a number of products, including enterprise. We scoped our analysis to a specific part of Struts, responsible for dealing with request parameters and cookies. This component automatically extracts parameter and cookie data from HTTP requests and passes it to the underlying application using the OGNL language processor (Apache's Object-Graph Navigation Language used for getting and setting properties of Java objects). This component has had a number of security vulnerabilities over the timeframe of our investigation which was 12 years, from 2004 to 2015. Effectively this was just a single security problem whereby Struts failed to handle the inputting of this data in a secure way. As a result attacker could manipulate the application, execute custom code and so forth.

How did we collect the data? The first, obvious source was official advisories. Many (but not all, as we later found) of these vulnerabilities have been published with CVE numbers and brief descriptions. This provided a base line and gave us an idea how many and what kind of security problems have been fixed by Struts developers. ¿From that we looked at the source code changes. We reviewed the entire source code evolution over the 12 years that related to the security control under study. That process was not particularly easy as the code moved between repositories and within the application structure number of times during the timeframe. Eventually we identified each code change related to every vulnerability. Having done that, we aggregated all the code changes into key categories. The details are included in the paper, but effectively there has been number of distinct areas of the code in which the security control operates: number of white lists and black lists, and different additional mechanisms and so forth. While identifying and aggregating code changes was the first step, we had already observed that the key code changes did not necessarily matched the actual vulnerability reports. This inaccuracy would make us question the veracity of (quantitative) studies that are based on this data alone for tracking vulnerability evolution.

Further, we looked at the bug reports in the project's bug tracking system, these often contain much more information than the public advisories. In particular, the developers comments on the reported issues were of interest. In many cases, we observed lengthy discussions regarding whether a particular issue should be considered a vulnerability, whether it requires a fix and what it should it be. Sometimes, bug reports on security issues were dismissed, only to become acknowledged as vulnerabilities later, and in some cases, years later.

We also investigated a number of blog posts that discussed Struts security. Sometimes the vulnerabilities were discussed into high detail. Usually the authors of the posts were the people who discovered the vulnerabilities or people who performed some post-advisory analysis. An interesting element of the blog posts were the reports on author interactions with the Struts developers, the process they followed, their reactions to the report, and so forth.

Having all of these key code changes identified and correlated with findings from other raw data we identified common phenomena related to vulnerability fixing and security control development. There's not time to go through all of them now, but I will just give you an example of the repeating patterns we have observed. All of the phenomena are discussed in the paper.

One of the findings is that security metrics are notoriously assigned incorrectly. For example, the (effectively) same vulnerability, with almost the same title has been reported three times over four years. Each of the security advisories describes a vulnerability with exactly the same impact and almost identical attack vector. First is for the original vulnerability discovered, while the other two for incomplete fixes that did not remediate the bug completely. Even though, each time the vulnerability has been reported with different severity score, higher each time.

Simon Foley: You could say that as they repeatedly tried to fix the same problem their understanding increased and as a result it was that increased their subjective opinion on the CVSS measure.

Reply: Yes. There were two vulnerabilities, one after another, one being a more general and having an incomplete fix, and the other having fixed to the gap. As you can see the CVSS metrics and the actual severity on the advisory were completely different.

Another phenomena is opportunistic fix. At the slide, you can see several code changes over a number of years related to the same security control. As the request parameters in Struts are interpreted as OGNL statements, and OGNL allows executing arbitrary code, it has to be restricted. Rather than properly disabling certain OGNL features, initially the restriction was enforced using regular expression on the parameter string. Over time, a number of security vulnerabilities related to this was fixed using the same solution that was easily available. However, it was rarely the right way to fix. For example, at one point the developers discovered that an expression for invoking constructors was allowed by the filter. The fix was to remove the white space from the white list as it effectively prevents the constructor expression that requires a space after "new" keyword. While this makes it technically impossible to invoke constructors it definitely is not the proper solution for such a critical vulnerability. However, it only required a single character change in the existing code. We observed that often this, opportunistic of way of fixing bugs led to more security problems later on. Another effect was that, over time, the regular expression became completely incomprehensible. Eventually after number of incomplete fixes the developers decided to apply a proper remediation, that is, disable expression execution at OGNL processor level.

The phenomena we discovered tend form a particular pattern in themselves. Once developers gain more understanding of what the problem is, what is the vulnerability that they are dealing with, what should be the proper solution, they would make different type of mistakes, than they had done at the beginning. It evolves over time and as larger software components are built from smaller, the issues repeat. The improper mechanism implementation on one side increases the misunderstanding of what the software can do on the other side. We find that this repeating nature in the phenomena particularly useful because it may be possible to turn it into a checklist that may be used during the software development process. This helps to understand more on how and why software vulnerabilities appear and evolve.

Simon Foley: For those of you who were at the workshop last year, you might remember the presentation that we gave. We claimed that developers introduce flaws into their code as a result of using APIs in a complete way, and we called this the *dark side of the code*. In that presentation we gave a simple example that nicely illustrated the problem (a developer forgets that a URL 'web address' can have the file method). The example was conjecture in that it seemed reasonable but we didn't have systematic evidence that these kinds of vulnerabilities truly happen, *in the wild*. Today's paper provides the systematic evidence that developers really do make these kinds of mistakes: we looked at the detail of over 300 code changes in struts and found repeated concrete evidence that developers were programming in the dark side. This qualitative result is not note something that can be easily discovered using quantitative techniques.

Reply: Our experiment, at a small scale, provided evidence to support some of the hypotheses of our previous work. Similarly, the developers blind spots phenomena, has been proposed in the past based on a controlled experiment involving interviewing developers. In our study we have seen this developer's blind spots phenomenon on real life made by real people in the real software.

As a closing point, I would like to remark why we think that using metrics is not fit for purpose for looking at security evolution. Over time, gaps in previous fixes appear as new vulnerabilities. This already creates a bias because one only counts vulnerability records they may think of them as independent issues, while in fact, often there are the same issues, just not fixed correctly in the past. Unless you spend time and effort to correlate them, you cannot really draw conclusions about evolution of the software security.

Also, security problems and vulnerabilities are often misunderstood by those who write advisories. Often, they only describe developers' interpretation of what the problem is rather than describe the actual problem. In the paper we have number of examples of advisories with too narrow scope or incorrect impact.

Finally, the severity metrics which we have shown are all often assigned incorrectly and not corrected when true nature of the issue is discovered later on. As we have shown in the example, subsequent instances of the same problem usually have higher severity because they are better understood. It does not mean that software has more severe vulnerabilities, it just means that the previous vulnerabilities had incorrectly assigned low severity which never got corrected.

Any questions? Comments?

Simon Foley: We should consider the debate about the relative values of qualitative versus quantitative research; both can be equally useful or lacking. If you would display again the picture depicting the phenomenon (Fig. 3 in the paper). Remember that these phenomena emerged as a consequence of looking at very large amount of code, vulnerability reports, and so forth, in great detail. Carrying out this qualitative analysis we can point to concrete evidence of developers programming in the dark side, that developers make opportunistic fixes rather, and so on. Now compare that evidence, with the examples that you gave at the start of the talk on results from quantitative studies based for example on CVSS scores. One example was *"In this paper, we examine how vulnerabilities are handled in large-scale, analyzing more than 80,000 security advisories published since 1995. Based on this information, we quantify the performance of the security industry as a whole.* and I ask you, which is the more useful?

Reply: Yes. My message is do less of these (quantitative studies) and do more of that other one (qualitative studies). Of course qualitative studies can be much harder to do, but even doing them in a small scale can give you much better results. Thanks.

Novel Security and Privacy Perspectives of Camera Fingerprints

Jeff Yan(✉)

Security Lancaster,
School of Computing and Communications,
Lancaster University, Lancaster, UK
jeff.yan@lancaster.ac.uk

Abstract. Camera fingerprinting is a technology established in the signal processing community for image forensics. We explore its novel security and privacy perspectives that have been so far largely ignored, including its applications in privacy intrusion, in handling new sociotechnical problems such as revenge porn, and in building a novel authentication mechanism – any photo you take are you.

Keywords: Authentication · Internet-scale privacy intrusion · Revenge porn

1 Introduction

Imaging sensors (CCD or CMOS) are a digital camera's heart. Due to sensor design and imperfections of the sensor manufacturing process, systematic artefacts (usually known as *sensor pattern noises*) form an equivalent of a digital fingerprint that can identify a camera. Such fingerprints are intrinsically embedded in each digital image and video clip created by a digital camera.

Sensor photo-response non-uniformity (PRNU), introduced in [4] in 2006, is a commonly used camera fingerprint to identify a specific camera. Not all pixels demonstrate the same sensitivity to light, and the PRNU captures slight variations among individual pixels in their capability of converting photons to electrons. PRNU fingerprints have good properties for forensic purposes. For example, they are unique to each camera; they are stable and they survive post-image processing and compression, and they do not age.

The research on camera fingerprints have been nearly exclusively done in the signal processing community [1], with a focus on forensic analyses in laboratories such as source camera identification (which camera was used to produce this image?), device linking (were two images produced by the same camera?) and detection of digital image forgery [4,5].

Here, we attempt to initiate and stimulate discussions and investigations surrounding camera fingerprints out of the box of signal processing.

J. Anderson et al. (Eds.): Security Protocols XXIV, LNCS 10368, pp. 90–95, 2017.
DOI: 10.1007/978-3-319-62033-6_11

2   A Novel Authentication Mechanism

Our first idea is that camera fingerprints can be built into various security or cryptographic protocols. In the following, we discuss how to build camera fingerprints into authentication protocols.

The ubiquity of smart phones (each with an embedded camera) provides an interesting opportunity for conceiving a new scheme that authenticates a user to a remote service, and which is both secure and usable. First, for people who use smart phones, their phones are a hardware token that is handy and available nearly all the time. Second, the existence of camera fingerprint makes it feasible to uniquely identify the camera, and consequently the phone and its owner (i.e. the user). Third, if a new scheme requires little hardware modification of phone sets, it has the potential of being deployed quickly and easily to hundreds of millions of users. We name this scheme 'any photos you take are you', which can be either a password alternative, or a secondary authentication method that can be used together with another mechanism, known or to be invented. This scheme can be a building block for mutual authentication protocols, too.

Basic protocols. In its simplest form, our proposal works as follows. In enrolment, each user takes a number of pictures using their phone. For each picture, we subtract a denoised image from the original one to get an estimate of the camera's PRNU. We average multiple PRNU estimates, each obtained from one of the pictures, to derive a reference PRNU, which serves as a unique identification fingerprint for the camera. In authentication, a user takes a new photo using her enroled camera (i.e. phone). A PRNU estimate will be worked out from this new photo, and it will be compared with the reference PRNU. For example, a normalized cross-correlation can be calculated, and if the correlation exceeds a predefined threshold, the user will pass authentication.

This scheme does not impose any memorability burden to users, and it appears to be highly usable and provides cool user experience. It is interesting to empirically evaluate its usability aspects.

However, there is a security problem. If a user has posted online photos taken with the same camera, either before or after she enrols her camera to the authentication system. Bad guys can peel off her PRNU from those photos, and replay it for their own authentication. Even if a challenge-response mechanism is in place, the attack still works. For example, during authentication, the server generates a one-time-use image or a visualized version (e.g. a barcode) of cryptographic materials as a challenge, and requires the user to take a photo of it and send it back as the response. The attacker follows this protocol, but she removes her own PRNU from the photo, adds a legitimate user's PRNU, and then sends the image back to the server. The server can verify the challenge image. However, this freshness verification is no use in verifying that the PRNU sent in the response is freshly read from a camera. It is a challenge to enforce a liveness test of PRNU.

Any phone users are entitled to post any photos taken by their phone camera. To accommodate this premise and in the meanwhile make our authentication mechanism work, one possible solution is to disallow old camera/phones but enrol only new ones. This way, fingerprint leakage before enrolment will not be a concern, and what we will enforce is that fingerprints will not be leaked after enrolment. That is, a photo taken by a camera for user authentication will be sent to the authentication server with the camera fingerprint intact in the image. If a photo is taken to be shared publicly, the camera fingerprint should be removed before the image is posted online.

This solution does not require modifications of smart phones' hardware or operating systems. However, it can face some security usability issues: although we can have a software program in place to alert each user that she should remove the camera fingerprint from each image that is to be publicly shared, she might not comply with the policy or simply forget it.

An alternative solution is to involve phone manufacturers and operating system vendors – Apple is both a phone manufacturer and an OS designer, anyway. A key modification is to enable and enforce a separation of context in smart phones' OS: before a photo is to be posted in the wild, the phone should remove its camera's PRNU from the photo without involving the user; otherwise, the PRNU stays in the picture.

It is a bad idea to grant discretion to a phone owner with regard to when she should tell the phone to remove PRNUs from photos produced. A common lesson from security usability: people have compromised security due to poor usability designs, and they will in the future.

It is better to enforce system-wide low level controls that do not require end user involvement (vs. App level). On the other hand, our proposed application effectively suggests that camera sensors become security critical, and thus they should be accessible only to critical processes, and not accessible to other processes any more. Camera manufacturers and OS designers are in a better position to enforce such policies for both security and usability. For example, they can be implemented with a security API, where keywords such as *for_anth* and *for_others* can be used to separate security context from non-security ones.

We now cannot impose a liveness test on a hardware fingerprint. Probably a step further is for smart phone manufacturers to build in some hardware circuits in their products to solve this problem.

Server side considerations. Several issues will impact the scalability of our solution, and therefore they matter. For example, it is computationally expensive for a server to handle a large number of PRNUs. Efficient fingerprint storage, retrieval and comparison can all contribute to a scalable solution.

Privacy-preserving mutual authentication. In a world where camera fingerprints are critical for user authentication, we will not allow a server to store them in plaintext, as they can and will be leaked and they can be misused by untrustworthy system administrators, too. In this regard, fuzzy hashing designed to handle noisy biometric-type data, instead of cryptographic hashing, can provide some protection. We do not want users to leak their camera fingerprints to a spoofing service (e.g. a phishing site), either. Therefore, a fingerprint should never be sent to a server in plaintext. We envisage that a privacy-preserving protocol is a good solution, where a secure computation of a fingerprint matching algorithm is run to compare a candidate fingerprint with a database of enroled fingerprints. The matching is done in a secure way in that both the privacy of the user and the confidentially of enroled fingerprints are protected. In the end, the matching algorithm will either authenticate or reject a user, but otherwise reveals no information to neither of the parties.

Most camera fingerprint matching algorithms operate on data representations over the real numbers, and thus cannot be used as is in secure computation, where common methods inherently work over finite fields of integers. A straightforward attempt to quantize the real values might lead to unsatisfactory matching performance. Another important factor to consider is the computational power (as well as battery power) available on a mobile phone to execute the protocol. A good design will be a privacy-preserving protocol that is lightweight for the client side. Non-trivial innovations in algorithm and protocol design are warranted.

Evolving (in)security. We are not aware of any perfect algorithm for removing PRNU signals from an image. Typically, image quality after PRNU removal is an important trade-off to considerate. This means, each photo allowed by the system to be posted in the wild contains residual PRNUs. There is a possibility for an adversary to collect such images to reconstruct a useful PRNU, which is potentially a security threat to our design. However, this accumulative PRNU leakage can be measured, and upper and lower bounds for the life cycle of the system to remain secure can be worked out in advance.

An alternative solution is to build some leakage-resistance mechanism in the protocols.

3 Privacy

Most if not all users have posted an enormous amount of footage online without realizing that each of them contains an inherent camera device fingerprint. Such a vast amount of 'unnoticed' fingerprints can be harvested for a consequence, either good or bad. Here, we briefly discuss that camera fingerprints are useful both for privacy intrusion and privacy protection.

Privacy invasion at the Internet-scale. It has been a hot topic in security and privacy communities in the recent several years to apply stylometry (i.e. writing style analysis) to identity-level identification and similarity detection on the Internet, e.g. [2,3]. Camera fingerprints can achieve similar effects, alone, and when used together, they can augment the power of stylometry. However, there is no single such study in the literature yet. We envisage that camera fingerprint will prove an effective method for privacy invasion in many contexts, for example:

- Revealing people who post photos anonymously;
- Linking multiple digital personas, e.g. multiple accounts on social networking sites, owned by the same people;
- Complementing stylometry for cybercrime and forensic investigations.

What else threat models are interesting and relevant?

Fight against revenge porn. As a relatively new socio-technical problem, revenge porn is sexually explicit footages (images or video clips) that are publicly shared online, without the consent of the pictured or videotaped individual. These materials are typically uploaded to the Internet to humiliate and intimidate a former partner, who has broken off an intimate relationship. Victims of revenge porn often suffer devastating consequences, due to its nature of psychological abuse and domestic violence. With the increasing number of reported incidents, several countries including the UK, Australia and some states in the USA have gradually had laws in place to outlaw the practice of revenge porn, but most countries do not (yet).

Camera fingerprints provide a viable technical solution for identifying and detecting revenge porn online. For example, if you worry about an ex-partner to upload revenge porn, you can pass on some other footage produced with a concerned camera to an engineer, who will then extract PRNUs and search online images and videos that have similar PRNU fingerprints.

We are not aware of any other technical solution that is available on the market or in the literature for the same purpose. A seemingly reasonable approach is to combine porn detection, face detection and face recognition. However, it is challenging for these techniques to achieve low false positives and negatives. As such, our proposal is likely the best solution for quickly locating revenge porn online. Then the victim can request to take down the offensive materials, use them as prosecution evidence, or whatever suitable.

Camera fingerprints provide a simple 'side channel' approach to an otherwise complicated problem.

4   Concluding Remarks

Camera fingerprints provide an interesting case, where forensics, security and privacy issues interplay with each other. The ubiquity of digital cameras implies that the issues facing camera fingerprints are not just of academic interests, but of important practical relevance. Security and privacy issues surrounding camera fingerprints have been largely ignored, but they are bound to lead to a large body of interesting technical research in the future. It is also interesting to see policy debates around camera fingerprints. For example, what and how will Facebook do with camera fingerprints embedded in the large amount of user-generated photos on their popular website?

Acknowledgements. I thank Mike Bond, James Lei, Laurent Simon, Bingsheng Zhang and the workshop attendees for discussing some of the ideas.

References

1. Liu, B.B., Wei, X., Yan, J.: Enhancing sensor pattern noise for source camera identification: an empirical evaluation. In: Proceeding of 3rd ACM Workshop on Information Hiding and Multimedia Security. pp. 85–90 (2015)
2. Afroz, S., Caliskan-Islam, A., Stolerman, A., Greenstadt, R., McCoy, D.: Doppelgänger finder: taking stylometry to the underground. In: IEEE Security and Privacy (2014)
3. Narayanan, A., Paskov, H., Gong, N., Bethencourt, J., Stefanov, E., Shin, R., Song, D.: On the feasibility of internet-scale author identication. In: Proceedings of the 33rd Conference on IEEE Symposium on Security and Privacy. IEEE (2012)
4. Lukas, J., Fridrich, J., Goljan, M.: Digital camera identication from sen-sor pattern noise. IEEE Trans. Inf. Forensics Secur. **1**(2), 205–214 (2006)
5. Chen, M., Fridrich, J., Goljan, M., Lukas, J.: Determining image origin and integrity using sensor noise. IEEE Trans. Inf. Forensics Secur. **3**(1), 74–90 (2008)

Novel Security and Privacy Perspectives
of Camera Fingerprints
(Transcript of Discussion)

Jeff Yan[(✉)]

University of Lancaster, Lancaster, UK
jeff.yan@lancaster.ac.uk

I will talk about three very simple ideas about camera fingerprints. I didn't have time to put all the details in my slides, so please feel free to ask for any clarification or any question anytime. I didn't realize until it was too late that my laptop charger didn't work, and Ross came to my rescue just a while ago. I borrowed his charger and did some quick-hack slides.

First of all, some quick backgrounds about camera fingerprints. On the left-hand side, this is human fingerprints which is used for many security applications. On the right-hand side, this is a camera fingerprint which can be used to identify individual digital cameras.

The first question: Where does this camera fingerprint come from? We know that CCD or CMOS sensors are a digital camera's heart. Most cameras use CCD sensors, but some use CMOS sensors. All these sensors are made in semiconductor foundries. The sensor manufacturing process is critical, but never perfectly controlled.

Therefore, each sensor in a CCD or CMOS chip responds to light differently. The difference is not huge, and each pixel responds to light in a slightly different way. The effect collectively is that all pixels in the camera will leave systematic artifacts in each image created by this particular camera or video camera.

A way of modelling or capturing this slight variation under illumination is called PRNU or Photo Response Non-Uniformity. Basically, PRNU captures variations among each individual pixels in their capability of converting photons to electrons. That's actually the physical nature of camera fingerprints.

A high-level concept is like this illustration. The first image is an image produced by a camera, and we can consider that this image is a combination of a perfect image, or a pure image, and a camera fingerprint. This camera fingerprint captures the variation of pixel responsivity under illumination for all pixels. That's why the dimension of a camera fingerprint is large, the same size as the image.

If we want to get the camera fingerprint, we apply signal processing methods to the original image to get a pure (sort of) image without noise. When we remove this pure image from the original image, the remaining image is mostly of noise signals, which are the camera's fingerprint. That's the high-level concept.

This line of research was started in the electronic engineering community and there are several known applications. For example, source camera identification.

© Springer International Publishing AG 2017
J. Anderson et al. (Eds.): Security Protocols XXIV, LNCS 10368, pp. 96–102, 2017.
DOI: 10.1007/978-3-319-62033-6_12

The question to answer is, if the police have confiscated some cameras, they'd be interested to know: which camera was used to produce a known porn image?

You have an offensive image, and you have a set of suspicious cameras. Then via camera fingerprint you can trace back the source camera which was used to produce the image. The police have particular interest in this application of source camera identification.

Another application that the police are interested is device linkage. You might have physical access to cameras or might not, but you are interested to answer this question: whether two images are produced by the same camera.

The third application is detecting digital image forgery. If you modified some images, by examining camera fingerprints in the images, you can detect this kind of forgery. All these known applications are for forensics purposes. Good algorithms for extracting camera fingerprints are important for these applications.

When I became interested in camera fingerprint, I had a look at the literature, which unfortunately was very chaotic, to say the least. Many fingerprint extraction algorithms had been published by then, but it's funny enough, nearly everybody claims that, "My method is the best." When you look at a single paper, by looking at its experiment results and curves and figures in the paper, the numbers in the paper do suggest that their method looks like the best. But when you put together all these papers, you don't know which one you're going to trust.

Another problem is, all the studies are hardly comparable because their experiment configurations were never consistent. Images used are different. Extraction methods are different. Comparison metrics, different too. It's very surprising and chaotic.

I decided to do a controlled experiment, which is expensive and meticulous, but I wanted to understand whether this line of work is indeed useful or not. We spent quite some time, but I think we got some good results with this experiment. At least we understand a lot of misconceptions in the literature and we also understand how to best extract camera fingerprints.

We wrote up a paper, which on one hand is well-received. It's highly commended by the PC committees and the leading researcher of camera fingerprints. They all say that this is a very good piece of research. On the other hand, this paper was hated by some people because we basically put together all those competing methods under the same testing condition to see which is indeed good. Of course, our results contradict many research teams' claims.

We had our paper published last year at ACM Information Hiding and MMSec, which was started by Ross 20 years ago as Information Hiding Workshop, but has evolved into a premium venue in the fields of information hiding, and multimedia security and forensics. I think the most important output from our experiment is that we've gained confidence that indeed, camera fingerprint is not snake oil.

The reason that I decided to do this very expensive experiment (in terms of human resources) was simple: I had three simple ideas which I wanted to build on the experiment.

Jonathan Anderson: Did the fingerprints survive transformations like RAW-to-JPEG and re-scaling and things like that?

Reply: Yes, the fingerprints survive all those image processing procedures.

Frank Stajano: Frank Stajano. I have a maybe related question. In moderately high-end cameras like prosumer and that thing, there are facilities to eliminate noise on the sensors, as you have hair or dust, by taking picture of a blank screen and then, if we are presenting, the camera then subtracts that. Would that remove also the camera fingerprint?

Reply: No. Those kind of operations will not remove the fingerprints.

Frank Stajano: Why is that?

Reply: Because camera fingerprints are unlike noise caused by hair or dust. As PRNU captures slight variations among individual pixels in their capacity of converting photon to electrons, camera fingerprints come from such a low-level effect. That's, the thing is deep at the bottom of an image, and manifests intrinsically in each pixel.

Frank Stajano: If each picture taken by the camera is then corrected by this presumably static bias that you examine by taking natural picture, how would this not also eliminate these differences?

Reply: The reason is that you need the specific algorithms to extract this fingerprint. You can decrease the quality of the fingerprint by doing some random processing, but the fingerprint will not be destroyed unless you know exactly their extracting algorithms. If you know this algorithm, indeed you can remove the fingerprints.

To give a history background, many years ago, actually before electronic engineers started this topic, this phenomenon of camera fingerprint was known in astronomy. Why? Because they had huge cameras. They wanted to capture images of outer space. In these areas, their image signals are very weak. If you allow weak noise signals like PRNU, then the pictures taken by those huge cameras would be useless for astronomy researchers.

Thirty years back, those people actually had to spend a lot of money to suppress noise signals like PRNU. For hugely expensive cameras, they can claim camera fingerprints do not exist because they're suppressed, but for consumer cameras, PRNU fingerprints are there.

Frank Stajano: You test after the dust removals?

Reply: Yeah.

We tested 50 different models of cameras.

The first idea we want to explore is to build camera fingerprint into security protocols. For example, an obvious application would be authentication. We've had in mind a new authentication scheme, 'any photo you take are you'.

The motivation is simple because now actually a lot of research efforts aim to get people to use hardware tokens for authentication in their daily lives. But deployment is a challenging issue. In our case, it's good for us because camera phones are everywhere. If our authentication scheme works well, it's easy to have a large-scale deployment.

To explain how our idea works, let's look at a simplified basic protocol. There is first an enrolment process, where each camera is enroled to our system. Each camera will take many photos, and each of these photos will be used to extract a fingerprint for the same camera. Each extracted fingerprint will be averaged to produce a high-quality fingerprint. We want keep high-quality fingerprints as reference fingerprints.

Then, when the user comes for authentication, she takes a photo of anything, and send the photo to an authentication server. The server will extract a camera fingerprint from the photo, and the fingerprint will be compared with a reference fingerprint stored.

This comparison can be complex. It's not a yes or no binary decision, but calculating a pixel-wise correlation, typically called a normalized cross correlation, which involves with some matrix manipulations.

Of course, there are many issues with this basic protocol. For example, fingerprint leakage would be a serious problem, because a lot of people use their cameras, use their phones to take photos and post them online, but these images will contain camera fingerprints. Adversaries can easily do a fingerprint replay attack. Initially, I thought a challenge–response mechanism might work against such replay attacks, but it doesn't.

The main lesson is the following. The common techniques for verifying message freshness in security protocols don't guarantee a camera fingerprint's liveness.

One possible solution is not to allow a user to enrol an old camera. If we enforce a policy that a user can enrol his camera only when it's fresh, i.e. a new camera, then we would not worry about images leaked before enrolment. Then afterwards, we'll enforce that fingerprints will not be leaked from the system.

This means, for authentication purposes, the system will keep a camera fingerprint intact in each image and send the image to the authentication server, but otherwise, if a user wants to post a photo online, then this image should be processed first – effectively, the fingerprint should be removed before the image leaves the camera.

The advantage of this solution is that it doesn't require hardware modification. It doesn't require a modified operating system, either. But there could be some serious security usability issues because users might forget to remove fingerprints. Although we can have a software program to alert each user that she should remove the camera fingerprint from each image that is to be publicly shared, she might not actually comply with the policy or she might forget it.

To address this problem, a solution is to introduce system level controls deciding for which images their camera fingerprints should be removed and for which the fingerprints will stay. Basically, this intends not to involve with any users in this decision-making process. The good thing, compared to the previous solution, is that we will have good usability and security, but the disadvantage is that we might have to modify a phone's operating system.

Of course, there is space to design a lot of fancier authentication protocols. For example, we shouldn't allow servers to store camera fingerprints in plain text because they are very sensitive materials, and we want to prevent the servers from leaking those camera fingerprints. We also should prevent users from leaking their camera fingerprints to a phishing site. It's important to protect a users privacy as well as the confidentiality of reference fingerprints. A common line of research on privacy-preserving authentication protocols is highly relevant here.

So far it's all about our first idea.

The second idea is about privacy. The motivation is very simple. A lot of digital images and video clips are available online, and most people do not even realize the existence of camera fingerprints in these images. We can conceive some privacy intrusion studies.

For example, we can use camera fingerprints to reveal people who post photos anonymously and we can link people who have multiple digital personas, for example, multiple accounts on social networking sites. We can link them together by exploring camera fingerprints.

In the security literature, there are a lot of papers talking about writing style analysis (or stylometry) for privacy intrusion, but there is not a single paper looking into privacy invasion based on camera fingerprints. Camera fingerprints can also complement stylometry for cybercrime investigation.

Frank Stajano: Frank Stajano. I guess, unless people go to extreme lengths to scrub their photos before posting them online, in fact, the metadata that's embedded in the JPEGs or whatever already has the serial number of the camera, the model and blah blah blah, so you don't have to go to very fancy things for de-anonymizing 99% of photos.

Reply: Some sites do remove those metadata, but they do not remove camera fingerprints.

Frank Stajano: Which sites remove metadata?

Jonathan Anderson: I think Flickr is an option.

Reply: Flickr, Yes. I'm not sure of Facebook because I do not use Facebook.

Frank Stajano: I thought that Flickr made a big deal of showing you all the metadata on photos. [inaudible] Interesting.

Reply: What I'm interested is, what are other interesting threat models in this study of privacy invasion. The result could be alarming if we have a number of interesting threat models and if we show this privacy intrusion method is very effective.

Bill Roscoe: It seems to me that anyone with whom I authenticate myself using this method will know my fingerprint and therefore potentially be able to steal my identity, so there's not really a strong form of signature, if you like, as with many cryptographic primitives.

Reply: Yes. You're right. Camera fingerprint can be used to trace you, and identify you.

Bill Roscoe: In other words, if anybody comes to verify, if I reveal my signature, he will know my signature. Therefore, potentially, forge photos with my signature.

Reply: That's true. If we use camera fingerprint for authentication, your camera becomes very sensitive, like biometrics. Therefore, privacy-preserving protocols are important for protecting the fingerprint, as I mentioned earlier.

Jiří Kůr: I was wondering if a server could use the fingerprint for remote attestation of an application platform, and the server connects to the application, takes a picture, and okay, then the fingerprint [inaudible]. The server can authenticate the remote device by taking a picture and verifying if the fingerprint is there.

Reply: Yeah, that's actually the first idea I was talking about, using the fingerprint as an authentication mechanism.

Jiří Kůr: I was talking about maybe a different context, that basically the server authenticates the device. Yeah. Sorry, probably you're right. I'm not sure.

Reply: Never mind. We can actually discuss that offline.

Jiří Kůr: Okay.

Reply: The last slide.

My third idea is using the camera fingerprint to fight against revenge porn. What's revenge porn? It's a relatively new socio-technical problem, where an ex-partner posts online a victim's sexually explicit photos or video clips. There are many incidents reported in the news.

Several countries now outlaw revenge porn, but many do not. There's no technical solution to this problem. A possible defense is to combine porn detection, face detection and face recognition, but they all have false positives and false negatives, and will not offer a good solution to the detection of revenge porn.

I think camera fingerprint looks like a good and simple solution, because if you have a concerned camera or you have access to other images produced by the camera, then you can extract their fingerprints from those devices or images. Then you do online search. Sort of like camera fingerprints provide a simple 'side channel' approach to an otherwise complicated problem.

Hugo Jonker: How would you technically identify that this is a malicious posting?

Reply: I think that's not my concern, because I assume the victim or anybody who worry about the sexually explicit photos or videos posted, will come to ask for help, and I will ask her for other images taken by the same camera, the concerned camera, or I will ask for her camera so that I can establish a camera fingerprint from there. Then I use this to . . .

Hugo Jonker: I understand that part, but I'm just wondering, if you find a bunch of pictures but you wouldn't know if those were consensual or non-consensual.

Reply: The victim would know.

Hugo Jonker: The victim would know, and you wouldn't. So you're not proposing a technical method to automatically determine whether or not it's . . .

Reply: No. You are right.

Hugo Jonker: So this is essentially a search service. . . ?

Reply: You are right. This can be a search service that help the victims.

Hugo Jonker: So this is essentially a search function . . . find porn starring you online?

Reply: Yes.

Frank Stajano: You'd mostly find all the other photos that this camera has taken of deserts and flowers and so on that were ever posted on Flickr, right?

Reply: Yeah.

Audience: Would the platforms that are used for this revenge porn be interested in collaboration? Why would they care? As a way to fight this problem as a whole, why would the platforms care . . .

Reply: Victims care.

Audience: But if they make money on high volumes of people viewing their content, then they don't really care. They are used to . . .

Reply: Victims care, and this is also actually a crime in some countries. The law enforcement there would care, too.

Audience: Yes, but the offender, if they want to use this kind of revenge on somebody, they may use the platform that's not interested in collaborating, in a country where jurisdiction doesn't really prosecute this kind of activity.

Reply: You're right, but that still can be tackled with our technical approach, right? We can identify revenge porn for the victims and then take the proper measures, for example, taking down those images.

Hugo Jonker: I think this will provide evidence in civil court cases.

Reply: Yeah. Exactly.

Hugo Jonker: You can show it's your camera, it was coming from your camera, and now the photos are there.

Reply: Yeah. For countries where revenge porn is outlawed, of course this service will produce evidence, so you can sue the bad guy.

Exploiting Autocorrect to Attack Privacy

Brian J. Kidney[✉] and Jonathan Anderson

Department of Electrical and Computer Engineering,
Memorial University, St. John's, Newfoundland and Labrador, Canada
{brian.kidney,jonathan.anderson}@mun.ca

Abstract. Text prediction algorithms present in many devices use machine learning to help a user type but they also present the opportunity to leak information about the user. This raises privacy and security concerns for users that are trying to remain anonymous. We present an attack inspired by IND–CPA to demonstrate how autocorrect could be used to identify a user. We show that, with prior knowledge of the user, they could be identified with as little as 512 kB of written text with a probability of 95%.

1 Introduction

Predictive text systems are a staple of modern mobile operating systems. Designed to help speed up the process of typing, these systems use both the current input and knowledge gained about the user over time to predict or correct the word that is being typed. This is often seen as a benefit to the end user, however there are security implications that should be considered. In this paper we show that the learning abilities of this class of software can be exploited to reveal personal information or even the identity of a user.

Predictive text systems are not a new concept. In 1970, Smith and Goodwin discussed a prediction system for touch tone phones which worked in environments where the possible inputs were limited [1]. The first universally available algorithm used on mobile phones was T9. This algorithm uses a dictionary to predict the most likely word typed on a standard 10–digit keypad, offering alternatives if the guess is wrong [2].

Modern text prediction systems go further, starting with a standard dictionary and adding a user–defined dictionary where words are added as they are used by the end user. These additions can be made in various ways depending on the capabilities of the system. Basic systems will learn new words as they are used or corrections as they are made. Words commonly typed that are not part of the base dictionary will get added over time. Likewise, common corrections made by the user will get added. More sophisticated systems can even analyze the user's online writings to populate the custom dictionary.

Using these dictionaries, these algorithms can employ multiple machine learning techniques for prediction but are generally based on a model of the language using hidden Markov models that adapt to the user's choice of words over time [3]. These models, however, can leak information about the user, especially

© Springer International Publishing AG 2017
J. Anderson et al. (Eds.): Security Protocols XXIV, LNCS 10368, pp. 103–109, 2017.
DOI: 10.1007/978-3-319-62033-6_13

when said user is trying to remain anonymous. For example, consider the scenario of a whistleblowing scientist communicating with a journalist. The scientist could take many precautions to conceal their identity, such as temporary email addresses and anonymizing proxy such as Tor. However, if the whistleblower was to use their standard keyboard on their mobile device, prediction models could result in unique text patterns that could identify them. For instance, if autocorrect was to mistakenly change a common word to a technical term specific to the whistleblower's field. If sent unnoticed by the user the incorrect prediction could reveal to the journalist that the author worked for the Department of Health and not the Department of Defense, for example.

In this paper we consider the implications of text prediction with machine learning. We enumerate multiple attacks that can be made on these systems – with physical access to the device and without. Finally we propose an attack inspired by Indistinguishability under Chosen Plaintext Attack (IND-CPA).

2   Attacking Predictive Text Systems

The most direct way to exploit predictive text systems is through the user dictionary. If an adversary can get access to this dictionary, they can extract all the words added to reveal information about the user. Although this could be done with physical access to the phone, there are some engines which sync their database with the cloud, where the dictionaries could also be compromised. Once the attacker has access to the dictionary, the contents of the file can reveal personal details about the victim based on the words and phrases they most commonly use. For example, a user with a drug addiction may have a dictionary that contain words used in drug culture, not usually found on a standard user's device.

Access to the dictionary file itself is not a requirement to exploit the text prediction system. In many implementations an attacker with physical access to the phone can simply start choosing the default suggestion for each word when entering text. In a well trained system, this will reveal the most common phrases typed by the victim.

In the following section we outline an attack that does not require physical access to the phone. We present a theoretical attack that can identify a user through autocorrect text and known writings that have been acquired in advance. We then propose a more practical extension of the attack for real world implementation.

3   Chosen Message Text Attack

Our attack on a predictive text system is inspired by the game procedures for indistinguishability under chosen plaintext attack (IND–CPA) [4]. Under the rules for IND–CPA, an adversary submits two plaintext, M_0 and M_1, to a challenger. The challenger secretly chooses which message, M_0 or M_1, will be encrypted for all rounds, encrypts and returns it. The adversary can then submit additional plaintext pairs for encryption until they feel confident in guessing which message is being encrypted.

In our attack the challenger is presented with two sets of training data from which to train a predictive text system. The challenger chooses one of the two sets to use throughout the game. The attacker then sends the challenger text which must be processed through the prediction system with the default suggestion chosen. The attacker can send as many texts as they like until they are ready to guess the "identity" of the challenger.

The attacker can use any method necessary to identify the training set chosen by the challenger. To make the attack more realistic, we assume the attacker does not have access to the same prediction model trained with identical data sets as the challenger. In that scenario it would be trivial for the attacker to reach the correct guess. All that would be required would be to find a small piece of text that, when input into both models, results in different outputs. We assume the attacker has access to a subset of the training data used for the challengers models, representing their ability to find writing samples from outside the attack scenario (previous conversations, publicly available written works, etc.) In our experiments the attacker uses this data in a naive Bayesian classifier to determine the author presented by the challenger.

4   Implementation of Attack

In order to implement our chosen message text attack two programs are required, a text prediction engine and a text classifier. For the prediction engine we chose the autocomplete Python library by Palacios [5]. This engine is based on the work of Norvig [6] and uses a hidden Markov model, a technique commonly found in autocomplete engines. It also allows for the user to provide their own corpus with which the model is trained.

We chose to use a naive Bayesian classifier to classify the resulting text output from the prediction engine. This type of classifier is commonly used as a part of anti–spam engines to separate wanted and unwanted emails. In our implementation, the naive Bayesian technique is used to separate between two possible authors. We use a version of the algorithm by Graham–Cumming [7].

For our proof of concept we chose to try to detect between predictions engines trained using the works of Mark Twain and Jane Austen, loosely representing the differences between American and British English. Text of their works were downloaded from Project Gutenberg and used to train both the prediction engine and classifier. In the case of the classifier, the corpora were truncated to the same size. This step was taken to ensure that there was no bias between the possible classifications due to a better trained classifier.

For our initial testing, we used a naive approach to choosing the text for the attack. The material was taken from ten contemporaries of Twain and Austen such as Dickens, Doyle, Joyce, and Woolf. This material was chosen as it would have a broad use of vocabulary and is from a time period that would not include references to newer technologies or concepts not found in the works of Twain or Austen.

Project Gutenberg texts have a standard format at the beginning of the file and a license agreement at the end. These portions of the texts have been stripped from the files. Additionally, the first chapter of each text has been stripped to avoid repetition they may occur in the authors styles. The modified texts are used to provide baseline numbers for the probability of success.

5   Results and Discussion

For our experiments we trained the predictive text engine with two megabytes of data for both the American and British variants of English. The naive Bayesian classifier was provided with varying lengths of training data in an effort to determine the amount of prior knowledge required to successfully identify an author. The results of the experiments are summarized in Fig. 1.

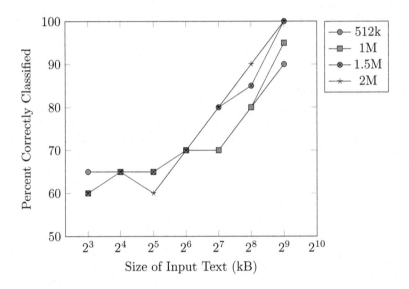

Fig. 1. Results of experiments with varying training data sizes.

Experiments were run restricting the input to the prediction engine to four characters (or less for smaller words). The prediction function used employed both the current word and the previous, so by limiting the current word input it was assumed the function would have more opportunity to expose language pattern. This could also increase the number of errors in the final text; in practice this is not unusual for autocorrect systems.

The attack presented shows that a user can be identified using the output of their text prediction system. These is an 80% chance of identifying a user using one 256 kB of data, if one megabyte of training data is used for our naive Bayesian classifier. This percentage increase to 95% with 512 kB of text from the user. We also show there is 80% chance of correct classification with as little as 128 kB of data, if the attacker has the full corpus used to train the user's autocorrect engine. This scenario is considered impractical but it is presented for comparison purposes.

With smaller amounts of data it is expected that the technique would get the classification right with a 50% probability. However as can be seen in Fig. 1, the technique works slightly better with 512k of training data in all but one case. The entropy of the training data and the experiment's sensitivity to certain word are the cause. As can be seen in Fig. 2, the entropy of the data is consistently higher for the works of Mark Twain even through the training set are of the same size. This produces a bias toward classifying text as American when small amounts of data are used. Additionally, the approach is sensitive to the existence of the "our" words like "favourite" in the input texts from Doyle, which increases the likelihood of a correct classification with low amounts of data.

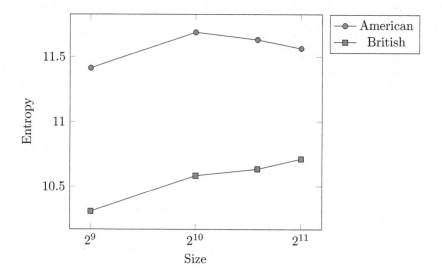

Fig. 2. Entropy of Naive Bayesian training sets

The text prediction system used was based on the fundamental techniques employed when implementing these systems. It is conjectured by the authors that prediction systems with more sophisticated methods would be easier to exploit. Using a prediction system that takes into account longer phrases could better identify an author. This is particularly true in areas with unique dialects and sayings. Having greater knowledge of the end user would only result in a more unique output, making the user easier to identify.

Similarly, better techniques could be used by the attacker. Naive Bayesian classification was useful for the initial implementation due to its simplicity.

Similar to the prediction engine, we could employ algorithms that process entire phrases. More powerful techniques such as deep learning used for author attributions may lead to better results [8].

Our examples were constructed with public domain texts as a proof of concept for the attack. A more sophisticated attacker should work to craft more specific inputs to the prediction engine. Since we were looking to identify the difference between American and British English, we could improve our attack by increasing the use of words were spellings difference in this variants for English. For example use of words such as colour (color), honour (honor) and specialise (specialize) would increase the likelihood of correctly identifying the author.

6   Conclusions and Future Directions

We have presented a theoretical attack on the privacy of an autocorrect user, inspired by IND–CPA. A proof of concept implementation shows that an attacker has a 95% chance of uniquely identifying an author with as little as 512 kB of text using this technique. These are initial results of our work and arise from experimentation with little optimization.

It remains as future work to investigate the optimization of this attack with various approaches for text prediction, classification, and message crafting. More sophisticated autocorrect engines, such as those used in Android and iOS, need to be tested for comparison to our simplified algorithm. Different classification techniques may also lead to better results, requiring less text from the user. Finally, we could look at better crafting our attack messages to expose the difference between the authors we are identifying.

Based on our results we believe that text prediction should be a concern where privacy is required or simply desired. In many situations where precautions have been taken, naive use of an autocorrect engine could negate the user's safety nets and leak identifying data. Although there are applications and services that offer communication with anonymity (for example, Whisper and PostSecret) their scope does not usually include the user's keyboard. In order to ensure the privacy of their users, service should disable predictive text where possible and where not advise their users to do so.

References

1. Smith, S.L., Goodwin, N.C.: Alphabetic data entry via the touch-tone pad: a comment. Hum. Fact. J. Hum. Fact. Ergon. Soc. **13**(2), 189–190 (1971)
2. Grover, D., King, M., Kuschler, C.: Patent no. US5818437, reduced keyboard disambiguating computer. Tegic communications, Inc., Seattle (1998)
3. Rabiner, L.R., Juang, B.-H.: An introduction to hidden Markov models. IEEE ASSP Mag. **3**(1), 4–16 (1986)
4. Goldwasser, S., Micali, S.: Probabilistic encryption. J. Comput. Syst. Sci. **28**(2), 270–299 (1984)
5. Palacios, R.: Autocomplete or: how I learned to stop spelling and love our AI overlords. https://github.com/rodricios/autocomplete. Accessed 29 Jan 2016

6. Norvig, P.: How to write a spelling corrector. http://norvig.com/spell-correct.html. Accessed 29 Jan 2016
7. Graham-Cumming, J.: Naive Bayesian text classification. Dr. Dobb's J. **372**, 16–20 (2005)
8. Bandara, U., Wijayarathna, G.: Deep neural networks for source code author identification. In: Lee, M., Hirose, A., Hou, Z.-G., Kil, R.M. (eds.) ICONIP 2013. LNCS, vol. 8227, pp. 368–375. Springer, Heidelberg (2013). doi:10.1007/978-3-642-42042-9_46

Exploiting Autocorrect to Attack Privacy
(Transcript of Discussion)

Brian J. Kidney[✉]

Memorial University, St. John's, Canada
brian.kidney@mun.ca

So motivation here: Ms. X contacts a journalist with some classified information, a classic whistle blower. Precautions have been taken toward to conceal location and to conceal the traffic. Some burner email addresses, the sort of stuff that, I don't know, if I'd know everything you have to do but if you're gonna get into this, you'd probably do a better research about. Access the internet using a mobile phone at random cafes, so never tied to a single internet access point or what not. Report breaks in the news, heads must roll. Authorities can narrow a suspect list based on the type of information. Who might have had access and stuff like that. But no one's breaking, they can't figure out who it is. And this is a bit of a contrived example but it's a motivation for this. The question is, did the suspect make a mistake?

The mistake if anyone was paying attention to the previous slide that I think they made is I put mobile phone in italics. Because mobile phones have an interesting, property in that they use predictive text. So, MS. X did not consider cell phones autocorrect. This is, this is my hypothesis. There's, there's a security concern here based on autocorrect. Predictive text just for a matter of history, it's been around since the 70's. We've, some of the earlier systems that were described were using phones to connect to servers and potentially do certain operations on them. They were very limited based on, you know, where you were on the server and the types of operations you could do and you only had so many keys. So it would try and figure out what you wanted to do. When texting became popular these old style phones had a system called T9 and people got very fast at typing messages using T9. People that were much better with phones than me. But it was very much dictionary based.

It was preloaded dictionary and this set of keys was probably going to be this word. When we moved to smart phones and we got keyboards and more specifically virtual keyboards where things could go wrong. You're not hitting a key or not getting that tactile response, we started adding newer systems. And these newer systems began to learn more and more about their users in order to help the user. It was the idea we will teach my phone or an online service or whatever it happens to be as much as I can about me, and my phone will be able to predict what it is I was trying to say. So can we exploit the autocorrect's engine to reveal the knowledge about the end user? It knows a lot about you. It is, you know, based on your corrections over time, it is learning your hobbies and your language patterns. You know, it learns that you commonly mistype one word and you mean something else. It learns a lot.

© Springer International Publishing AG 2017
J. Anderson et al. (Eds.): Security Protocols XXIV, LNCS 10368, pp. 110–118, 2017.
DOI: 10.1007/978-3-319-62033-6_14

So when I first started the research, I sort of proposed a chosen message attack, and it's in the paper. It's inspired by the game mechanics of indistinguishability chosen plain text attack. It's not really based on the attack itself, just sort of the game mechanism. So if you're familiar with it, you'll see the similarities here. The challenger has two training sets to train a particular text engine, and must choose from one of those to use for the entire game. So the challenger decides it's going to be person X or person Y for the entire game. The adversary submits text snippets and the challenger must enter them into the engine choosing the default result. And we will repeat until necessary until the adversary is ready to guess which training set or which user is being used. I thought this might be an interesting way to sort of attack the thing but before we could do that, I needed evidence. At, at this point in time, this was, oh, sorry, yeah.

Frank Stajano: So one thing you said on the previous slide is it would accept the default result. Now one of the most known things about these autocorrect is that it is suggesting that most of them are wrong. And so you have to say I didn't mean for you to correct that, I would not be correct if I didn't correct the autocorrect, why would they never do that?

Brian Kidney: This is based on the fact that most people are very much unlike you. There are a lot of websites dedicated to the humorous examples of what happens when you just keep typing. A lot of users of Smartphones, it seems to me that I, I don't have any statistics on this. But they will just type and type and type and autocorrect just solving the problem as they go and then they hit submit and you get a website called damn you autocorrect. Where you get all kinds of crazy examples. I've, I know a couple who constantly post the messages that the husband wrote because he's really bad at typing and he doesn't pay attention. And for years he's been making the same mistakes but he doesn't, he wants to get something out quick. So it is based on that sort of behavior. If you are very careful there's, there might be a bit of a flaw in the attack, if you're very careful. But most people aren't going to be that careful about it.

Frank Stajano: We are talking about the user who was going to the cyber caf on purpose and doing this and using those?

Brian Kidney: Yeah, but it, it seems to me that when you read a lot about, like if, there is a great article, it's not the Guardian, it might have been the Guardian, on what Snowden, Edward Snowden did to cover his tracks. And it even actually admits that he made one mistake along the way with an email address that he used for too long. But it talks about a lot of what he did but it doesn't seem to talk about like being careful about other things. We commonly think about not being tied to a certain IP address encrypting all the communications. We don't sort of think about the things that are in our phones commonly so let's say we have a non-technical person, they know that there's a bit of trouble. They may do enough research, they might read that article and then realize there's a few things they have to do but they won't see other things that could potentially be a problem.

Frank Stajano: I guess this ties in with history talk that is not here. Until it's pointed out as something that will be part of the attack then it would not look about it. But not if a publisher thinking he could say maybe I should send a thousand needs.

Ross Anderson: So for, for us, so maybe this is another reason to always use burner phones. Never let it be around long enough to get to know you. That's the reason.

Brian Kidney: And the burner phone, the problem with the burner phone is if it's just a phone, that's okay but the Sims trying to get Sims that aren't tied to yourself and that are getting much harder to do. If you're looking for just a separate number and what's not, you normally have to, it's getting much harder to get a phone without providing ID to tie it to you. So from my proof of concept, I came up with a pervasive ease drafting attack and this is a very, very simplistic model that makes very few assumptions just to see if I could figure out, see if I could start identifying people sort of ball park numbers around data and stuff that I might need. I took a simple predictive text engine, I actually got one off GitHub. It's based on the work of Peter Norvig but it uses, it's based on the work from him in his, in his artificial intelligence book. It uses a lot of the simple techniques that were in the early text engines. They've gotten better since.

It's trained with a large sets of text and used to predict other works. Then for the classification, I just took the simplest method I could find, a naive Bayes classifier, commonly used in early spam systems. Train those with smaller amounts of text and used that to guess the author of the predictive text. The text that I use were taken from Project Gutenberg. I needed big samples of text and I wasn't sure where to get them so it was suggested to me to just go find some authors on Project Gutenberg. The authors for training the two, my user X and user Y are Mark Twain and Jane Austen. And they were specifically chosen because they represent the difference between American and British English. This is something that I thought might be something that could trip up people with an autotext engine. You may be typing along and trying to hide but like it's commonly honor, it's putting the -our in the honor in your British word -or in your American. All though Canadians will put the -our in there too. We sort of use an English in between somewhere.

Text, the text that I use for that, that were predicted were of a similar time period. They sort of fell in the, the time period between Twain and Austen or they were about their times of writing so authors like Kipling, Dumas, Arthur Conan Doyle, F. Scott Fitzgerald. Part of the reason for choosing those so I had Twain and Austen and they were sort of in a similar time period with sort of similar technologies and experiences and I didn't want to have things that got into later time periods that might start talking about technologies that don't exist or that didn't exist back then and just sort of confuse things. So I just picked everything to sort of be in the same time frame.

Hugo Jonker: Over here, I have a question.

Brian Kidney: Oh it's hard to see. Sorry, yes.

Hugo Jonker: Dumas wrote in French I think?

Brian Kidney: Sorry?

Hugo Jonker: Dumas wrote in French language?

Brian Kidney: I used English versions of the text. He was a bit of an outliner with the text so I used the English translations of his works so

Hugo Jonker: The translations from where?

Brian Kidney: Sorry, the Project Gutenberg translations so

Hugo Jonker: When were the translations created? Were they kind of created around the time of Jane Austen and Mark Twain or were they created in the 2000s based on the original package?

Brian Kidney: Honestly actually I don't know the answer to that.

Hugo Jonker: Because at the time used could bias.

Brian Kidney: It, it was bias with maybe some of the speech patterns but not necessarily the words themselves. So it wouldn't introduce any sort of, I don't think it would introduce any sort of concepts and stuff because when they do these translations they try to stay as close to their original works so you know you wouldn't have talks of structures that didn't exist in that time period and stuff like that. But that's my belief, I actually don't know when the translations were done.

Simon Foley: The same thing with Joyce would be unflattering as well, it seems to be tied to devoting [laughs].

Brian Kidney: It's the style

Simon Foley: In your translation it doesn't reach.

Brian Kidney: I'm not sure. I've, I've read a bit of Jane's and I never found it of like the, The Dead and stuff like that wasn't

Simon Foley: Was it something like the Ulysses [laughs]?

Brian Kidney: Ulysses, yeah that might be an outlier, outline that was used so yeah. I haven't read that text myself to be honest so. It turned out that the one, the only one that really caused an issue was Sir Arthur Conan Doyle and I can explain that when I get to the results. Oh wait, hold on a second, I really like this. I apologize, this doesn't actually project very well and it looks okay onscreen. I guess I should look at the resolution as one way. This is just sort of an overview of what I was doing. So you start here with these predictive text engines and you just train them with some Mark Twain, some Jane Austen various sizes for various tests. And I'll take this sample text, or in this case it was just bodies of text from Doyle and Fitzgerald and what not and feed them through the text engine.

And that gave me the predicted samples and then individually that's why there's only one line here because I do this one first and then I do this one.

I would take the American sample, run it through my naive Bayesian classifier that has been trained with smaller subsets of text from the authors. And then see what the classification was and then just count the number of ones that correct and the number of ones that are incorrect.

Frank Stajano: I have a very basic question of not understanding what is being done. I saw that, that seeing that we're using as the corrections that were made when people made a typo. And so when dopes the type of the corrector applies some correction based on what it has learned you have already typed? Now where are the typos being corrected in here? Okay, I assume that all the text was already correct.

Brian Kidney: All of the, all the text is correct so what I did just to sort of simulate typos was I bounded the amount of text for each word that went into the prediction engines. I believe it was four characters. So it would take the result after four characters and output. It does lead to these sample text. Again, this, a lot of just simplifications were done as a method to see if we could find, find out some things. These texts could be unreadable because you'd have a lot of four character words. There was no word that sort of mapped to that four characters from one author to the other. So it would just what it does but it defaults.

Frank Stajano: So you are articulating like Jane Austen would write the first four characters which were passing through space and her phone correctly is to say.

Brian Kidney: Four characters so quick four characters, four characters, four characters. So words like the and is and that, they would be slated in their longer words that really I was trying to get these, -ours, the -ise, the -ize things in there, to see if we could classify. So basically I would truncate how much was allowed into the prediction engine. It doesn't produce a result that you'd be able to transmit and someone will be able to read but it just produces sort of that prediction mechanism because it's really hard to you know. I could have given a lot of text to people and try to get them to type it but you know that's a much bigger experiment. I was looking for a proof of concept here. Some results. So you can see in the graph here. This is to present the, to present correctly classified by the size of the input text and each line is a different amount of training texts of the predictive, the prediction engine itself. Sorry, to the classifier.

So if we only had 512 K of actual data to put into our classifier you know we get this line down here that isn't very represented of anything good [laughs]. You know, it's, it's not what we want. However, if we start putting in 1 Meg, Meg and a half, two Megs, we start to very quickly need less input text to start getting a decent classification rate. 80% probability of success with only 256 K of attack text. We can get 90% with 512 as long as we trained our naive Bayes classifier with enough data.

We did expect the base, I did expect the baseline to be at 50%. There's a little oddity in that number that sort of pops up in this line here in that amount of trunk here to text from Sir Arthur Conan Doyle there's one extra word in there that sort of just throws things off a little in the British English, it matches really easily. And the other thing, we noticed was there's an issue with the entropy of the training text. So if I trained with, if I trained the prediction engine with one meg of Mark Twain and one meg of Jane Austen, there wasn't the same amount of entropy in those two sample sizes. I actually mapped it out here.

Apparently Jane Austen was somewhat repetitive in her writing. I haven't read enough Jane Austen to know but consistently there is more entropy in the American samples which were Mark Twain than there was with Jane Austen. So with that fact, generally you had a much better chance of guessing the American one right. And I explained the bump wrong and I apologize for that. The fact that the baseline seems to be at 55% is that Arthur Conan Doyle extra -our word that seems to fit in the text that I was able to locate at the lower end sort of just jumps out. And there is another phrase that happens that nullifies that with this amount of train data. So it's a little bit sensitive in the lower end of the, the data, it's just very sensitive the way you actually put in there. That sensitivity sort of goes away as you train more.

So some discussion about this: we use basic techniques for text prediction it's based on like the simple hidden American off models that were used in the earlier engines. Newer algorithms with better training would probably leak more data. They do a lot of things these days with these algorithms. They'll even tie them to your Facebook, in your Twitter and it will go online and will start to sort of create speech patterns for you based on everything you've ever written online and then update your engine.

Similarly the classification technique could be improved. I've talked recently to a deep learning researcher and naive Bayes classifier is just sort of an introductory classification mechanism. He's seen some work with respect to text classification and the deep learning that if you spit, if you put the data in, it will start to find features that aren't necessarily going to be picked on a naive Bayes and not necessarily going to be picked up by handcrafting some samples. And deep learning, I was talking about this in the coffee break, is a little odd in that you can actually feed it the same piece of text over and over and it will learn more and more. I've seen in an example in an algorithm that outputs Shakespeare and if you train it 20 times with this corpus of text, it's not very good. But if you train it 100 times with the same corpus of text just over and over and over, it gets much better.

So it would have potentially decreased the amount of data that we need but this is a further avenue for investigation. But even with these simplifications, the proof of concepts still show that there is something here. There's, there's something that, you know, you would potentially be exploiting. More sophisticated attacks would really craft the inputs or, use some words like color versus colour and just a lot more of them rather than just taking random pieces of text. And in the real world, you can't really demand prediction, you know, you can't say, "Oh I need to identify this person so please type this for me." But there could be some sort of social engineering that could happen especially if this is in an actual active conversation. So they're trying to identify someone in active conversations trying to remain anonymous. You can sort of steer the conversation towards potentially some words that could get miscorrected into other words in certain fields. You know it'll require a fair bit of ahead, a fair bit of work ahead of time but it could be worth it.

So some conclusions, the predictive eavesdropping attack of privacy using autocorrect was presented. Showing that it can be successful 90% of the time with little as 512K of data. The experiment had very little optimization and it really remains as an, as some further work to investigate more sophisticated techniques and see what you know, that's going to require me learning about some technologies that I don't have a lot of experience with, so, we just sort of simplified things for proof of concept.

Frank Stajano: So you appear, you appear to distinguish Mark Twain and Jane Austen as American and British and so were you're distinguishing between Mark and Jane or were you distinguishing between American and British? If you had two Americans subjects, would you have been able to distinguish between the two?

Brian Kidney: So to show...

Ross Anderson: Or do you think it's something that's very far apart in this place where you think it's very well I can distinguish them?

Brian Kidney: Yeah and that would, that helped in our simplistic example. So, I believe if we wanted to take two Americans, if those two Americans were say in different fields. So, some data about a government program came out and you've narrowed it to someone who could be in the department of health and someone who could be in the department of defense, their language patterns could be distinct enough that you would be able to differentiate between the two. If they were very close, you may need more samples of data to input. Although I would hope, the hope is that these more advanced techniques would, would limit the amount of data you need to input into the attack to sort of differentiate between the two. It's very early work.

Frank Stajano: I would like to understand the extent to which my dictionary is personal to me only if I actually correct its mistakes.

Brian Kidney: If you, sorry, if you?

Frank Stajano: So if I just always accepted the font which it is must be rough, am I going to be much different from Ross or am I going to be different from Ross only if I make the corrections and he makes the corrections?

Ross Anderson: No, my dictionary for example picks up the names of family members simply because I've typed on them.

Brian Kidney: Yeah.

Ross Anderson: Yours won't have that.

Brian Kidney: So one of the things it will do for training is it will put distinct exceptions in for things you've corrected. Especially if you keep typing a five letter word that it think it's more.

Frank Stajano: Please be specific because you must have corrected the family member's name the first time that it was

Ross Anderson: Not clear.

Brian Kidney: No and if you...

Ross Anderson: Not, not clear and just take it two or three times and it, and it,

Brian Kidney: It learns the other words that you type. So it does have distinct exceptions for when you correct. If you type a lot and keeps thinking you mean this and you keep correcting it, then it will learn that okay it's not this, it's then. However, if you just keep typing words that aren't within the dictionary and what not, it will learn those along the way. So it starts off with a fairly, you know, it's not a, it's not a limited dictionary but it's, it's a very general dictionary and then it starts adding things that you consistently type over time. Family names, if you're in the security field there's probably some terms that you use that you know your children don't use and stuff like that.

The last point there is the authors believe that text prediction is a liability where privacy is required. One thing that anyone who's implementing systems that require some privacy or anonymity could do is just turn off the predict, the text prediction in your thing. And in some applications that happens, Google Chrome on the Android devices, when you go into incognito mode, will actually turnoff text prediction. On iOS it won't. Why, that may have to do with Apple having the engine as versus Google having control over the engine on the iOS device but I'm not sure. But there are other applications out there like PostSecret and Whisper and stuff like that are sort of posting anonymously that don't turn off the text prediction. So it's, it's basically a suggestion that you, you know, if you were designing something with privacy in mind, it's to turn off one of the most invasive things on your phone.

Frank Stajano: I guess I should be asking this, to the extent that these corrections are done in the cloud especially with the Siri type things, they don't want to send their info to the cloud in the first place?

Brian Kidney: Yeah, I looked specifically at the keyboards and not Siri because that's a whole different.

Frank Stajano: But the keyboard Swift Key or whatever, it, it doesn't send these stuff, doesn't it?

Brian Kidney: Some of them

Frank Stajano: To improve the models on the machine.

Brian Kidney: No, it, I don't know if some might but it doesn't require it because I have no internet connection while I'm here unless I find WiFi and I could still use that system. It's still

Frank Stajano: No but there is instance, but it, it doesn't it periodically try to improve vibrance or single text for instance.

Brian Kidney: I believe in most phones that's an opt in thing because of other privacy concerns. A lot of people don't like when parts of a phone, phone home so to speak.

Frank Stajano: And so in summary is making lots of vibrant, maybe they are better off using dictionary there./I reckon there's guidance because the typos made could make them you know distinguish them.

Audience: If someone is making the same typos, right, maybe they are better using the dictionary and correcting the typos because their typos make them, you know, distinguishable. I may be better off you know using that correction and get them correct. So it flattens you know the patterns of my typos [laughter].

Brian Kidney: Yeah, I, I can't disagree with that. I can't disagree with that [laughs].

Ross Anderson: Yeah, I think the intention must be read through what you write before you send it, you know and add the influence [laughs]

Brian Kidney: Of course.

SMAPs: Short Message Authentication Protocols

Khaled Baqer[1(✉)], Johann Bezuidenhoudt[2], Ross Anderson[1],
and Markus Kuhn[1]

[1] Computer Laboratory, University of Cambridge, Cambridge, UK
{khaled.baqer,ross.anderson,markus.kuhn}@cl.cam.ac.uk
[2] Leonine Initiatives (Pty) Ltd., Roodepoort, South Africa
jb@leonine.biz

Abstract. There is a long history of authentication protocols designed for ease of human use, which rely on users copying a short string of digits. Historical examples include telex test keys and early nuclear firing codes; familiar modern examples include prepayment meter codes and the 3-digit card verification values used in online shopping. In this paper, we show how security protocols that are designed for human readability and interaction can fail to provide adequate protection against simple attacks. To illustrate the problem, we discuss an offline payment protocol and explain various problems. We work through multiple iterations, or 'evolutions', of the protocol in order to get better tradeoffs between security and usability. We discuss the limitation of verifying such protocols using BAN logic. Our aim is to develop usable human-friendly protocols that can be used in constrained offline environments. We conclude that protocol designers need to be good curators of security state, and also pay attention to the interaction between online and offline functions. In fact, we suggest that delay-tolerant networking might be a future direction of evolution for protocol research.

Keywords: Security · Protocols · Usability · Offline · Authentication

1 Introduction

Mobile payment systems have transformed the life of people in less developed countries (LDCs), bringing a convenient means of exchange and store of value to people living far from any conventional banking service. For rural people, phone payments enable everything from pensions to farm subsidies to be paid directly and efficiently, reducing the possibility for corruption and extortion. Even for people living in large cities, phone payments have greatly cut the cost of financial services. A further key application is remittances: migrant workers who have moved from the countryside to the city can send cash home to relatives. However the currently deployed systems, such as M-PESA (Kenya), use SMS or USSD as their carrier, and they stop when the network does. This leaves hundreds of millions of the world's very poorest people stranded. Living off-network in

© Springer International Publishing AG 2017
J. Anderson et al. (Eds.): Security Protocols XXIV, LNCS 10368, pp. 119–132, 2017.
DOI: 10.1007/978-3-319-62033-6_15

mountains, forests and small islands, they still have to use cash for transactions in their village, and are fully exposed to the depredations of dishonest officials.

There are four major limitations of current phone payments. First, both merchant and customer have to be online, so they don't work in areas without network coverage. Second, the cost of the SMS is unnecessary when half the customer's transactions are with the same village merchant. Third, existing systems are mostly locked in to a particular telco and bank as they rely on SMS or USSD. This lock-in increases costs and prevents inter-scheme payments, which is a problem for migrant workers. Fourth, most payment systems operate online. Resilience is not considered thoroughly, at least not beyond providing redundant servers to process requests. When networks go down because of power cuts or congestion, or rural networks close at night because base stations depend on solar panels and have no batteries, payment services cease.

Electronic purses for offline payments exist in the academic literature, and are also fielded, whether as standalone systems or EMV extensions (e.g. UEPS [1] and Germany's Geldkarte[1]). However they have not been implemented by LDC mobile providers, who can install SIM-toolkit applets. There are both engineering and business issues; we are less concerned with the latter here, as they vary widely between countries.

The engineering issue is that existing purse systems are designed for complex messaging between the purses (e.g. between the purse in a smartcard and another purse embedded in a parking meter or ATM) while phone-to-phone payments conducted in the absence of a network or direct link (NFC, Bluetooth, infrared, etc.) must by default rely on users copying numbers between their phones. The protocols must therefore be redesigned for usability, which means minimising the number of digits that need to be typed while supporting robust error handling and recovery.

In this paper, we show how security protocols that are designed for human readability and interaction can end up vulnerable to simple attacks. To illustrate the problem, we discuss our attempt to design an offline payment protocol, and the various problems we had to deal with. We present multiple iterations, or 'evolutions', that the protocol went through as we sought to get reasonable tradeoffs between security and usability. Our target demographic is phone users in LDCs, many of whom are illiterate.

2   System Model

The concept of operations is similar to existing phone payments, except that payments also work when the phone is offline. Sam is a GSM SIM card issuer who may also operate the offline payment system described in this paper, which allows payments between SIM purses in areas with intermittent network coverage. In the following examples, Alice will play the role of a paying customer and Bob will be the shop owner receiving payment, but these roles can be reversed. Sam issues a SIM_A to Alice and SIM_B to Bob.

---

[1] https://en.wikipedia.org/wiki/Geldkarte.

The SIMs of Alice and Bob interact with each other only via human decimal number entry and comparison. Therefore, this protocol has to carefully ensure that SIM_A and SIM_B agree on their transaction history, in spite of the low entropy of the manually-executed challenge–response round trips. The SIMs send records of past payments back to Sam whenever they detect network coverage, for reconciliation between their bank accounts.

In some applications, the network may be intermittent rather than absent, and so a side benefit of our protocols is that they can enable payment networks to support delay-tolerant authentication (see Sect. 4.2).

Where both Alice and Bob have smartphones that can communicate directly (Bluetooth, Wi-Fi, NFC, etc.), a very capable offline payment system can be built with conventional tools. However, many poor people use simple GSM phones that cannot communicate with each other directly in the absence of a GSM network. Then the only way for SIM-toolkit applets to communicate across phones is that their users copy sequences of displayed decimal digits. Numerical transactions are already familiar from other systems such as airtime purchases and prepayment utility meters. It is well known, for example, that even illiterate people can cope with twenty-digit sequences provided these are arranged as five groups of four digits, which is enough for a 64-bit ciphertext, and is used in prepayment meters, but is about the usable limit [2].

3   Design Evolution

The following setup is required in each iteration of the protocol. SIM_A and SIM_B are identified in the protocols by unique, human-recognisable decimal numbers A and B respectively, typically their phone numbers. Sam embeds an individual symmetric 128-bit private key K_A into SIM_A and K_B into SIM_B, which are tamper-resistant to some extent. (Sam could generate these keys from a master key K_S using a key-derivation function, such as $K_A = h_{K_S}(A)$, $K_B = h_{K_S}(B)$). These per-card keys are each known only to Sam and to one single SIM card.

3.1   Basic Protocol

The basic payment protocol proceeds as follows:

1. Alice agrees to pay Bob X and each of them enters both this amount and the other party's phone number into their phones.
2. Bob chooses a 3-digit nonce N_B and forms a 3-digit MAC C (using the shared secret key K) of B and X. He tells Alice the values

$$(N_B, C) \quad \text{where} \quad C = \mathsf{Mac}_K(B, A, X, N_B) \bmod 10^3 \tag{1}$$

with Mac being a 64-bit message-authentication-code function.
3. Alice verifies C. She now believes that she and Bob agree on the amount X and the payer and payee phone numbers A and B (with probability 0.999).

4. Alice authorises the transaction by entering her PIN; her purse decrements its balance by X and generates a 3-digit nonce plus a 4-digit MAC to bind her name and nonce to the data contained in the challenge C:

$$(N_A, R) \quad \text{where} \quad R = \mathsf{Mac}_K(A, N_A, C, N_B, B) \bmod 10^4 \qquad (2)$$

5. Bob enters N_A and R into his purse, and checks it increments by X.

Verification. We then analysed this protocol via the Burrows–Abadi–Needham (BAN) logic [7]. We idealised the protocol as:

$$B \longrightarrow A : \{B, A, X, N_B\}_K \qquad (= C)$$
$$A \longrightarrow B : \{A, N_A, C, N_B, B\}_K \qquad (= R)$$

We wished to prove that Bob the shopkeeper should trust the payment amount X, i.e. $B \models X$. This can only be deduced using jurisdiction rule, for which we need $B \models A \Rightarrow X$ (B believes A has jurisdiction over X) and $B \models A \models X$ (B believes A believes X).

The former follows from our trust in the software, which has the property that it only creates ciphertexts that start with its own identifier. The value X is contained in the challenge C (but see Sect. 3.2). The latter, that $B \models A \models X$, must be deduced using the nonce verification rule from $\sharp R$ (R is fresh) and $B \models A \mid\sim X$ (B believes A uttered X).

Now $\sharp R$ follows from the fact that $R = h(K; A, N_A, C, N_B, B)$ and contains the nonce N_B Bob just generated. B believes A uttered X from the software constraint already mentioned.

In our original design, we did not include N_B in Bob's challenge, and as a result could not get the protocol to verify. This is in effect what happens with EMV, which in consequence is vulnerable to the preplay attack [6]. In our initial design, we also wondered whether C should contain Alice's phone number too: $C = \mathsf{Mac}_K(B, A, X, N_B)$. The BAN analysis showed this is superfluous. However we include it for error-detection, as discussed later.

However, despite the fact that the protocol verified, there was an attack.

3.2 Evolution 1: Eliminating Narrow Pipes

A crooked merchant Bob can perform the following attack against Alice:

1. Alice agrees on price X and Bob receives Alice's phone number A.
2. Bob now chooses a higher price X'.
3. Bob then repeatedly feeds X and X' to his SIM_B, which will generate a new nonce N_B each time and output a MAC C. Bob continues until he finds a colliding pair with the same MAC (X, N_B) and (X', N'_B) such that

$$\mathsf{Mac}_K(A, X, N_B, B) \equiv \mathsf{Mac}_K(A, X', N'_B, B) \equiv C \bmod 10^3.$$

This will take just a few dozen trials for a 3-digit MAC.

4. Bob aborts all the trial transactions except for the last one for (X', N'_B).
5. Bob then gives (N_B, C) to Alice, but asks his own SIM_B to proceed with the last one, using N'_B and X'.

This way, Alice makes a payment for X, but Bob receives one for $X' > X$, violating conservation of money.

The vulnerability is that R only includes C, not X, and while C depends on X, C does not have enough entropy to prevent an online collision attack by Bob against SIM_B that allows X' to replace X. Once this is noticed, the fix is easy: include the amount X in the input to the payment MAC R, rather than the challenge C.

Such attacks are beyond the scope of BAN, which was only intended for protocols involving cryptographically long nonces and MACs, and does not keep track of guessing entropy or collision risks. Some more modern cryptographic verification tools (e.g. CryptoVerif [5]) can quantify such probabilities.

Anyway, the repaired protocol now runs:

1. Alice agrees to pay Bob X.
2. Bob chooses a 3-digit nonce N_B, forms a 3-digit MAC C with B and X, and sends Alice:

$$(N_B, C) \quad \text{where} \quad C = \text{Mac}_K(B, A, X, N_B) \bmod 10^3 \qquad (3)$$

3. Alice verifies C to ensure they agree on payer, payee and amount.
4. Alice authorises the transaction by entering her PIN; her purse decrements its balance by X and generates a 3-digit nonce plus a 4-digit MAC:

$$(N_A, R) \quad \text{where} \quad R = \text{Mac}_K(A, N_A, X, N_B, B) \bmod 10^4 \qquad (4)$$

5. Bob enters N_A and R into his purse, and checks it increments by X.

The verification proceeds as before, although by now we might place less reliance on a BAN-logic verification of a short message authentication protocol.

3.3   Evolution 2: Transaction Chaining

The revised protocol still raised security concerns:

1. Bob could try to add money to his SIM card by faking transactions with fake customers and just guessing the response R. Each attempt will succeed only with probability 10^{-4}, and repeated attempts can be blocked by a retry counter. We can also mix up R with N_A. However the detailed design is far from trivial. For example, Bob could connect SIM_B to a PC to automate an attack, and interleave guessing attempts with real payments from a customer SIM he controls. In the worst-case attack, Bob is the local payment service agent, and has hundreds of customer SIM cards in stock. We need to make the fraud probability acceptably low without making the authorisation code too long or otherwise making operations too complex or fragile.

2. Alice can similarly fake a transaction with probability 10^{-4}, but this may be less of a concern in practice, as Alice cannot repeat thousands of transaction attempts against SIM_B without the collaboration of Bob. But a colluding Bob could just run the attack without Alice (see above).

3. Bob can also try to fake transactions with real customers A, by keeping a record of their $Mac_K(A, N_A, X, N_B, B)$ replies. In such a fake transaction, Bob can choose A and N_A, and if the real Alice has already paid n times in the past for a regularly bought item of fixed price X, then Bob has enough data to be able to look up a valid pair (N_B, R) to complete a fake transaction with probability $n \cdot 10^{-3}$.

The last attack is of particular concern if Alice makes daily purchases of the same price X for years, as the probability of Bob being able to fake a transaction response R from SIM_A approaches one. Our solution is to establish a payment session between Alice and Bob that maintains additional shared entropy stored in both SIM_A and SIM_B. We include this state in the MAC inputs, such that knowledge of past MAC responses no longer helps Bob guess future ones. We also replace N_A and N_B with MACs of the transaction data that only the bank Sam can verify. Then even if a fake transaction is accepted by a SIM, it will still be spotted when one of the parties eventually uploads it to Sam.

Most phone payment transactions in LDCs are to familiar recipients. A villager will do most of their shopping at the one village store; a migrant worker will make most remittance payments to his wife or perhaps his mum back in his home village. So the obvious next evolution is to look for ways in which subsequent payments can be made easier. This has been a familiar strategy in established online banking systems for about 30 years now.

If the security of payments authenticated using short codes must depend on maintaining as much shared security state as possible, then why not use a hash chain of all transactions in the current session, rather than just the current transaction context?

Let a payment session be a hash chain maintained in both cards. Its state is kept in each card as a 256-bit value S_i, along with a transaction counter i. When A and B start a new series of transactions, both their SIMs initialise this session as a hash state of

$$T_0 := (A, B) \tag{5}$$
$$S_0 := H(0, T_0) \tag{6}$$
$$i := 0 \tag{7}$$

where H is a collision-resistant hash function with 256-bit output (e.g., SHA-256 or SHA-3). The transaction counter i records how many payments have been committed in this session. Alice and Bob now should have the same value of S_0.

SIM_A and SIM_B also set up a shared transaction key K_{AB}. At this stage we can assume it is simply derived from their phone numbers using a key derivation function and the universal shared secret K: $K_{AB} = h_K(A, B)$. (In Sect. 4 we discuss options for mitigating the risk of a shared master secret.)

Once the payment session is established, Alice can pay Bob as follows:

1. Alice and Bob agree on a price X.
2. Alice and Bob then select the payment session to be used, and their SIMs retrieve not just A and B but also the hash chain values (i, S_i).
3. SIM_A checks that X is within limits agreed with Sam, and that Alice's on-card purse value M_A has enough funds for the transaction, presumably $M_A - X \geq 0$. It aborts the transaction otherwise. Likewise, SIM_B checks whether both X and its purse value $M_B + X$ are within limits agreed with Sam, and aborts if not. (Transaction limits agreed with Sam may be variable, and depend on for example X, i, A, or B.)
4. Bob's SIM_B generates and displays a challenge of $n_{c,1}$ deterministic digits that Alice and Sam can verify, $n_{c,2}$ deterministic digits that Sam can verify, as well as $n_{c,3}$ digits of random entropy to help ensure that payment sessions do not repeat – an $n_c = (n_{c,1} + n_{c,2} + n_{c,3})$-digit decimal challenge message

$$C_{i+1} = E^{n_c}_{h_{K_{AB}}(S_i)}[(\mathsf{Mac}_{K_{AB}}(i, S_i, X) \bmod 10^{n_{c,1}}) \,\|$$
$$(\mathsf{Mac}_{K_B}(i, S_i, X, F_B) \bmod 10^{n_{c,2}}) \,\| \, N_B] \tag{8}$$

which Alice copies into her phone. Here $0 \leq N_B < 10^{n_{c,3}}$ is a number picked by SIM_B and $\|$ is concatenation of decimal digits. E^{n_c} is a pseudo-random permutation over $\mathbb{Z}_{10^{n_c}}$ (see [4]), to ensure that adversaries cannot be certain about the function of individual digits without knowing K_{AB}. F_B is optional other information that can be included and that SIM_B will eventually transmit to Sam (but not to SIM_A) such as M_B or a timestamp, added as an entropy source and as forensic evidence of disputed transactions.
5. Alice's SIM_A then calculates an $n_r = (n_{r,1} + n_{r,2} + n_{r,3})$-digit response

$$R_{i+1} = E^{n_r}_{h_{K_{AB}}(S_i, C_{i+1})}[(\mathsf{Mac}_{K_{AB}}(i, S_i, X, C_{i+1}) \bmod 10^{n_{r,1}}) \,\|$$
$$(\mathsf{Mac}_{K_A}(i, S_i, X, C_{i+1}, F_A) \bmod 10^{n_{r,2}}) \,\| \, N_A] \tag{9}$$

containing $n_{r,1}$ digits that Bob can verify, $n_{r,2}$ digits that Sam can verify, and $n_{r,3}$ digits N_A chosen by SIM_A. F_A is optional other information that SIM_A will record and eventually transmit to Sam, such as M_A or a timestamp.
6. SIM_A then updates its non-volatile state and on-card transaction records:

$$M_A := M_A - X \tag{10}$$
$$i := i + 1 \tag{11}$$
$$T_i := (S_{i-1}, X, C_i, R_i) \tag{12}$$
$$S_i := H(i, T_i) \tag{13}$$

7. SIM_A finally displays its response message (9).
8. Bob types R_{i+1} into his phone, which reports the success or otherwise of the transaction.

The point of hash chaining is twofold:

– Even if someone gets lucky and guesses a correct authentication code R_i for an individual transaction, this will still leave the underlying security state S_i inconsistent between Alice and Bob, between whom subsequent transactions will then fail with high probability.
– The entropy of the security state S_i makes it less likely that a query to $\mathrm{Mac}_{K_{AB}}$ is ever repeated. This reduces the risk that knowledge of past values of R and C can help an attacker to predict future such values, and use these to set up fake transactions.

There are various attacks to consider, for example Bob can complete a fake transaction on SIM_B with probability $10^{-n_{r,1}}$, or duplicate sessions to double-spend Alice's responses. To fine-tune such risks, we can vary the number of digits allocated in the exchanged messages C and R between the first transaction and later transactions in a session, for example:

	$n_{c,1}$	$n_{c,2}$	$n_{c,3}$	$n_{r,1}$	$n_{r,2}$	$n_{r,3}$
First transaction	1	1	3	6	3	3
Later transactions	1	1	1	4	3	0

In addition, we need to limit the number of failed transactions:

– A SIM can keep a record of failed transactions and can ensure that only a fraction of all transaction attempts per session are allowed to fail. For example, a payment session can be terminated once 5 of the last 10 transaction attempts have failed. Such retry limits should be implemented only on a per-session basis, to reduce the risk of denial-of-service attacks, where an adversary deliberately exhausts a SIM-wide retry limit.
– If retry limits apply per session, we then also need to limit the total number of sessions that a SIM can participate in, to well below $10^{n_{r,1}}$, e.g. a few thousand. This way, Bob cannot iterate fake transactions across many non-existing customers.

The exact limits and number of authentication-code digits can be tuned based on risk analysis and usability studies. They could also be made variable, though the usability consequences would have to be carefully tested. Likewise, the content of F_A and F_B remain for further study.

4   Mitigating the Risk of a Shared Master Secret

4.1   Evolution 3: Group Key Scheme

If smartcards were perfectly tamper-resistant, then the initial design would be largely complete at this point. They are certainly more resistant than was the case twenty years ago, when large-scale compromises of pay-TV smartcards were pretty well an annual occurrence. This is partly due to technological improvements such as side-channel countermeasures, top-layer sensor meshes, and randomised place-and-route; and partly due to minimising the value that can be extracted by cloning a single card. In EMV, for example, the keys authenticate transactions on a single account, so the extractable value is typically in the low tens of thousands of dollars, rather than the millions that could be made from cloning a pay-TV card. As long as reverse engineering a card costs tens of thousands of dollars and the attacker needs perhaps a dozen identical cards to work with, this is probably enough.

The overlay SIMs used in our field trial are not certified to EMV standards, though the vendor assures us that an EMV compliant overlay product will be available in due course. So in the short term we might deploy a two-tier system in which merchants get a high-security EMV-certified SIM card containing a master key while customers get a medium-security overlay SIM card containing a derived key, namely their phone number or card serial number encrypted under the master key to provide a diversified key. This is the approach used for some 20 years in UEPS and for a decade in Geldkarte. It would thus have the advantage of being familiar to banks and their insurers, with a zero loss history and the comfort that comes from reusing existing standards and business processes. If anyone seeking to monetise a break of a card needed, as a practical matter, to extract money from merchants (as the other users are too dispersed and too poor) then it could make perfect business sense.

The downside with this approach is that a substantial volume of LDC phone payments are migrant remittances, where neither the sender nor the receiver is a merchant.

A second approach is combinatorial keying, which was proposed in the 1990s in the context of satellite TV, where it was known as 'broadcast encryption', and attempted to give each pay-TV subscriber a set of keys of which some suitable subset could enable her to decrypt each programme. If a card were cloned, then that particular subset could be blacklisted without this affecting the great majority of other subscribers; only a small number of subscribers with the same subset of keys would have to be issued with replacement cards.

A similar idea can be adapted here, where the communications are many-to-many. For example, we can divide all users into $d = 100$ key groups, give everyone 100 out of 5,050 keys, and thus require an attacker who wanted to impersonate any user to clone 100 cards rather than just one.

In more detail: Sam generates a set of shared 128-bit group keys, in the form of an upper triangular matrix of $d(d+1)/2$ keys $(K_{i,j})_{0 \leq i \leq j < d}$. (Sam could again generate all these from a master key K_s using a key-derivation function, such as $K_{i,j} = h_{K_s}(i,j)$).

Each interoperable SIM issued by Sam also contains a common private 128-bit key K_g. Sam uses K_g to assign each SIM to one of d key groups ($d \approx 10^2$), using a pseudo-random function applied to its phone number:

$$g_A := h_{K_g}(A) \bmod d \tag{14}$$

$$g_B := h_{K_g}(B) \bmod d \tag{15}$$

Sam stores in each SIM in key group g_A the d group keys

$$G_A = \{K_{0,g_A}, K_{1,g_A}, \dots, K_{g_A-1,g_A}, K_{g_A,g_A}, K_{g_A,g_A+1}, \dots K_{g_A,d-1}\}. \tag{16}$$

(and equivalently for SIMs in group g_B, etc.).

SIM$_A$ and SIM$_B$ can now secure their message exchanges using the key

$$K_{AB} = \begin{cases} h_{K_{g_A,g_B}}(A,B) & \text{if } g_A \le g_B \\ h_{K_{g_B,g_A}}(A,B) & \text{if } g_A > g_B. \end{cases} \tag{17}$$

K_{g_A,g_B} or K_{g_B,g_A} will be available in both SIM$_A$ and SIM$_B$, and both can use K_g to select it. Any other SIM$_U$ picked at random (for reverse engineering) by someone who does not know K_g will contain it only with probability $2d^{-1} - d^{-2}$ (i.e. $2d^{-1}$ if $g_A \ne g_B$ and d^{-1} if $g_A = g_B$).

This is straightforward to do if each user gets a SIM card issued by a payment service provider that is also the phone company. Where the two are different, and especially if the payment service runs on an overlay SIM independent of the phone company's SIM, it isn't so straightforward, because of the need to establish a trustworthy link between the user's phone number and her key group. This can be done by an online protocol if the phone is online as the overlay SIM is first fitted, but otherwise might require copying quite a few digits.

4.2   Evolution 4: Delay-Tolerant Needham–Schroeder

In many applications of interest, both Alice and Bob will get network connectivity from time to time as they travel to town or through areas with mobile service. There is significant research in more general store-and-forward mechanisms or delay-tolerant networks for extending service in LDCs. Even in the few cases where one of the parties does not ever travel to town, connection can be established via a *data mule*. For example, if Bob is old and housebound, while his daughter Alice works in the big city and sends him money, a neighbour who travels past Bob's hut can take data to and from a point of network presence. This should let us establish authenticated key exchange, although it appears to be unexplored territory from the protocols community's point of view.

An initial idea is to turn the bug in the Needham-Schroeder protocol [8] into a feature. The fact that Bob has no guarantee of the freshness in Alice's initial exchange with Sam, and that she can therefore pass on a key packet to him a month or even a year afterwards, can be used to create a delay-tolerant version of the protocol. In order to preserve the original notation of [8], we reverse the roles in this iteration whereby Alice (A) is the merchant travelling to the city (data mule), and Bob (B) is the housebound villager who requires relayed messages from Sam (S). We assume that Alice and Bob have just done the first transaction in a new payment session, and want Sam's help to set up a K_{AB} that is present only in their SIM cards and thus cannot be compromised if any other card is reverse-engineered.

1. Alice catches the boat into town, and SIM_A detects a connection. SIM_A automatically uploads transaction logs to Sam (to update shadow accounts for reconciliation). She also sends a request to authenticate with any new counterparty, in this case Bob[2]:
$$A \rightarrow S : A, B, N_A$$

2. Sam sends K_{AB}, via SMS or USSD, encrypted with the shared key K_{AS}:
$$S \rightarrow A : \{N_A, B, K_{AB}, \{K_{AB}, A\}_{K_{BS}}\}_{K_{AS}}$$

3. When Alice returns to the village, SIM_A can display, during transactions discussed below, the authenticated shared key:
$$A \rightarrow B : \{K_{AB}, A\}_{K_{BS}}.$$

4. The final two steps of the Needham–Schroeder protocol are performed offline between the transacting parties, by showing authenticated nonces to obtain agreement:
$$B \rightarrow A : \{N_B\}_{K_{AB}}$$
$$A \rightarrow B : \{N_B - 1\}_{K_{AB}}$$

Note that an implementation would be likely to optimise this somewhat, for usability reasons. The final two steps can be reduced to challenges and responses of a few digits each using the methods in earlier sections, but the key packet $\{K_{AB}, A\}_{K_{BS}}$ is harder. If K_{AB} were a 128-bit key that alone would require copying 40 decimal digits. Users of prepayment utility meters (including illiterate users) regularly copy 20-digits strings that represent DES-encrypted commands, so perhaps 40 digits can be done as a very occasional procedure. More likely, an operator might take the view that 30 digits are enough; an 80-bit key would not be the weakest link. Again, this requires real testing in the field. Where users interact with merchants directly, the merchant can perhaps help (subject to worries about the merchant ripping off vulnerable customers). But where a helpful neighbour is acting as a data mule for an elderly and housebound Bob, and carrying messages scribbled on bits of paper, 40 digits may well be too much.

More research is needed about how to integrate online payments, offline payments, data mules, and delay-tolerant networking in general. The value of this research is not just to extend and enhance payment systems per se, but also all sorts of other electronically enabled services, from pay-as-you-go solar panels to agricultural subsidies and payments from aid donors.

To evaluate such systems we need to gain insight into what transactions are taking place online versus offline; which transactions are critical (e.g. large transactions or cash-outs); incentives for contacting back-end systems; incentives for carrying data on behalf of other users; and realistic threat models. Should we assume that everyone in a village would happily conspire to cheat a bank, or that the headman or store owner in a village might be happy to be responsible for the village's good behaviour, or that villagers might vouch for each other?

---

[2] The notation here follows the original Needham–Schroeder protocol [8].

5   Usability

Our goal was to achieve the most usable design that is acceptably secure. We present here a cognitive walkthrough and error recovery analysis.

First, both customer and merchant have to enter each others' phone numbers. This happens anyway in phone payment systems, and there is a mistake every few attempts. Even trained people who are alert make about one digit-entry error per 200 digits [3], and so we expect at least one in ten attempts to sync phone numbers to be problematic. In existing systems, error recovery can waste a call or a text. In our proposed system, an error is detected when Alice verifies Bob's challenge.

After Alice has entered Bob's six-digit string and got an "OK", she enters her PIN to authorise the payment, just as at present. She then shows, or calls out, the seven-digit payment code to Bob. If it's accepted by his SIM card, his phone will show "OK". If she reads it wrong, or he types it wrong, then neither has the money: her value counter has been decremented while his hasn't been increased yet. With good faith, they both have an incentive to retry until they get it right; Alice wants the goods, after all, and Bob wants her money. Even if Bob's phone battery suddenly goes flat, they can write down the seven digits and complete the transaction later.

If they are interrupted or never complete, then when Bob and Alice later upload their transactions, Sam will have the data needed for dispute resolution.

If Bob is trying to cheat Alice by getting her to pay twice, he can report an "OK" as a failure. Alice will detect the cheating on reconciliation. There is however an issue here about whether Bob might abuse a position of power, or Alice's illiteracy. Similar attacks are possible on many other payment systems (e.g. pension payments) and are mitigated by social rituals. We will experiment with poster instructions that Bob should show Alice the results of typing in the payment code; if this is overt so that everyone in the shop can see it, the exploitation risk should be acceptable. Another possibility is a close-out code from Bob, which we plan to field test.

6   Conclusion

Phone payments have been transformative in Africa, South Asia and elsewhere, helping millions of the very poor to raise themselves from poverty, and helping the less poor too. Extending them to areas without network service will continue this process but will also give disproportionate benefit to the very poor as the existing networks have been rolled out first to the less poor regions. The Gates Foundation advertised for a technology to do this and we won a grant from them to build a prototype.

The mission is to design an offline electronic purse system optimised for use in less developed countries. Unlike existing systems such as Geldkarte and Proton, our design aims to maximise usability in off-network transactions by minimising the number of digits a user has to speak, hear and type, while providing robust recovery mechanisms for the inevitable errors and making sure there isn't any scalable attack that is large enough to care about.

In this paper we have set out the evolution of our proposed core payment protocol. There are a number of lessons already for protocol researchers.

First, when we start dealing with authentication protocols with short strings of digits, our intuitions about security can fail us, and formal verification doesn't always help. Our first attempt at a protocol was vulnerable to a simple collision attack, because we used the entropy that was visible rather than all the entropy available. Worse, the defective protocol verified just fine using the BAN logic. That doesn't imply that BAN is useless (as we did find another design flaw) but just that it's not enough in this context. We leave to future work whether other verification tools can find such flaws.

Second, when dealing with very short authentication codes, transaction chaining can be useful, and is a reasonable next step once we've learned to use all the available entropy. It had already appeared a generation ago in EFT-POS systems in Australia, where MAC residue was used for key updating, but then apparently had been forgotten.

Third, when a system is offline part of the time, then the interaction between the offline component and the online one bears careful study. If much of the world will have to live with delay-tolerant networking, then it's time to start thinking about how to incorporate delay tolerance into the infrastructure, rather than its being an occasional hack that developers will often get wrong. This may seem counterintuitive to some providers, given that banks in the developed world spent the first half of the 1990s ripping out offline capabilities from ATM systems, and the second half reducing merchant floor limits for credit-card transactions. Yet it's noteworthy that when they introduced EMV in the 2000s, offline capabilities reappeared, and they did so by placing carefully calibrated amounts of trust in largely tamper-resistant smartcards and terminals.

A lot of services are going to have to coexist with network outages. That means, we suggest, that the next challenge for the protocols community will be to work out ways to build support for delay-tolerant networking into the infrastructure. We hope the examples here will help start the discussion.

References

1. Anderson, R.J.: UEPS – a second generation electronic wallet. In: Deswarte, Y., Eizenberg, G., Quisquater, J.-J. (eds.) ESORICS 1992. LNCS, vol. 648, pp. 411–418. Springer, Heidelberg (1992). doi:10.1007/BFb0013910
2. Anderson, R.J., Bezuidenhout, S.J.: Cryptographic credit control in pre-payment metering systems. In: Security and Privacy, p. 15. IEEE (1995)
3. Baddeley, A., Longman, D.: The influence of length and frequency of training session on the rate of learning to type. Ergonomics 21(8), 627–635 (1978)
4. Black, J., Rogaway, P.: Ciphers with arbitrary finite domains. In: Preneel, B. (ed.) CT-RSA 2002. LNCS, vol. 2271, pp. 114–130. Springer, Heidelberg (2002). doi:10.1007/3-540-45760-7_9

5. Blanchet, B.: CryptoVerif: computationally sound mechanized prover for crypto-graphic protocols. In: Dagstuhl seminar Formal Protocol Verification Applied, p. 117 (2007)
6. Bond, M., Choudary, O., Murdoch, S.J., Skorobogatov, S., Anderson, R.: Chip and skim: cloning EMV cards with the pre-play attack. In: IEEE Symposium on Security and Privacy (SP), pp. 49–64. IEEE (2014)
7. Burrows, M., Abadi, M., Needham, R.M.: A logic of authentication. Proc. Roy. Soc. Lond. A Math. Phys. Eng. Sci. **426**, 233–271 (1989). The Royal Society
8. Needham, R.M., Schroeder, M.D.: Using encryption for authentication in large net-works of computers. Commun. ACM **21**(12), 993–999 (1978)

SMAPs: Short Message Authentication Protocols
(Transcript of Discussion)

Khaled Baqer[✉] and Ross Anderson

University of Cambridge, Cambridge, UK
{khaled.baqer,ross.anderson}@cl.cam.ac.uk

Khaled Baqer: What I'd like to do first is to highlight the background and motivation for the payment project that we're working on at Cambridge. I'll do a ten-minute introduction and Ross will take over to discuss some of the attacks and the interesting parts of this paper.

The story begins with the mobile payment revolution. This is not Apple Pay, Google Pay or whatever extension of EMV you have on your phone. These are mobile payments in LDCs, less developed countries. So top right, you have M-Pesa in Kenya, top left you have bKash in Bangladesh. These systems work by providing a menu for the user on the phone's SIM toolkit (applet running on the SIM), so they can access, for example, 'send money', enter the amount and the recipient's phone number. Usually this is saved in the user's phonebook, so all you have to do is to enter the amount. The phone sends a message to the server, and the server replies with a confirmation back to the user, and the recipient gets a confirmation of the transaction.

This has been transformative in bridging the gap and providing financial inclusion. Millions of people don't have bank accounts, and even if they do, these accounts are dormant and nobody really uses them. Because of social reasons we can discuss offline, people don't want to go to banks. Some of them don't even know how to use their accounts, and they don't want to walk miles to the closest bank branch.

The first big use for M-Pesa was remittances: someone working in Nairobi sending money back home to their relatives in a remote village, and then they can cash out with the local agent. Store-of-value, of course, and personal safety, these are big ones: you don't want to carry cash in some regions, it's unsafe. It also provides a means for governments to deliver payments directly to users. Meaning if they want to have a direct financial relationship with the users they can directly send the funds to their phones and not send cash that can be lost along multiple hops, if it gets delivered to the intended recipient at all.

What we started out with are the challenges listed here: can we extend this to areas where there is no network? Because mobile payments work beautifully if they work, but they stop when the network does, and so we have people in some places walking miles to the closest area where they can get reception on their phone, just to make a phone call.

This is not only limited to LDCs. There was the blackout in the US years ago, and more recently, in the UK you have regions that were offline because of

© Springer International Publishing AG 2017
J. Anderson et al. (Eds.): Security Protocols XXIV, LNCS 10368, pp. 133–140, 2017.
DOI: 10.1007/978-3-319-62033-6_16

a power outage and people could not use their cards, they could not use mobile devices to pay, they were running out of cash, and it was getting horrible.

Another reason we want to do this is to cut network charges. We think that transaction fees are a big hindrance to increasing the uptake of mobile payments in less developed countries. When the transaction fee is a big chunk of the transaction itself, people will just use cash.

The main constraint is that we have to design this for basic phones. They're called feature phones, but really they lack any features: no cameras, no NFC, no Bluetooth, absolutely nothing. These are £20 or less no-camera phones.

I'm sure you can come up with more examples than the ones shown on the slides about short message authentication protocols, but they're familiar from the three-digit CVV codes that you can find on the back of your bank card. Of course, it's familiar to the audience of this workshop that usability and security go hand in hand. We're limited with regards to what security mechanism we can provide, based on the usability of the system, and if the users see that there's a point of using something like this. I talked about the offline constraint environment, and now we will discuss all the problems in the context of offline payment systems in less developed countries.

We have existing offline purse systems. We have Geldkarte in Germany, we have UEPS, if you're familiar with Ross's work. These systems can be implemented in SIM toolkits, which is what we want to do. The first problem, then, is how do we access the SIM toolkit, because feature phones have one SIM slot and that's already taken by the mobile network operator (MNO), and we don't have access to that.

This is the initial barrier for entry, because we can't access a trusted zone in the user's phone. Another problem is that these protocols are designed for complex messages back and forth between the devices and coupled with the third problem, that the phones don't have any bandwidth for communication, this becomes something that we cannot implement while maintaining some sort of reasonable usability.

So, how do we solve the first problem? We now have the enabling technology to bypass the MNO's restriction on the device. This is a SIM overlay, that Ross, I think, has one of them, if you care to see it. It's a trusted element, it acts as a SIM and looks like a very thin SIM. It's a sticker. You can peel it off, you can put it on the existing SIM (the MNO's SIM), then insert it back into the phone. This gives the user access to two SIM toolkit menus.

Now we have a trusted zone that we can program. It's a Java card, and it's very simple to program. We can load our own keys, we can do whatever we want in this trusted element. That's the first problem solved.

What we want to present here is DigiTally, the offline payment system that we're working on. We want this to be free and open-source to get the largest adoption possible; no patent issues with the systems that I mentioned before. We want this to be implemented as SIM toolkit applets. Smartphone apps would make life a lot easier, but we want something deployable today, not in five to ten years when Android phones become more popular than they are right now. So we want to implement them in overlay SIMs, as a proof-of-concept to demonstrate that an MNO's restriction is not an obstacle.

The name, DigiTally, and I credit Ross for that, is due to the fact that the system works by means of tallying the digits that are exchanged between the users. So how does this work? I will now describe the basic protocol. You can probably see a lot of problems here that Ross will definitely summarise for you, but this is the strawman stuff.

Alice and Bob want to pay each other X. They know their identities, A and B, and they agree on X. What Bob the merchant does first is to generate a nonce N_B. He MACs the transaction and gives Alice N_B, B (if unknown to Alice) and C which is a subset of the MAC (a few digits), not the entire MAC. Alice receives this verbally from Bob, or the code is shown to Alice. She enters the digits in her phone, and if the MAC verifies on both devices, she authorises the transaction with her PIN. Her device does something similar: she generates another nonce N_A, and she generates the response R to Bob's challenge C.

In this response, she includes the two nonces, N_A and N_B, she includes the challenge MAC that she received, and she includes the two identities A and B and she MACs all these parameters producing R. She provides N_A and a subset of R to Bob. Bob enters the digits into his phone, if everything checks out, then Alice's balance was already decremented by X, and Bob's device is incremented by X (after entering R). I will let Ross go through the interesting attacks and development of the protocol.

Ross Anderson: Well, so we've got a protocol that appears to work. This being the protocols workshop, one of the first things that you do is try to verify it. So can you verify it, for example, using the BAN logic? Summarising the protocol here, the challenge is a MAC of Bob's phone number, Alice's phone number, the amount and Bob's nonce; and the response is a MAC of Alice's phone number, Alice's nonce, the challenge that was just seen, Bob's nonce, and his phone number.

The reason for the challenge is that you want to make sure that both of the parties agree on the sender phone number, the recipient phone number and the amount. The reason for the payment nonce is, of course, to show that the payment was authorised. Now this can be built into the standard transaction flow for M-Pesa and the other mobile phone systems with the addition of the challenge and response. I should perhaps mention that most of these mobile phone payment systems use essentially the same transaction flow, because they started off using software from a firm called Fundamo that ended up being bought by VISA. So we take the standard system, and we put a small modification on it: the challenge and response.

What we need is that Bob trusts X, if Bob believes, Alice believes X, and if Bob believes that Alice has jurisdiction over X. Why should Alice believe X? Well, if Alice uttered X and X is fresh, according to the nonce verification rule, and all of these trace back to the software constraints, so this appears to be fairly straightforward.

Jonathan Anderson: Where does K come from?

Ross Anderson: K is the key that they share, and I'll discuss that later. To begin with, you can think of it as being a universal shared master secret, and we'll refine that concept as we go on. In fact, our version 0 design didn't verify, because we didn't put N_B (Bob's nonce) in R, and this meant that it failed to verify. Then we realised this is exactly the same vulnerability that you have in EMV, which leads to the pre-play attack. The use of the BAN logic in this case enabled us to avoid a common error from which millions, billions of bank cards in the west suffer, and which leads to fraud. Are we all sorted then? Have we got a verified protocol?

Bill's shaking his head, and of course that's absolutely right.

Bill Roscoe: I've read the paper.

Ross Anderson: He read the paper. He cheated. That's cheating! [laughter]

Can anybody else see what the vulnerability is? It turns out that the vulnerability is the challenge C is only three digits long, and so you can do, basically, a birthday attack on that, which is outside the scope of the BAN logic. The BAN logic assumes that all nonces, all keys, all MACs and so on, are infinitely long. It doesn't take account of entropy, and in fact that's the case with most verification tools with the exception of CryptoVerif.

How do you do an attack? Well, Bob chooses a higher priced X'. Say X is 500 Kenyan shillings for a bag of rice and X' might be 50,000 Kenyan shillings, and so Bob generates a series of new nonces $N_{B'}$ and he finds a collision such that the MAC of A, X, N_B and B is the same as MAC of A, X', $N_{B'}$ and B. As C is only three digits, that means that you have to make several dozen attempts, which is quite feasible – even on a phone with a rubber keyboard.

Bob then aborts all of the trial transactions except for the last one of the colliding pair, and he can give N_B and C to Alice, but in his SIM he uses $N_{B'}$ and X'. This means that when the transaction goes through, Alice pays 500 Kenyan shillings, and her value counter is decremented by that much, while Bob receives 50,000 Kenyan shillings and his value counter is incremented by that much. This violates the law of conservation of money, on which banks are understandably rather keen. So this is a significant failure.

This is one of the interesting things from the scientific point of view that comes out of considering short message authentication protocols. You can't just use your raw, out-of-the-box verification tool kit, because you have to start keeping track of entropy as well.

Incidentally, it was our colleague Markus Kuhn who spotted this 'man in the middle' attack, which is how he joined the paper as an author.

Then we got together and we started thinking about other issues around entropy. And the obvious thing is that Bob could try to add money to his SIM card by faking customers and just guessing the response R. If you're guessing a four-digit response, then that means that you might have to make 5,000 guesses. Are you worried about that? How hard are people prepared to work, in a country where people earn a dollar a day, in order to make some upper transaction limit?

And how feasible is it for you to implement on your SIM card, velocity checks as to how many bad MACs can be verified before you have to go online and refresh the system? That's a bigger design issue that we discuss in the paper.

What we can also do is look for collisions among transactions with real customers. Is it possible to confuse a former transaction X with former transaction Y? Now there's a generic fix to these kind of attacks, which is that you generate all the nonces with a key K_{AS}, known to Sam the banker. Alice's nonce N_A is some counter encrypted under K_{AS}. K_{AS} is present in Alice's overlay SIM card and also in Sam's hardware security module in Nairobi. This way, when transactions are uploaded, Sam can check the nonces as well as the MACs, and if something is wrong then he can alarm on that.

That is basically a variant of trick that was already used in UEPS 20 years ago, in that of the things that get uploaded, you have some things that could be checked by the merchant and other things that could be checked only by the bank. This is one of the ways of dealing with the risks of such systems.

The second thing that we start to think about as a second evolution, is why don't we chain transactions together? We started thinking about this, because typical mobile phone payment transactions in the third world very often go to people to whom you have paid before. Either you are paying the village storekeeper again and again and again, buying shopping bags full of household necessities; or else another big application of such systems is remittances. You go and work in Nairobi, and you send money back to your wife or to your mum, or whoever, in the west country once a week.

If you can establish a long-lived session between payer and payee, then perhaps in the case of small repeated transactions you could use fewer MAC digits, say when you're making your hundredth purchase from the village store for 500 shillings. You could then see to it that you can block various attacks which involve guessing or finding collisions with past MACs. What you can do is replace N_A and N_B with MACs of the transaction data, and you can keep shared state between Alice and Bob, which means that if somebody gets a fortuitous collision on a MAC, it will only work for one transaction.

The sort of thing that you do is have the payment session being a hash chain, and the status is a hash digest and a counter. When Alice and Bob start a new transaction, the SIMs initialise a session, and then whenever you do another transaction, you update the state. I'm not going to read through this equation. You can get the details in the paper.

This means that you can tune the transaction parameters for the number of MAC digits you want on initialisation, the number of MAC digits you want at each transaction, and the risk of fraud. How you go about verifying protocols like this, we don't really know. We suspect that you have to write down some kind of game and use game theory to look for equilibria – circumstances under which some particular fraud strategy might give a payoff. That we leave for future work. And again, that's the second part of the transaction chaining. Then what you do is update the state and decrement the value counter, and the transaction proceeds as before.

The third evolution that we considered is: what about group keying? If overlay SIMs had enormous storage, you could simply give every SIM card a unique K_{AB} for every other SIM card. Right? Then you would have unique pair of keys and bank rules generally say something like that for an EAL4 verified card you can do transactions up to 20 Euros or 20 dollars, or whatever. With a universal shared secret key, but for larger transactions you're expected to have a unique key per transacting pair of Alice and Bob.

Is there a useful halfway house? Well, broadcast encryption schemes from about 20 years ago had the idea that you could prevent the break of a single pay-TV card from being used to generate a universal solution to a satellite TV system simply by dividing your subscribers into groups. The same idea happens here. What you can do is use combinatorial keying whereby you divide users into a hundred key groups, and you then give each SIM card a hundred keys out of a total ... sorry, that's a mistake. That should be 4,950 keys: half n, n minus one. That means that an attacker who breaks one card could then only impersonate one percent of the card fleet. He can't impersonate a hundred percent of the card fleet. The idea here is that you can push out the costs of somebody doing a group break.

Why do we care about this? Fraud happens when it's industrialisable, and how is somebody going to industrialise an attack on a system like this? Do you extract value from a small number of merchants who happen to have a lot of cash on the premises, or do you attack the system by handing out SIM cards that enable lots of people to go and take small amounts from their village merchant? One works with these case studies and comes to the conclusion that in many of these cases, a class break would involve drilling keys out of more than one card if you use group keying.

This isn't, however, a magic solution, because this is easy to do in the case where the bank is the phone company, but a system like this is more likely to be taken off in cases where the bank isn't the phone company, because then the bank is having to pay the phone company for SMSs, and has got an incentive to deploy a system like this.

Now here's the really interesting bit: Delay-tolerant networks. There's a lot of places in the world where people have to deal with intermittent network service. One case: we came across a story of a village in the Finmark, in northern Sweden, where there isn't GSM service and there is a helicopter service in the nearest town, so what people do is they get their phones and give them to the helicopter driver, and rather than paying for a helicopter ride yourself, which is several hundred Euros, you just get your phone taken into town and it gets your email updates, your Facebook updates and all the rest of it. There are similar things apparently done in villages in Brazil, where you have to get on a speedboat for an hour or two into Manaus, in order to check your Facebook.

Wouldn't it be neat if you could have a PC in the village which would enable local sharing, and which could also be upgraded by means of a USB card carried every day by the speedboat driver? Getting the Internet and getting online service to the last billion people is probably going to involve thinking about the infrastructure for delay-tolerant networks.

So is there any general mechanism that might be applicable here, and that we could use in our case of off-network payments in Africa and South Asia? Well, the case that's perhaps of most interest is where people want to do relatively high value payments, again and again, to the same recipient. Again, think the guy who goes into Nairobi and gets a job, and wants to send money home to a remote village once a week, over the ten pound limit. So what you want to do is have a means whereby after some initial protocol or handshake, Alice and Bob end up with a high-quality, long-term shared key which they can use to authenticate transactions above that universal key limit.

Remember Needham-Schroeder? The shared-key version? We all tell our students that this was one of the first crypto protocols, but it's got a bug. Right? Alice says to Sam, I want to speak to Bob and here's my nonce. Sam says here's a key encrypted for you, and here's the same key encrypted for Bob. Alice goes to Bob and says, here's a key packet from Sam which enables you to speak to me. And of course the bug is that Alice could wait for a year between the second message and the third message, and so you've got no guarantee of freshness, at least from Bob's point of view. And this is considered to be a bug that was fixed in Kerberos by moving to timestamps.

But we realised, in the delay-tolerant network environment, this isn't a bug. This is a feature. A well-studied protocol, well out of patent, does exactly what we want! Because Alice and Bob want Sam's help to establish a unique shared key, K_{AB}, so that they can then do transactions above the twenty dollar limit. One party starts a Needham-Schroeder protocol with Sam once they get connectivity, okay? Alice and Bob do their first ten dollar transaction, or whatever, using the shared key that's in every SIM card, but then both of the SIM cards remember, and Alice's SIM card says, 'I remember I've done a transaction with Bob. Opportunistically, I should get a K_{AB} whenever I can next speak to Sam.'

Alice then goes online, and you get the key packet. The thing that you then have to work on is how do you exchange the digits offline for the key packet K_{AB} encrypted by K_{BS} – that's the third message there – with the other party? If you're going to encrypt something in a single AES block, but that's 128 bits, which is 40 decimal digits, which is perhaps a bit of a pain. How many digits do you actually need for K_{AB}? How many bits do you need for K_{AB}? Will 80 bits be enough? Are 64 bits enough? How big does the key packet have to be?

Well, one of the things that we do know is that from the work in pre-payment electricity meters we did 20 years ago, that people – even people who can't read and write – can easily manage 20-digit codes, because 20-digit codes presented as five blocks of four digits are how people buy electricity in many less developed countries. That we know we can make work. Is that good enough? Can people deal with 30? Can people deal with 40? That's for experimentation.

The next step in payment networks, we believe, is to extend them to areas where the network stops, and what we hope to do this year is a realistic field trial so we can figure out whether people can use this stuff, and what the usable parameters are for challenges, for responses, for key packets, for delay-tolerant Needham-Schroeder, and the constraint here is the user interface. That's what we're designing out from. The crypto, we assume we can do. Okay, we may need two or three goes and great care over the verification, but what we've got to do is have something that people will actually use in the field. We need to think about scalability and recovery and so on, if it's going to be acceptable to banks.

What we've shown in the paper, which I hope you'll read, is how we evolved the protocols to deal with entropy problems which the BAN logic missed, and which other verification techniques mostly miss – dealing with transaction sharing, dealing with mitigating the risk of shared keys. And the future research direction is what do we do with delay-tolerant networks in general, because these are going to be important. They were important in the past, when a lot of stuff was offline. We've tended to forget them over the past 20 years, but we're now seeing more and more stuff require some delay-tolerant capability – EMV for example. How much more is going to be needed and how do we as protocol engineers go about delivering on that requirement?

That's what we've been up to, and that's what we're planning to do in field trials during the summer. Any questions?

Vashek Matyas: How low-level is the mobile that you are considering in this scheme?

Ross Anderson: The mobiles that we're considering are the mobiles that you buy for $8.00 in Tesco's. They have no camera, they have no touch screen, they've got rubber keyboards, and they've just got a little LCD display with several lines of ASCII text. That's what most people have in the demographic that we're trying to reach. You see, the reason we did this is that the Gates Foundation had a call for proposals for how to do payments off-network, and so we've come up with this idea and won a small grant which should pay for the field trials.

Vashek Matyas: But with a camera you can rely on bar or QR codes?

Ross Anderson: With anything like that, you're easy. If you've got NFC or Bluetooth or anything like that, you just do all this in an app. But given that we've got the mechanism, you can use the same mechanism whether it's in an app or whether it's being done by manual copying of digits.

Jeff Yan: You actually answered my question already. I was curious on what motivated the design and how did you get realistic requirements.

Ross Anderson: The Gates Foundation has funded dozens and dozens of mobile payment networks in LDCs. They found it transformative for growth and development, but it runs out where the network does, and there's lots of villages that are off-network.

Explicit Delegation Using Configurable Cookies

David Llewellyn-Jones[(⊠)], Graeme Jenkinson, and Frank Stajano

Computer Laboratory, University of Cambridge, Cambridge, UK
{david.llewellyn-jones,graeme.jenkinson,
frank.stajano}@cl.cam.ac.uk
https://mypico.org

Abstract. Password sharing is widely used as a means of delegating access, but it is open to abuse and relies heavily on trust in the person being delegated to. We present a protocol for delegating access to websites as a natural extension to the Pico protocol. Through this we explore the potential characteristics of delegation mechanisms and how they interact. We conclude that security for the delegator against misbehaviour of the delegatee can only be achieved with the cooperation of the entity offering the service being delegated. To achieve this in our protocol we propose configurable cookies that capture delegated permissions.

1 Introduction

Everybody hates passwords. They are insecure in theory and even worse in practice; complex passwords are slow to use and prone to error. The Pico Project[1] [10] aims to provide a secure, privacy-protecting hardware token replacing all of a user's passwords while avoiding the need for trusted third parties and eliminating phishing attacks. To be successful, Pico must give not just the same level of usability, but also the same level of flexibility as passwords. It must do this even where the functionality is currently achieved by subverting security mechanisms to such an extent that the security benefits of passwords are essentially lost. This is quite a tall order.

A case in point is that of *delegation*. For most websites there is no formal approach for delegating access to an account, but users still successfully manage to do so on a quite routine basis. How do they do this? They share their password with the person they're delegating to.

It will be immediately obvious that this provides little-to-no security above that offered by the delegator's trust in the person being delegated to. This delegatee is granted full permissions to the account, to the extent they could quite easily lock the rightful owner out by changing the password.

Users aren't doing this because they lack a basic security understanding. They do it because they trust the people involved or societal pressures, because it's convenient, because they have no alternative, and because it works [9]. Sharing of passwords is even used as an expression of trust [7,8].

---

[1] https://mypico.org.

© Springer International Publishing AG 2017
J. Anderson et al. (Eds.): Security Protocols XXIV, LNCS 10368, pp. 141–152, 2017.
DOI: 10.1007/978-3-319-62033-6_17

The challenge is to provide a more secure approach that users will be willing to adopt. We ask the question of how Pico, building on top of the incumbent infrastructures of the Web, can offer similarly simple delegation but without destroying its security benefits in the process. We will explore this question, showing that a simple delegation protocol is not only possible, but is in fact a natural evolution of the existing Pico design. We claim the following contributions in this paper.

1. A technical solution for delegation offering security, minimal reliance on the goodwill of the delegatee and using Web technologies for easy deployment (Sect. 2.1).
2. A taxonomy to explore the space of possible delegation solutions (Sect. 3).
3. A claim that you cannot delegate securely and revocably without introducing technical changes to the verifier (Sect. 3.1).
4. A discussion about open questions, including how best to deploy evolvable solutions: better to provide a formal mechanism early that relies on trust, or a more secure solution requiring changes to website back-ends (Sect. 4)?

2   Pico the Delegation Device

In its broadest terms delegation is an arrangement between three parties: the *delegator* user, the *delegatee* user and the *delegated* service. We will refer to them respectively as *Rebecca* and *Eric*, accessing the *DumpIt* cloud storage service. The semantic relationship between the parties involved is shown in Fig. 1.

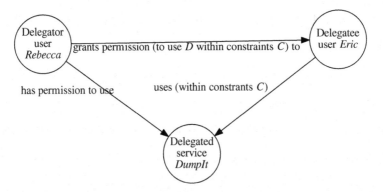

Fig. 1. Semantic relationship between the actors.

A critical observation for us was that, in its existing form, Pico is already performing delegation according to the relationship as shown. To see this, consider the standard Pico protocol for logging in to an account on the Web shown in Fig. 2 and which is documented in more detail by Jenkinson *et al.* [6]. The process is initiated by Rebecca entering a URL on her browser with the Pico

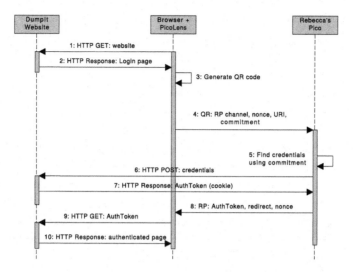

Fig. 2. The standard Pico protocol.

Lens installed. On receiving the login page, the Lens displays a QR code then scanned by the Pico. This provides the Pico with the necessary information to log in to the DumpIt site.

At this point the real authentication begins. The authentication takes place between DumpIt and Rebecca's Pico, with the end result that Rebecca's Pico has the digital *AuthToken* (a session cookie) for accessing the site. But even though Rebecca's Pico has authenticated, this is of no use to Rebecca. She doesn't want to access the site using her Pico, she wants to access it on a more convenient device with a decent browser. Hence Rebecca's Pico *delegates* the AuthToken to the browser in step 8 of the protocol.

So Pico is already a delegation device, but with a pool of delegatees restricted to lenses it's already paired with. We can generalise this to allow delegation to other humans by breaking step 8 into two and placing another Pico in the middle.

2.1 Delegation Protocol Using Cookies

The resulting split protocol is shown in Figs. 3a and b. This allows an authorisation token (the session cookie) to be delegated from Rebecca's Pico – which has an account with the DumpIt service – to Eric's Pico, allowing Eric to access DumpIt as if he were Rebecca (and even if Eric has no account with DumpIt himself).

The process involves Rebecca passing the AuthToken to Eric that he's then able to present to DumpIt for access to the service. As can be seen in Fig. 4a, the actual delegation step is initiated when Rebecca selects the option on her Pico. Her Pico displays a QR code which Eric scans, instigates the transfer of the AuthToken from Rebeca's Pico to Eric's Pico where it can be stored for

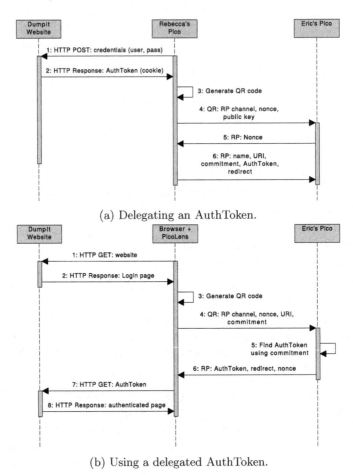

(a) Delegating an AuthToken.

(b) Using a delegated AuthToken.

Fig. 3. The delegation protocol, slightly simplified for clarity.

later use. The use of a transient QR code is intended to encourage Eric to be in physical proximity with Rebecca when the transfer takes place, although in and of itself it can't guarantee this. In the background Rebecca is POST-ing her credentials to DumpIt, which returns back a session cookie. This session cookie is the AuthToken passed to Eric.

Some time later Eric will want to make use of the delegated token. Eric can make use of the existing Pico approach for logging in to websites: he scans a QR code presented on DumpIt's login page, providing the Pico with the information needed to complete the login. As we've seen the usual Pico approach would have Eric's Pico POST login credentials (username and password) to the website, which would reply back with a session cookie for access to the site. The Pico then installs this on the browser. However, the AuthToken held by Eric's Pico is already such a session cookie. Rather than POST credentials, Eric's Pico sends

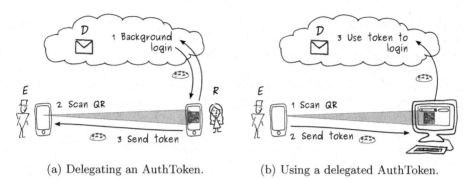

(a) Delegating an AuthToken.   (b) Using a delegated AuthToken.

Fig. 4. Delegation in practice.

the AuthToken to the browser, which uses it for access to the site without the need to log in. Figure 4 illustrates how the process appears to the end user.

We have implemented this on top of the existing Android Pico App and Pico Lens Firefox Plugin. This has provided us some insight into how effective the approach is, and its prospects for providing improvements in the future. It has also raised important questions about whether users would make use of the functionality even if Pico made it available. Is delegation a practical function?

3   Delegation for End Users

To answer this question we believe the social characteristics of delegation are key. The goal of delegation typically falls in to one of five categories as shown in Fig. 5. We offer an example of each.

Value-sharing involves multiple users all gaining non-exclusive benefit from a service through delegation of access. Netflix allows the legitimate sharing of an account for simultaneous streaming (ideal for adults sharing a flat). It supports multiple profiles but credentials still have to be shared to allow access to content. Sharing the credentials for simultaneous access multiplies the value of the account to its users.

		Shareable	*Exclusive*	
Grant access		Effort-sharing	Effort-transfer	*Task*
		Value-sharing	Value-transfer	*Benefit*
Restrict access		Self-delegation		

Fig. 5. The five categories of delegation.

Effort-sharing is similar, but now multiple users are able to share a task amongst them through access to a service. A reviewer assigned multiple papers to review through a conference website might delegate some of the reviews to a colleague by sharing access[2]. A similar example is that of a corporate social media account[3]. The communications team will need access to a single company account, with the only way of doing so by sharing the credentials between them. The effort of running the media feed is divided between all of those involved.

Effort-transfer involves the delegation of a specific task from one person to another and is similar to effort-sharing, but with the addition of exclusivity. If I want my local computer-shop to health-check my laptop I'll have to hand over the admin password. We can't both work on it simultaneously and ideally I'd like to give them access only while they're performing the task on my behalf. I'll have to give them admin access too, even though they don't need to see my photos and emails.

Value-transfer shifts the process back from activity to consumption again. Your account credentials represent the key to accessing some value you may want to 'gift' to someone else. For example in the past parents would hand over cash to their children to buy sweets from the local shop. Now they send them out with a credit card and PIN [9]. Either way, once the money is spent it can't be used again.

Clearly there can be some blurring of boundaries between these categories. For example a social media account will require effort to maintain, but allows users to draw benefit from it at the same time.

Self-delegation reverses the role of delegation. Rather than granting access to others it can be used to *restrict* access for the owner of the account; useful for managing risk. For example while travelling abroad you might want to take with you access to only low-value and essential accounts. You can delegate just the accounts you need, limiting your exposure in case they are compromised. This is similar to buying a pre-paid cash card for travel.

One of these categories is not like the others. The first four are all *permissive*, whereas the last is *restrictive*. This is also reflected in how they can be performed. The first four can all be achieved using passwords, but self-delegation cannot.

For the permissive categories, password sharing is likely to be a simple way to achieve the objective. It is unlikely to be the safest or most secure way of doing so, but with an appropriate level of trust most people will accept this (essentially replacing technical security with personal trust).

It is worth noting that there is another form of delegation that implies an obligation on the party delegated to, as happens when a task is delegated from one person to another [5]. In spite of the terminology we use (*e.g. effort-sharing* and *effort-transfer*) we're only interested in technical enforcement related to delegation of permissions, not tasks. Although the two may go together (you

---

[2] In practice, most peer-review platforms provide a formal mechanism for delegating reviews, so sharing an account wouldn't be necessary.

[3] For example Twitter or Instagram.

may have to delegate some permissions in order for a task to be completed) we won't consider how such task obligations might be enforced.

Delegation, then, is a rich space in terms of user motivation and functionality. In creating an effective delegation process we must encompass this functionality with our technical protocol, but the design choices we make in achieving this will also affect other characteristics which are also important, such as usability and security. Mapping approaches to points in the space of relevant characteristics can provide us some insight into compromises that might incentivise users to choose one approach (password sharing?) over another (Pico delegation?).

3.1 Constraints

By definition the process of delegation enforces certain constraints in what any protocol must involve, such as the fact that Rebecca must be involved in the set up of the delegation step, and both Eric and DumpIt must be involved in the use of the delegated privilege.

However there remain several areas that are open to interpretation. Table 1 presents our attempt to define the possible variables that can be used to categorise different delegation approaches. The table summarises the variables but requires some explanation in places.

Table 1. Delegation scope. A spanning arc $\widehat{XY}$ implies a physical proximity constraint, described further in Sect. 3.1.

Variable	Type	Values
Usability	Continuous	Low – high
Expressiveness/flexibility	Continuous	Low – high
Security	Continuous	Low – high
Trust required	Continuous	Low – high (of E by R)
Accountability of E	Discrete	$\emptyset$, E, R, D, ER, ED, RD, all; *i.e.* $\mathcal{P}(\{E, R, D\})$
Plausible deniability of E	Discrete	Full, RD, ED, ER, D, R, E, $\emptyset$
Involvement at creation	Discrete	$\widehat{ER}$, ER, ED, $\widehat{ERD}$, ERD
Involvement at operation	Discrete	ED, EDR
Revocable by	Discrete	$\emptyset$, R, D, RD

Expressiveness relates to the use of a language to specify the permissions granted (contrariwise, specifying limits to their use). For example, Rebecca may want to delegate only a subset of the available functionality of DumpIt, to allow reading but not writing, or to apply a time restriction on how long the service can be accessed.

The trust required implies the extent to which Rebecca must trust Eric not to abuse the delegated permissions. Allowing more precise permissions specification and support for revocation will reduce the level of trust needed.

The values for accountability list those actors with the potential to account for Eric's actions in a provable way. Plausible deniability represents the inverse of this. It indicates whether Eric can deny responsibility for an action to a particular set of other entities.

Whether a party is involved at the creation determines how the process of delegation takes place (by definition delegation always occurs from Rebecca to Eric). A spanning arc $\widehat{ER}$ implies Eric and Rebecca must be in physical proximity to perform the delegation (otherwise conducted remotely via the network). Both the delegatee and delegated service must always be involved when the permission is used ("involved at operation"). Requiring the delegator to be involved implies that every action can be permitted or refused in real time.

Finally, revocation implies that Eric's permissions may be withdrawn without affecting those of Rebecca.

Ideally a developer could simply select the best for each variable and forge a new protocol to suit. Unfortunately there are also constraints between them to prevent them being selected à la carte. We capture these in the following claim.

Claim 1. The following relationships are intrinsic to the nature of delegation.

1. There is an inverse relationship between expressiveness (supporting a richer language for expressing rights delegation) and usability.
2. There is a direct relationship between expressiveness and security.
3. There is an inverse relationship between security and trust.
4. Accountability is the precise inverse of plausible deniability. Therefore if Eric can plausibly deny some act, then he cannot be accountable for it.
5. Revocation implies accountability. If a party can revoke Eric's permissions without revoking Rebecca's, then that party must be able to tell which of the two is performing an operation.

A number of further relationships would seem to immediately derive from these, such as that there is an inverse relationship between usability and security. For discussion and examples relating trust, security, delegation, plausible deniability and authentication together, see Christianson's insightful paper [4]. We also claim the relationship between security, trust and expressiveness to be of crucial importance, which we express as follows.

Claim 2. For Rebecca to minimise her exposure she must restrict the permissions entrusted to Eric to just those needed for him to carry out his task.

A more expressive rights language will allow permissions to be expressed more specifically and therefore reduce trust. Since the permissions are dependent on the functionality offered by the service, and the gate to this functionality must also be provided by the service, this immediately leads us to our final claim.

Claim 3. The security-trust balance of delegation can only be achieved if the verifier offers a means of expressing fine-grained permissions.

We'll return to this in Sect. 3.3 where we discuss the practical implications of this in relation to cookies. Since the baseline case in terms of both functionality and usability is that provided by password sharing, we will consider how this fits within these constraints in the next section.

3.2 Characteristics Using Passwords as Tokens

As we've seen, delegation is already perfectly possible just by sharing passwords. In their seminal paper of 1999, Adams and Sasse recommend shared passwords as an important way for authentication to match workers' sense of responsibility: "Shared work and responsibility require users to perceive that they are using shared passwords" [1]. They also identify that it can impact security and more recent advice from GCHQ emphasises this unequivocally: "You should never allow password sharing between users. Sharing accounts, or even occasional use by anyone other than the account holder, negates the benefit of authenticating a specific user." [3].

In practice, for most websites, sharing of passwords is the only practical way for an end user to delegate access. If our claims in the previous section concerning the constraints on delegation are valid, we should be able to place password sharing into the space and demonstrate how a more formal approach could move it to a 'better' place. We use the variables from Table 1 to summarise the characteristics as follows.

$$usability = \text{high}, \quad flexibility = \text{min}, \quad security = \text{min},$$
$$trust = \text{max}, \quad accountability = \emptyset, \quad deniability = \text{full},$$
$$creation = \widehat{ER}, \quad operation = ED, \quad revocable = \emptyset.$$

Our underlying claim is that without a formally defined or approved way to perform delegation, users will continue to simply share passwords as a means to achieve it. And yet password sharing is inherently insecure (as indicated by the *security* and *trust* assignments). For delegation to evolve positively, we must supply sensible protocols for performing delegation that increase *security* and decrease *trust* while having minimal negative impact on *usability*.

In the next section we will consider our proposed protocol using cookies as tokens and discuss how it provides a framework that can evolve to support this.

3.3 Characteristics Using Cookies

The characteristics depend heavily on the contents of the AuthToken. To take a common example, a WordPress admin cookie contains the following fields[4].

$$cookie = username \mid expiration \mid token \mid hash.$$
$$hash = SHA256(username \mid expiration \mid token,$$
$$MD5(username \mid passfrag \mid expiration \mid token)).$$

---

[4] See https://developer.wordpress.org/reference/functions/wp_generate_auth_cookie/.

In all cases *expiration* is the same ASCII string representing the time in Unix epoch format and *token* is a random session token stored against the user in the WordPress database. The *passfrag* string is a four character fragment of the base64-encoded hashed password.

The key points to note are that the data – including the expiration time – are all HMAC-ed and that the cookie includes a per-session random token. Consequently there's no way for Eric to extend the expiration time without invalidating the cookie, and DumpIt can revoke the cookie by disassociating its database entry for the session token from the user. Finally, although DumpIt isn't able to distinguish between normal and delegated sessions, Rebecca can do so since every AuthToken (each with unique session token field) has to pass through her Pico. If DumpIt were to record activity against sessions it could, in collaboration with Rebecca, account for Eric's activity.

Under this scheme we therefore have the following properties for cookies, which are also summarised in Table 2 for easy comparison against passwords.

$$usability = \text{medium}, \quad flexibility = \text{medium}, \quad security = \text{medium},$$
$$trust = \text{medium}, \quad accountability = RD, \quad deniability = R, D$$
$$creation = \widehat{ER}, \quad operation = ED, \quad revocable = D.$$

Table 2. Property comparison.

Scheme	Usability	Flexibility	Security	Trust	Accountability	Deniability	Creation	Operation	Revocable
Passwords	High	Min	Min	Max	$\emptyset$	Full	$\widehat{E}R$	ED	$\emptyset$
Cookies	Med	Med	Med	Med	RD	R, D	$\widehat{E}R$	ED	D

This can all be achieved by leveraging the existing site's cookie mechanisms. WordPress offers a particularly robust cookie structure; other sites are less thorough, for example relying on the default HTTP cookie expiration fields which are not cryptographically tied to the cookie (and can therefore be changed).

The only flexibility WordPress offers when generating cookies is whether they last for two days or two weeks[5]. This would allow Rebecca some control over how long Eric is granted access, but doesn't offer more expressive control over the admin capabilities delegated to him. Nevertheless this is an improvement on

---

[5] These values are hardcoded and chosen using the `rememberme` form value; see https://developer.wordpress.org/reference/functions/wp_set_auth_cookie/.

password delegation. As such we describe this property as *medium*, although a different cookie structure could allow greater flexibility (*low* to *high*).

This is an example of our Claim 3 above. The security is limited by the expressiveness of the permissions supported by the verifier. In our Pico implementation the website takes on the role of verifier, and so the website must be updated to support fine-grained permission and to allow Rebecca to bake configurable cookies expressing them to her specification. In theory the website could choose any rule language for this, but in practice Rebecca specifies the rules using an interface on her Pico, so some agreed interaction is required.

4 Open Questions

Question 1. Until websites support configurable cookies with more fine-grained permissions, the Pico implementation can still offer all-or-nothing delegation. Given the prevalence of password reuse across sites, this represents an improvement on password sharing. Is it therefore appropriate to make this functionality available even in this sub-optimal form, or better to wait until sites offer the configurable cookies required for proper security?

Question 2. Our implementation using Pico offers some insight into what is achievable. But would real people actually use the functionality? A user study by Bauer *et al.* [2] found people "are most likely to pick the [delegation] option they understand the best, even when they know it is not the option they want.". Will users take the time to learn about and apply tight delegation rules?

Question 3. In the form of password sharing, delegation is an expression of trust [8]. If I give you my password I'm not just granting you access, I'm also making a statement. Is there a way to avoid formal delegation processes becoming a mark of distrust?

Question 4. Delegation is transitive in our implementation. Therefore an Auth-Token granted to one user is easily transferred to another. The delegatee doesn't even need an account with the delegated service. Can we enforce non-transitive delegation while still supporting this, and without conflicting with plausible deniability?

Question 5. Many sites offer REST-ful APIs intended for delegated access by trusted apps. Developer tokens or delegated authorisation (*e.g.* OAuth) are often used to allow access. Do these provide a better starting point than cookies for user delegation?

5 Conclusion

Password sharing is widely used as a means of delegating access, so providing a more formal method seems like an obvious next step. We have described an approach that is a natural extension to the existing Pico protocol. We found the most important lever for controlling security to be the expressiveness of the language used to describe permissions delegated, and that configurable cookies are a means for achieving this. Exploring this space has uncovered many questions that still need to be answered.

Acknowledgements. We are grateful to the European Research Council for funding this research through grant StG 307224 (Pico). We also thank the workshop attendees for comments.

References

1. Adams, A., Sasse, M.A.: Users are not the enemy. Commun. ACM **42**(12), 40–46 (1999). http://doi.acm.org/10.1145/322796.322806
2. Bauer, L., Cranor, L.F., Reiter, M.K., Vaniea, K.: Lessons learned from the deployment of a smartphone-based access-control system. In: Proceedings of the 3rd Symposium on Usable Privacy and Security, SOUPS 2007, pp. 64–75. ACM (2007)
3. CESG: Password guidance: simplifying your approach. CESG, CPNI, January 2016. https://www.cesg.gov.uk/guidance/password-guidance-simplifying-your-approach
4. Christianson, B.: Living in an impossible world: real-izing the consequences of intransitive trust. Philos. Technol. **26**(4), 411–429 (2013)
5. Giorgini, P., Massacci, F., Mylopoulos, J., Zannone, N.: Modeling security requirements through ownership, permission and delegation, pp. 167–176. IEEE, August 2005
6. Jenkinson, G., Spencer, M., Warrington, C., Stajano, F.: I bought a new security token and all I got was this Lousy Phish—relay attacks on visual code authentication schemes. In: Christianson, B., Malcolm, J., Matyáš, V., Švenda, P., Stajano, F., Anderson, J. (eds.) Security Protocols 2014. LNCS, vol. 8809, pp. 197–215. Springer, Cham (2014). doi:10.1007/978-3-319-12400-1_19
7. Lenhart, A., Lewis, O., Rainie, L.: Teenage life online: the rise of the instant-message generation and the internets impact on friendships and family relationships, June 2001. http://www.pewinternet.org/2001/06/21/teenage-life-online/
8. Palfrey, J., Sacco, D.T., Boyd, D., DeBonis, L., Tatlock, J.: Enhancing child safety and online technologies, December 2008. http://cyber.law.harvard.edu/pubrelease/isttf/
9. Singh, S., Cabraal, A., Demosthenous, C., Astbrink, G., Furlong, M.: Password sharing: implications for security design based on social practice, p. 895904. In: CHI 2007. ACM (2007). http://doi.acm.org/10.1145/1240624.1240759
10. Stajano, F.: Pico: no more passwords!. In: Christianson, B., Crispo, B., Malcolm, J., Stajano, F. (eds.) Security Protocols 2011. LNCS, vol. 7114, pp. 49–81. Springer, Heidelberg (2011). doi:10.1007/978-3-642-25867-1_6

Explicit Delegation Using Configurable Cookies
(Transcript of Discussion)

David Llewellyn-Jones(✉)

University of Cambridge, Cambridge, UK
david.llewellyn-jones@cl.cam.ac.uk

This is really just very preliminary research around delegation, and in the context of the Pico Project it's all about replacing passwords. The comparison that we're making is between people delegating passwords to one another in order to delegate access to particular accounts, and using Pico for the same purpose.

Our starting point is this question of how people share passwords and our question is whether or not we can provide some better approach using something like a Pico token. The first question to ask is whether people really do actually share passwords? And of course, yes they do. This is an article from PC Mag from just over a year ago [2] which actually gives you tips for how you should go about sharing passwords if you wanted to. They say, for example, that you shouldn't send a password in an email you should split it into two pieces and send half using email and the other half using some other mechanism.

They also give some interesting use cases for when people might want to share passwords. For example, they suggest situations where you have a family and you want to all access the same Netflix account. Or situations where, for example, in a corporate environment you have a shared corporate Twitter feed or social networking account and you want multiple people to access that account and post to it. Another example they give is where you have a backup to allow someone else to access your account in case of an emergency. Arguably, they're valid cases for when you want to delegate responsibility for an account and, at present, for a lot of services there isn't really any other mechanism for doing so.

Can I ask, have any of you ever shared your account? Or been given an account by someone else to share?[1] Yes, so it's not that unusual; it does happen quite often. Of course, it happens but it's not the ideal secure situation.

We've got this setup (Fig. 1), which is essentially just the setup we're thinking about. We talk about *Rebecca* the delegator, *Eric* the delegatee and this service, *DumpIt*, that could be some kind of Cloud sharing service that Rebecca wants to delegate access to Eric to. In an ideal situation Rebecca would, probably, not want to delegate full access to Eric but perhaps only access to the particular parts that Rebecca wants to provide to him. It might be an account but it might also be, say, a credit card where a parent wants to give a child the credit card to go and make some payments or to get some money from an ATM. Or it might be a phone. We just heard from Ross Anderson[2] how people give phones to a helicopter pilot and that is essentially a delegation process where they're

---

[1] At this point, the majority of the audience raised their hands.

[2] "SMAPs: Short Message Authentication Protocols", these proceedings.

© Springer International Publishing AG 2017
J. Anderson et al. (Eds.): Security Protocols XXIV, LNCS 10368, pp. 153–164, 2017.
DOI: 10.1007/978-3-319-62033-6_18

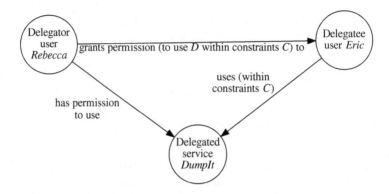

Fig. 1. Semantic relationship between the actors.

delegating responsibility for performing a payment to the pilot. Delegation comes in many different forms.

The idea is that, ultimately, once Eric has done whatever it is that he wants to do with the account, he forgets the password and then everything is secure again. Hopefully. Or maybe, he doesn't; we don't really know. It's not very secure but it's certainly useful and it's quite intuitive functionality and so therefore people use it. It fits with their mental model of how things work. We also find that it provides an element of trust acknowledgment as well. This has been suggested by various people, but in particular there's been a report by the Internet Safety Technical Task Force that shows that teenagers use password transfer from one to the other as a recognition of trust in each other. Of course, if someone asks you for access to your account and you refuse to give them your password or you use some other more restrictive technical means for doing so, then in some sense you're saying that you distrust them, so there's an element of social interaction involved as well.

Of course, delegation can go wrong, because Rebecca has to trust Eric. In the wake of the recent FBI iPhone case the British police very gleefully announced that they have other mechanisms for dealing with access to iPhones [3]. There was a suspected terrorist, Junead Khan, and they wanted access to his iPhone. So they posed as company managers saying they said didn't believe his work record, they wanted to see evidence of it, and so he then had to delegate his phone to them to give access to the records. He essentially gave them his unlocked phone and, of course, although he didn't want to give them access to his entire phone, just to the work records, he had to give them the entire phone at which point they arrested him and set the phone so that it wouldn't lock. A clever technique that worked for them but also an example of where this trust can break down. If you don't really trust the person you're delegating access to then there's a risk they may use it for other purposes.

In the context of the Pico Project, the obvious question is *can Pico provide a better mechanism for delegation?* We thought about how we would extend Pico to provide this kind of capability. There are password managers that will allow you to transfer passwords from one user to another. Of course, that still leaves you with essentially the same problem as before: it's basically the same technique as giving a password. Is there a more secure way to do this? Well, it turned out that Pico was actually already providing a delegation capability, it was just doing it in the background and without an extra party involved. So the protocol already supported it. I'll go through the protocol in a second or two.

Before I do that, I want to summarize the objective of the work and the motivations for the work as described in the full paper. I won't go through everything but, essentially, the contributions that we're claiming are the following: first of all that we have an approach that Pico uses and that we've defined. We also wanted to know is it actually any better than sharing passwords? We therefore developed a taxonomy to try and understand whether or not one is an improvement of the other. We also give a theorem – actually it's more of a claim – that you can't delegate securely and revocably without introducing some kind of technical change at the verifier which in this case would be the DumpIt service. Then we also introduced some open questions but our objective has been to provide a practical solution not necessarily something which is robustly secure all the way through.

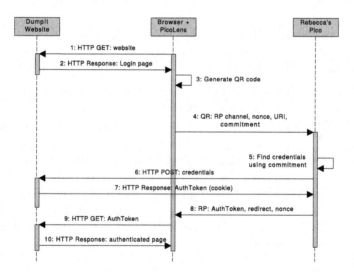

Fig. 2. The standard Pico protocol.

This is the standard Pico protocol (Fig. 2). I'm not going to go through everything but in broad terms the idea is that Rebecca wants to access the DumpIt website, Rebecca has a Pico and already has a trusted relationship with a browser which has a plug-in installed called the *Pico Lens*. Rebecca accesses the site, the Pico Lens recognizes that there's a password form there, and therefore produces a QR code. The QR code is then scanned by Rebecca's Pico which provides a means of establishing a secure connection between the lens and the browser plug-in, and over which the information needed by Pico about the page is transmitted. The Pico then logs into the service in the background via, for example, a mobile phone channel. It logs in to the site and the site returns a cookie. The cookie is the access token for the site, so the Pico then transmits this cookie back to the browser lens, the browser lens installs the cookie at which point the browser has access to the site.

I'm sure many of you have heard talks about Pico in the past and that's the standard Pico protocol as it works at the moment. Essentially what's happening is that the Pico is delegating access to the browser. The Pico logs in, and it then delegates access to the browser. Our new approach is to simply stick another Pico halfway along this process of transferring the cookie between the Pico and the browser [step 8 of Fig. 2].

Jonathan Anderson: In practice how transferable is that cookie between devices? Is the service looking at other fingerprinting of the browser that was used to generate the cookie, to confirm it's the same? That sort of thing?

Reply: Yeah, it's a good question. In our experience, not at all and I think it's actually a very hard thing to do. There isn't much fingerprint from a browser that appears to be very useful for doing that. In practice it seems not to be done very widely.

Jonathan Anderson: Even geographic regions? I could imagine that if you generate a cookie in a browser in Cambridge and then somebody starts using the same cookie in Malaysia ten minutes later that could raise an alarm.

Reply: I guess it could, but certainly not amongst the cookies that we looked at. I didn't look extensively at lots of different cookies but for the ones that we've tried it with that doesn't seem to be a problem at all.

Frank Stajano: There have been talks of people saying we will have more pinning down of cookies and the places they came from. But if you do that too aggressively then as people roam then their session stops working, so that may be why we have not observed this happening. We know that it's a hack, that in theory you should lock things down and not make it work because the thing that has passed identification is not the thing that is then using it, but on the other hand trying to make it too strict would break current usages beyond it.

Jonathan Anderson: Well, if I get off a plane and start using my Facebook session on a different device I would not be surprised if I had to type my password again.

Frank Stajano: On a different device yes, but if you had the webpage online and you start logging in through a changed network and now it doesn't work? If you hand over from one network to another, just because you move from this room to another, and then the Amazon purchase you were in the middle of doesn't work, that would be a bit annoying.

Reply: As it happened, Frank flagged up this issue of whether or not cookies work were locked to browsers as something that had been proposed. I did a search for it and didn't find any really convincing approaches that were proposed as being standard techniques for doing it. It's an interesting question in the long run but it certainly doesn't appear to be the case in general at present.

It is true that the big difference between this and the standard Pico approach is that the cookie that gets transferred is then transferred to another Pico and then kept also for a longer period of time before it's actually used. When Eric wants to use the delegated cookie he just goes through the standard process that Pico would normally go through to install it on the browser and then gains access to the site. This is what it looks like for the user (Fig. 3a). Rebecca wants to delegate a cookie, she clicks the button on her Pico, sets the criteria for the cookie, and it produces a scan code that looks like that shown in the diagram. Eric scans the code (Fig. 3b), the cookie is transferred, and then when Eric wants to use the cookie he just scans the site as he would have done with his standard cookie. It recognizes that it's a delegated cookie rather than a password and it sends that back to the browser. It's really quite lightweight for the user but, obviously, still more effort and more formal than simply giving someone a password.

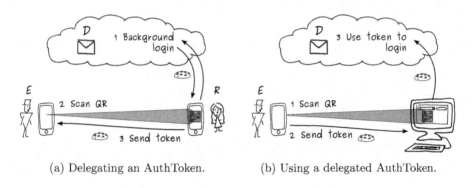

(a) Delegating an AuthToken.   (b) Using a delegated AuthToken.

Fig. 3. Delegation in practice.

This is what the interface looks like (Fig. 4). Rebecca simply clicks a button on her Pico, but then she also has to input some details about the restrictions that she wants set on the cookie. Ideally, your cookie would be slightly more restricted and in practice it *is* slightly more restricted than your password. I'll come back to that in a second. Ideally, you would refine it further to give better levels of access control. Then she clicks 'generate' and the QR code is generated. So it's a very lightweight procedure, which is the intention.

The implementation demonstrates that it's practically achievable but is it more secure than sharing passwords? That's something that we wanted to look into and so we tried to develop some kind of notion of what the features of delegation are and how they compare between different approaches. It also raised a number of questions. There's been some very interesting work done by Bauer and a number of other researchers at Carnegie Mellon on "Lessons learned from

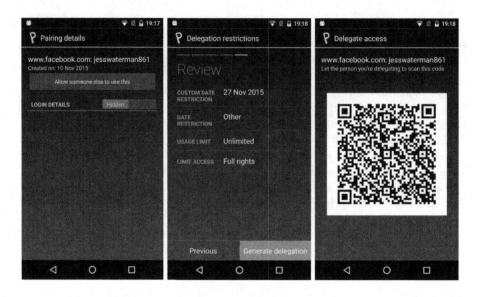

Fig. 4. Pico interface.

deployment of a Smartphone based access control system" [1] where they used a system over a long period of time. And they discovered that, although people could delegate access control to doors, and various other mechanisms, and they could provide restrictions on those access controls, they found that people invariably used the controls that they were familiar with rather than the controls which were what they actually wanted to apply.

For example, they might restrict access to the delegatee to just a week because there was a button that said '7 days worth of access control'. Rather than going through a more elongated process of saying, "I want to give them access to it just on a Wednesday when they have their tutorials in that room," for example. When they asked users why they were doing this, it wasn't necessarily because they didn't want to go through the process it was simply because they didn't realize that those capabilities were possible, that the options were there to make it more precise.

So the obvious question to ask is, would people really use this functionality? Would they go to the trouble of delegating only the access rights that they're really interested to delegate? Or would they essentially give people the same full access as a password would give? The other question which comes up is the question about trust. If providing a password is an acknowledgement of trust in the person that you're giving the password to, then does that mean that people actively don't want to use more formal techniques that restrict the level of trust required for the delegation that they're providing? Would that be acknowledgement that you don't trust the other person[3] and so therefore you

---

[3] See Helen Nissenbaum, 2001, "Securing trust online: wisdom or oxymoron?" Boston University Law Review, 81(3), pp. 635–664.

would not actually do this? The reports were invariably about how teenagers do this, in which context I guess these things are very important. These are some of the questions which we'd like to try and answer through a bigger user study. We haven't done that yet, we've only got some theoretical ideas about the differences between these various things and we've tried to understand them by looking at the different features.

Table 1. Delegation scope.

Variable	Type	Values
Usability	Continuous	Low – high
Expressiveness/flexibility	Continuous	Low – high
Security	Continuous	Low – high
Trust required	Continuous	Low – high (of E by R)
Accountability of E	Discrete	$\emptyset$, E, R, D, ER, ED, RD, all; $i.e.$ $\mathcal{P}(\{E, R, D\})$
Plausible deniability of E	Discrete	Full, RD, ED, ER, D, R, E, $\emptyset$
Involvement at creation	Discrete	$\widehat{ER}$, ER, ED, $\widehat{ERD}$, ERD
Involvement at operation	Discrete	ED, EDR
Revocable by	Discrete	$\emptyset$, R, D, RD

We have these nine different features (Table 1) and we tried to understand the delegation in terms of these features. They're either continuous or discrete but that doesn't really matter at this point. Some of them, perhaps, require a little bit of explanation.

Usability is pretty obvious: is the system more or less usable?

The expressiveness and flexibility represent how finely you can define the access control that you want to delegate. With a password the access control that you normally delegate is basically everything. You delegate the entire control of the account even allowing someone to wrestle control of the entire account by changing the password so that the original person, Rebecca, can't use it. Ideally you would want to express more fine grain access control.

The security level: is it a secure approach?

The trust required in Eric by Rebecca: does Rebecca trust Eric?

The accountability of Eric: is Eric accountable in terms of the question of whether the actions that Eric performs can be distinguished from the actions that Rebecca performs? And the reverse of that is plausible deniability.

And then various other things like who needs to be involved at the creation time? Who needs to be involved when the delegation is used? Who can revoke the credential?

In terms of the actual examples of how we look at these characteristics, this is for passwords:

$$usability = \text{high}, \quad flexibility = \text{min}, \quad security = \text{min},$$
$$trust = \text{max}, \quad accountability = \emptyset, \quad deniability = \text{full},$$
$$creation = \widehat{ER}, \quad operation = ED, \quad revocable = \emptyset.$$

I'm going to skim over this because I've got them on a later slide comparing them with how Pico works. Essentially, you can see it's high usability but very poor security, and very high levels of trust required.

In terms of how we compare it with a cookie, I've got an example of a cookie taken from WordPress and you can see that it contains various things:

$$cookie = username \mid expiration \mid token \mid hash.$$
$$hash = SHA256(username \mid expiration \mid token,$$
$$MD5(username \mid passfrag \mid expiration \mid token)).$$

It contains the user name, the expiration date, the token. The token is essentially a nonce that's generated and stored on the server as well and which the server checks when the cookie is used. A hash which contains a pass fragment which is actually pretty weak, it's just a four character truncation of the hash of the password so quite easy to spoof. Most of the security happens in the token part and crucially because the information is hashed the cookie can't be spoofed by someone else.

The cookie can't be less secure than a password because a password can generate a cookie but it can be more secure and in this case it's, probably, more secure because it doesn't allow people to change the password. Often you have to type the password in again to do that. We can provide the comparison and we see that essentially the usability of passwords is, probably, slightly more but the trust required is slightly less and so the security's slightly more for the cookie example. There are various other slight changes in the other features as well.

$$usability = \text{medium}, \quad flexibility = \text{medium}, \quad security = \text{medium},$$
$$trust = \text{medium}, \quad accountability = RD, \quad deniability = R, D$$
$$creation = \widehat{ER}, \quad operation = ED, \quad revocable = D.$$

Audience: Sorry, why is the flexibility *medium* there because the expressiveness is still kind of all or nothing? It's less than all, I suppose, but there's still no additional expressiveness in terms of, well you can access this section of the block but not that section.

Reply: Okay, so that's a really good question. The expressiveness is slightly more because most websites will allow you to have some choice over the flexibility of the expiration date. Invariably when you log into a website you can say, do you want your cookie essentially to last forever, or to last for a short period of time. That gives you some extra flexibility. But there's also an "in theory" future flexibility that you have with cookies that you don't have with passwords. You could, in theory, bake more expressiveness into your cookie that would then improve on what happens at the moment. Perhaps that should say "low to medium" or "low to high", there's a range that is potentially there. In some sense the point is that ideally you would have this expressiveness, at the moment it's only very slightly there. It has the possibility.

Frank Stajano: The metaphor of the cookies is not just because the cookie is what the browser is sending but it's that instead of being a password where you're basically *becoming* the other person, with a cookie the person who's delegating can bake your cookie with exactly the things they're willing to delegate to you but not any more. It's a special cookie made for you. That, as we promised to say later, depends on changes to the verifier but it would give much more flexibility than a password.

Reply: WordPress already has quite nice levels of access control. You can be an editor, you can be contributor, you can be an admin. If that were baked into the cookie then you could immediately have more levels of flexibility but it depends on the verifier as Frank says.

The claims we make are that there are actually some relationships between these different characteristics. I'm not going to go through all of these but the crucial relationship is between the expressiveness and the trust and security. The more expressive your cookie, the lower your trust requirement and the better your security, and that's the lever you essentially have in this case to control the security.

Claim 1. The following relationships are intrinsic to the nature of delegation.

1. There is an inverse relationship between expressiveness and usability.
2. There is a direct relationship between expressiveness and security.
3. There is an inverse relationship between security and trust.
4. Accountability is the precise inverse of plausible deniability.
5. Revocation implies accountability.

That leads onto the second claim that essentially if Rebecca wants to minimize her exposure to risk she has to restrict the permissions entrusted to Eric for him to carry out the task and that, crucially, has to be performed by the verifier. That access control check has to be done *by the verifier* in order to make it secure and that's where, currently, an essential piece is missing from the puzzle. And that needs to be improved.

We also raise a couple of questions. Is it appropriate to make the functionality available now, whilst the expressiveness isn't there, or would it make more sense to wait until cookies improve in terms of their expressiveness and then provide this functionality later? This approach provides, in some sense, a way to evolve the security, to improve the security in small stages, but not as it currently stands.

In summary our experiences were that we found that it certainly was possible and that this approach, perhaps, provides an evolution from passwords to cookies and then from cookies to expressive cookies. But this approach is certainly not perfect. You can't prevent someone else, for example, transferring a cookie to someone else and performing multiple delegations. Also you need this buy-in from both the end users and the verifier, and there are lots of questions around that.

Bruce Christianson: The easiest way of preventing people from telling other people their passwords is to make sure they don't know their own password and Pico gives you the power to do that.

Reply: Yeah, I guess, in theory it does... in practice it does in theory it doesn't. There's nothing stopping someone digging around inside Pico and extracting it out[4]. But yes, that provides a nice practical approach.

Bruce Christianson: And that could also allow you to prevent further delegation. If the cookie has to be used with a password that is specific to the Pico that the cookie is delegated *to* then you can't delegate it further.

Reply: Right. Okay. Yes. In fact one of the questions that I raised is, whether or not you can prevent multiple delegations without having the verifier involved. Do you have to have an account at DumpIt in order to do that? That would be a way to do it, but it would not give bulletproof security, I guess.

Frank Stajano: If we are allowing changes at the verifier end then we can certainly have an agreement that says "here is a cookie for doing this and nobody else can use it". But if we are just riding on existing Web technologies, which we are doing at the moment, then we are limited in what features we can exclude and which we can apply, because we have to do things without the cooperation of the Website.

Bruce Christianson: Are there any restrictions that you impose at the moment on the browsers or the Pico users?

Frank Stajano: Well the restriction is that the browser has to be equipped with a plug-in or you can't use it. This can be a serious restriction. We've had users complain, "Oh this feature is rubbish because I have to use Firefox and I don't like Firefox."

Ross Anderson: There's already one application area where people have a choice between monitored or unmonitored delegation, which is when reviewing papers for conferences. If I ask Khaled [Baqer] to review a paper for example, there are two ways I can do it. I can send him the paper in an email saying "Khaled what do you think of this?" and he sends back some text which I cut and paste into EasyChair[5] as my text, because it's less bother. Or if I can be bothered to use the full protocol I can fill in the form saying "I hereby wish Khaled – with email here – to be a sub-reviewer for this". Now I would suspect that many people don't use the formal mechanism simply because they can't be bothered; the extra fifty keystrokes would be too much work. And by doing a user study of academics and asking "how often do you bother to use the formal delegation mechanism?" you could answer question 2 on your slide and perhaps part of question 3.

Reply: Yeah. It'd be interesting to do that. I'm not sure the same security characteristics are in play. I'm not sure there's much of a security concern in delegating...

---

[4] Editor's Note: Although a user who relies on Pico tamper-evidence to protect against password theft is motivated not to extract their own passwords from the Pico.

[5] EasyChair is a conference management application: http://easychair.org/.

Ross Anderson: Well it's about accountability, it's about having all the boxes ticked, it's about having the facts of a big list of sub-reviewers at the back of the conference proceedings volume.

Frank Stajano: Yeah, but the difference with the situation that David is describing is that you're not giving Khaled your EasyChair password so that he can enter the review for you; you're only giving him the paper, so there's nothing bad that he can do.

Ross Anderson: Well he could write a completely outrageous review.

Frank Stajano: Yeah but you'll get the text yourself, that you wouldn't re-paste, right? So that's quite different from you giving him your password which was the alternative that you had without doing the proper delegation.

Audience: And in other collaborative editings that means you also have share-able links from collaborative docs and that sort of thing, where it's explicitly an anonymous capability that is generated. It can be revoked but it's an anonymous thing so the revocation mechanism consists of let's go back to the world in which you have to be logged in with a certain account in order to access it.

Bruce Christianson: But one of the issues with password sharing is that it erodes accountability, because you can't work out who did a particular thing, the delegator or the delegatee. This is the point Ross is making.

Audience: Sure, but I think in many of these cases – maybe not the Easy-Chair example but in a lot of these cases – I question whether accountability is something that we actually want, or if it's just the first thing that we think of. Whereas what we actually want is trust expressed through delegation, and if something happened through my access therefore it's my responsibility no matter who actually did it.

Bruce Christianson: Yes.

Frank Stajano: Well sometimes accountability is something that someone else wants, but I don't want.

Reply: In fact we identify these two characteristics *accountability* and the other one was *plausible deniability* which are reverses and they're both potentially positive in different situations[6], I guess it depends what you're really after.

---

[6] See for example Michael Roe, 2010, Cryptography and evidence, http://www.cl.cam. ac.uk/techreports/UCAM-CL-TR-780.pdf.

References

1. Bauer, L., Cranor, L.F., Reiter, M.K., Vaniea, K.: Lessons learned from the deployment of a smartphone-based access-control system. In: Proceedings of the 3rd Symposium on Usable Privacy and Security, SOUPS 2007, pp. 64–75. ACM (2007)
2. Duffy, J.: Tips for sharing passwords. PC Magazine, September 2014. http://uk.pcmag.com/password-managers-products/35518/feature/tips-for-sharing-passwords
3. Paul Cruickshank, A.C., Pearson, M.: British police tricked terror suspect into handing over phone, source says. CNN, April 2016. http://edition.cnn.com/2016/04/01/europe/uk-isis-terror-convictions/

Red Button and Yellow Button: Usable Security for Lost Security Tokens

Ian Goldberg[1], Graeme Jenkinson[2], David Llewellyn-Jones[2],
and Frank Stajano[2(✉)]

[1] University of Waterloo, Waterloo, Canada
[2] University of Cambridge, Cambridge, UK
`frank.stajano@cl.cam.ac.uk`

Abstract. Currently, losing a security token places the user in a dilemma: reporting the loss as soon as it is discovered involves a significant burden which is usually overkill in the common case that the token is later found behind a sofa. Not reporting the loss, on the other hand, puts the security of the protected account at risk and potentially leaves the user liable.

We propose a simple architectural solution with wide applicability that allows the user to reap the security benefit of reporting the loss early, but without paying the corresponding usability penalty if the event was later discovered to be a false alarm.

1 Introduction

Imagine this scenario. I go abroad on a trip. I get back and, on attempting to do some online banking, I can no longer find that all-important physical token that lets me log in. I know I brought it with me abroad, and I'm pretty sure I was always very careful with it, but now I can't find it. What should I do? I could, of course, report the loss to the bank, but then I'll have to go through the security rigmarole with the call centre operator (after I get through the automated voice menus and more than my Recommended Monthly Allowance of muzak), answer long-forgotten "secret questions" to prove that I am me, jump through various hoops to have them send a new device in the post to my registered home address, possibly pay an additional insurance premium for having lost a security token... all the while thinking that, thanks to Murphy's law, shortly after the request for a new token has been accepted I will find the old one in a hidden pocket of my suitcase (not that I didn't already check, of course).

So instead I don't report the loss, hoping that sooner or later I'll find the lost token at home, which on the face of it is by far the most likely outcome. But I'm feeling slightly uneasy, imagining that maybe some foreign crooks found it and are hacking into my current account as we speak.

I. Goldberg—On sabbatical at the University of Cambridge Computer Laboratory while working on this topic.

J. Anderson et al. (Eds.): Security Protocols XXIV, LNCS 10368, pp. 165–171, 2017.
DOI: 10.1007/978-3-319-62033-6_19

This example shows how the security procedures currently in use to deal with lost security tokens give me a rather powerful disincentive to report the loss immediately. If I still have any hope that I might find the token later, I might save myself a lot of hassle by pretending I never lost it and meanwhile continuing to look for it. Note that we take the term "security token" in its most general sense, to encompass not only calculator-like login devices but also credit cards and so forth.

The research question we address is:

can we devise a better procedure that might reconcile the two conflicting goals of the token user?

... namely not wanting to be hassled unnecessarily in the relatively common case that the lost token will be found again (= "I'd rather not report the loss, at least yet"), and not wanting to end up in trouble in the rare but not impossible occurrence that the token was actually stolen and misused (= "I'd rather report the loss immediately").

To be more precise, whether the token user ends up in trouble following the loss of the token and its misuse by criminals depends on the exact terms and conditions that regulate the agreement between the token user and the token issuer. In the banking case it is common for the liability of the user to be limited so long as the loss was promptly reported through official channels (e.g., declaration to the police), but this may vary by jurisdiction. In any case, whatever the arrangements, if value is taken out of the system by crooks who access the account without authorization, the legitimate actors in the system are going to incur a loss, however distributed, and it is reasonable to assume that, to avoid moral hazard ("I don't pay for it so I don't give a damn"), the bank will pass on at least some of the liability to the user if the user did not report the loss. So we assume that the user has *some* incentive not to leave the loss unreported.

From another viewpoint, one might observe that some banking tokens are protected by a PIN and allow only three attempts before locking up, and therefore that the user should not care about the possibility of misuse of a lost or stolen token unless the adversary is assumed to be able to overcome such protections. Not all tokens offer such protection, though; and, even for those that do, the probability of guessing a human-chosen PIN in three tries is significantly higher than a naïve calculation might suggest, because human-chosen PINs are far from uniformly distributed [1]. Therefore, by the "moral hazard" argument above, in our general discussion it still makes sense to assume that the user should have some incentive to report the loss of a token.

On a related note, we observe that there is a wide spectrum of possible strengths of the hardware tamper resistance mechanisms offered by security tokens, from non-existent through smartcard-grade to sealed and protected cells enclosing processor, memory and battery, and beyond. And, orthogonally, there is a wide spectrum of possible consequences for the loss of the token, from negligible to extremely serious. It is reasonable to expect that the appropriate countermeasure will depend on the threat scenario and that there will be a correlation between the two variables. It seems unlikely that a single solution will suit every possible case: for any given hardware implementation of a security token, one will always be able to construct horrendous threats for which the countermeasures will be insufficient and trivial threats for which the countermeasures will be overkill and too expensive. Any solution will only be optimal for a subset of the possible cases. Any general solution will be a trade off. This is basic risk management.

2   The Core Idea

Our core idea is to decouple the reporting of the loss from the reissuing of the token. We wish to encourage the token user to report the loss as soon as possible, and therefore we wish users to incur no penalty for doing so[1]. Reporting the loss should be a "no big deal" activity that gracefully tolerates false alarms.

We model our solution as two metaphorical buttons, a "pre-alert" yellow button and a "true alert" red button. The semantics of the yellow button are *"I don't know where the token is, but maybe I'll find it again soon. Please disable it temporarily."* Pressing the yellow button is a lightweight and no-hassle operation (involving no interaction with call centres) that has the effect of notifying the back end that the token has been lost: the back end should reject any attempts at authenticating with that token until otherwise notified. Pressing the yellow button should not, however, revoke the token or initiate any heavy-duty administrative actions such as issuing a new one.

The semantics of the red button are *"I really think I lost it now, and I have given up any hope of finding it again. But I need to use it, so please send me a new one instead."* Pressing the red button is a request to revoke the lost token permanently and to issue a replacement for it. It will involve cost in several dimensions, potentially including administrative actions requiring unpleasant interactions with voice menu systems and call centre operators, penalties, handling costs and delays, but will only be invoked as a last resort.

Pressing the yellow button (freezing the accounts) is a cheap action that can be undone, whereas pressing the red button (revoking the accounts) is an action that is both expensive and irrevocable. The advantage of this yellow/red strategy is that it lowers the cost to the user of taking protective security action and therefore it increases the likelihood that such action will be taken promptly, keeping the user more secure.

At this stage we are building a mental model for the user rather than a particular implementation: we said "metaphorical buttons" because we do not necessarily envisage them as physical buttons on a physical device. If they were, and they do not have to be, we would have to specify on which device they would appear (clearly not on the token whose loss we are considering reporting). It may well be, for example, that the yellow button is implemented simply by sending a

---

[1] To those objecting that reporting the loss freezes the account and prevents the user from logging in, we point out that, having lost the token, the user is unable to log in whether or not they report the loss.

particular SMS or email to a designated recipient. The red button, on the other hand, will involve similar procedures to those currently in use for revoking a lost token, because there must always be a hierarchy of more and more time-consuming but more and more powerful emergency procedures one can invoke even if every supporting piece of authentication evidence (including security tokens, passports, etc.) has been lost or has otherwise become unaccessible.

There is of course the question of how the red and yellow buttons are *themselves* secured, and how the yellow button is "unpressed"[2]. There are a number of plausible instantiations, but we present one next. The red and yellow buttons may actually just be codes generated at the time the token was delivered to the user (either initially or after the last press of the red button). These codes can be likened to GPG revocation certificates [2]: they should be stored in a way that the true owner is sure to maintain access to them, but it is not horrible if others also gain access. This is because if someone else accesses the red or yellow button, they can lock or revoke the token (just as they could publicize the revocation certificate to revoke a GPG key), but that is arguably the correct outcome given that the token is no longer in the hands of its legitimate owner. Storing the red and yellow button codes on one's phone is reasonable (as long as there is also a more permanent copy somewhere, say taped to the electricity meter at home).

When the yellow button is pushed, whoever pushes it is given an unlock code, which should be high enough entropy to be unguessable, so it is basically a capability to unlock *that particular yellow-button pressing*. The only ways out of the yellow state are with the unlock code issued when the state was entered, or by pushing the red button.

Some users may indeed be tempted to "keep the yellow button pushed" whenever they are not actively using the token (or perhaps whenever they get on an airplane), and this is not totally unreasonable. The downside of this conservative strategy is that it amounts to manual locking and unlocking of the token at every use, which negatively affects usability; moreover, the user is betting that he will not lose his copy of the unlock code—the risk to the bet is having to push the red button, as the only ways out of the yellow button state are with the unlock code issued when entering the state, or the red button.

---

[2] The yellow button is logically a switch with two states, "alert on" and "alert off"; so the "yellow alert" state stays on until explicitly revoked. The red button, instead, is logically more akin to a "trigger" button that can be used to fire off an alert but not to say when the alert is over (it will be over when the replacement token is shipped to the user). So if the yellow button is implemented by sending an SMS, then another SMS must be sent to unpress the button. A timeout would also work but would be less secure and would remove control from the user and we therefore advise against it.

This is only a sketch, rather than a full design addressing all the relevant issues of authentication to the freezing proxy or revocation proxy[3] after having lost the authentication token, of the trust relationship between the proxy and the user, of the possibility that attackers might go after the proxy instead of the token and so forth. We do however consider it an improvement over the status quo and a solution with wide applicability, and we therefore consider the idea worthy of wider discussion even at this preliminary stage.

3   Red/Yellow for Pico

Most banking tokens are dedicated, in the sense that each bank issues its own; if a person has accounts with three banks, they generally need to use three different tokens. This makes things easy for the bank, who has full control over the design and operation of both endpoints, but complicated for the user, who might accrue a keyring of tokens as bulky as that of a prison warden. From the user's viewpoint it would be much more interesting to use a universal token capable of granting access to several independently run accounts.

We originally conceived the red/yellow idea in the context of the Pico [3] project[4], which is indeed a universal authentication token: rather than being tied to one particular issuer or back-end service, it contains potentially thousands of independent login credentials for the same user, for accounts on many unrelated back ends. We shall now therefore discuss how to apply the red/yellow button idea to Pico, not so much because that is where the idea occurred to us originally but because doing so highlights the complications associated with the additional level of indirection required to deal with multiple independent back-end verifiers.

Within the Pico system, pressing either button requires contacting all the back-end servers on which the user has accounts. This in itself is a penalty to pay, at least in terms of privacy loss. While Pico allows the user to maintain a separate persona for every service (or even several personae with the same service), pressing the yellow (or, a fortiori, red) button would allow a global network observer to link the many simultaneous revocation requests back to the same Pico, thus deanonymizing the user. Temporal linking might give the user away even if mixes, remailers or other network anonymizers were used to obfuscate the source of the requests. Adding random delays of sufficient magnitude between the revocation requests, in an attempt to frustrate such relinking, would leave a window of vulnerability between discovery of loss and protection of account that somehow goes against the motivating principle of introducing the red/yellow button architecture.

---

[3] Defined as the in-cloud servers that the yellow and red buttons respectively talk to, and that consequently issue "account freeze" or "account revocation" commands to the servers on which the user accounts are hosted. This level of indirection is necessary when one token unlocks accounts on distinct servers. We shall explore this idea further in the next section.

[4] https://mypico.org.

An alternative strategy, geared towards privacy, exploits the Pico's "network share server" [3, Sect. 4.1] that must send a periodic keep-alive signal without which the Pico locks up. In this strategy the user who has lost the Pico sends the revocation requests (or at least the yellow ones) just to that server, telling it to stop providing its keep-alive signal, but without notifying the actual back ends. This has the security disadvantage of not locking the accounts immediately but only within the time interval (say half a day or one day) within which the Pico expects to hear the keep-alive signal again from its network share server. It also has the additional security disadvantage that, if the adversary managed to extract any credentials from the lost Pico (either through hardware attacks or by capturing it before it locked itself), then the block will be totally ineffective because the back ends won't know about it. This strategy offers some privacy at some cost in security and it is debatable whether this is the appropriate trade-off.

A variant of this strategy, geared towards both privacy and immediacy of revocation but with an efficiency cost for the user, is to require the network share not just once or twice a day but at every authentication request. This implements a different trade-off, with greater security (accounts are locked immediately) at the cost of greater energy consumption for the Pico, greater latency for every login and potentially lower availability as the user won't be able to log in whenever the network share server is unreachable, even if the server to which the user intended to log in is reachable.

Yet another strategy, also geared towards privacy and immediacy of revocation but with the inefficiency cost shifted towards the servers, might involve some kind of "anonymized" public revocation, by which we mean an architecture with the following properties. There is an append-only publicly writable bulletin board in the cloud (suitably protected against denial of service) where yellow and red button presses end up. Each button press is encrypted (with suitable randomization) with the public key of the service it intends to freeze or revoke, to ensure that a global network observer may learn that Alice froze or revoked something, but not *what*[5]. Each service is notified by the bulletin board whenever a write event occurs and must attempt to decrypt the new message in case it was addressed to that service (this inefficiency being the cost of privacy protection for the user). It is interesting to discuss the incentives of the parties involved, in search of a reward system that would motivate the services to incur this extra cost in order to protect the privacy of their users.

4   Conclusions

We have sketched a simple and very general idea for allowing users of security tokens to report loss of token without incurring the heavy penalty usually associated with doing so. This should in turn improve security.

---

[5] So when Alice loses her Pico and presses the yellow button, thus writing hundreds of revocations to the bulletin board, the NSA learns that Alice lost her Pico, but is none the wiser about what services she has accounts with.

The idea is still at an early stage and we have not implemented it yet. We are keen to discuss further architectural and scalability considerations with our peers at the workshop.

Acknowledgments. The authors with a Cambridge affiliation are grateful to the European Research Council for funding this research through grant StG 307224 (Pico). Goldberg thanks NSERC for grant RGPIN-341529. We also thank the workshop attendees for comments.

References

1. Bonneau, J., Preibusch, S., Anderson, R.: A birthday present every eleven wallets? the security of customer-chosen banking PINs. In: Keromytis, A.D. (ed.) FC 2012. LNCS, vol. 7397, pp. 25–40. Springer, Heidelberg (2012). doi:10.1007/978-3-642-32946-3_3
2. The Free Software Foundation: The GNU Privacy Handbook (1999). https://www.gnupg.org/gph/en/manual/c14.html#REVOCATION
3. Stajano, F.: Pico: no more passwords!. In: Christianson, B., Crispo, B., Malcolm, J., Stajano, F. (eds.) Security Protocols 2011. LNCS, vol. 7114, pp. 49–81. Springer, Heidelberg (2011). doi:10.1007/978-3-642-25867-1_6

Red Button and Yellow Button: Usable Security for Lost Security Tokens (Transcript of Discussion)

Frank Stajano[✉]

University of Cambridge, Cambridge, UK
frank.stajano@cl.cam.ac.uk

My name is Frank Stajano and, with my colleagues Ian Goldberg, Graeme Jenkinson, David Llewellyn-Jones, I'm going to speak about something we originally thought of last year. Ian Goldberg is a cryptographer and privacy specialist at the University of Waterloo in Canada. He was on sabbatical at Cambridge last year and Graeme Jenkinson was, until recently, working on the Pico project with me and with David Llewellyn-Jones, who just spoke. We were discussing various things you could do with Pico in various circumstances. This is a bit of a digression and it's somewhat more general than Pico, but we will get back to Pico in due course.

First of all a motivating story. A variant of this story happened to me a few months ago and to David's wife as recently as last week. Let's pretend that, on a trip to the Czech Republic, I happen to bring with me my online banking token, which is necessary for doing secure transactions with the banking website and to pay money to someone else. I brought it because I suspect that maybe, within the time I'm here, I will be required to pay a bill urgently. Everything goes well except that, when I get back home, in the mess that is my house after I've come back and have undo all my luggage, I suddenly can't find the token anymore.

Vashek Matyas: I'm used to tokens where you have to insert your bank card, so I just go to the bank and they give me a new token. I'm assuming this is a different one?

Reply: Yes, it's different: this one is basically the union of the one you have[1] and the bank card. It has some secret inside it and it's yours. It's personalized. It doesn't have a slot for the card. In fact, it's smaller than a card, but you can substitute everything I said about the token with "you can't find your credit card". That would also work.

So my question is: Did I lose this thing while I was abroad?, because then I would feel somewhat uncomfortable. Or maybe I did bring it back, but I just can't find it now. I don't know, and I'm not too sure what I should do about it.

Following the advice from the bank ("as soon as you don't know where your banking token is, tell us"), I do report the loss. As a reward, I get a barrage of voice menus and hours of muzak while I try to get through to the call centre. When I finally speak to an operator, it's not a full human being with an

---

[1] Which is stateless, and is the same for every customer of that bank, so we wouldn't actually call it a token.

© Springer International Publishing AG 2017
J. Anderson et al. (Eds.): Security Protocols XXIV, LNCS 10368, pp. 172–180, 2017.
DOI: 10.1007/978-3-319-62033-6_20

independent brain, it's a call centre drone who follows a script! So I have to go through lots of strange procedures. I have to answer security questions that I set up fifteen years ago, such as "what is your memorable date"; I can't remember the answer because, "for security", I didn't give them anything I would actually remember, like my birthday. Eventually they agree that I'm genuine, but while they reissue it I have to go for ten days without my token.

The general summary is that I get through a lot of pain.

After all this, as Murphy's Law would have it, as soon as I put the phone down I find the token somewhere I didn't expect, and I am somewhat annoyed. On the other hand, if I didn't report the loss, then some evil bad guys in this strange place I visited might be having a go at my account. They might even be trying to take my token apart; this is unlikely, but it is still scary for me to some extent. Especially when I listen to all of Ross's stories on how banks treat fraud victims. The customers say that something bad happened to them and the bank says, "You must be the bad guy then" and then they have to call for assistance and it's a very painful process.

From this comes our research question, which is:

Can we devise a better procedure that might reconcile the two conflicting goals of the token user?

The two conflicting goals are: number one, not wanting to call the call centre because it is a pain and so I'd rather not report the loss because I suspect I might find my token under the sofa; and number two, the other conflicting goal is that instead I do want to report the loss because if I don't then I might end up in trouble.

I have a few footnotes to what I just said. The first one is about this issue of trouble. Do I end up in trouble if I don't report my loss? To some extent this depends on the terms and conditions of the token issuer. In banking (it depends on jurisdiction of course) there is usually limited liability if I do report the loss, but it is unlikely that I will ever get away without any penalties of one form or another because otherwise there's the *moral hazard* argument that then I would not care at all: I would just be careless with my assets and not cooperate with the bank in protecting them; to prevent that, they will pass on some liability to me, perhaps in the form of higher fees, perhaps in the form of a raised insurance premium or whatever it may be. And so I still assume that, one way or another, I will have an incentive against loss imposed on me, so I will get into some kind of trouble if I don't cooperate by reporting the loss of a security token.

Another footnote is that sometimes (many times; certainly in the case of the token that's pictured) these security tokens are protected with something like a PIN. If they are also protected with some hardware mechanism such that after entering three wrong PINs it locks up, then I should think that I am safe, because even if someone finds the token then they cannot guess my PIN in three strikes. So, why should I go through any further trouble if there is already this protection?

However, as we have been taught by Joe Bonneau and his colleagues, who presented this graph at Financial Cryptography a few years ago [1], here we have a wonderful chart where four digit PINs are plotted as the first two digits against the second two digits, with colour intensity encoding the frequency of each PIN. You can see patterns that show that they are not at all chosen uniformly if they are picked by humans. You see patterns that come from symmetry (4545, the diagonal is popular) and patterns that show how people pick dates and you can see whether they are British or American depending on whether they say 21/3 or 3/21. You may have seen this graph before. If you haven't, it's worth studying. Given that humanly chosen pins are predictable, then, for the moral hazard argument given before, I would still have an incentive to report the loss.

Another footnote I wanted to mention is that there is actually a spectrum of many strength levels of tamper resistance of the tokens. You can go from something that is completely unprotected to something that is as hard to penetrate as a SIM card, all the way to something even more tamper proof. Orthogonal to that is another spectrum of how serious it is for me to have lost this token. In the two dimensional area that results from the cross product of these two axes I situate the situation of interest. This is too big a space to have a solution that works *optimally* in every possible case. It is always possible, for any given implementation of a security token, to find examples where it is totally overkill and it costs too much; or other cases where it gives insufficient protection against a sufficiently strong adversary. Any general solution will *necessarily* be a trade-off. This is basic risk management so I'm not particularly interested in discussions about the fact that "for this level of token then there is going to be someone who can still break it". Well, of course there is. There will always be.

What core idea are we offering here for resolving this trade-off between the two goals of the user who has lost a token? Until now the situation looks like this: a big red panic button that the user can press. If they press it, the semantics are: "sorry, I lost the token; please reissue the token". Pressing this button gets me out of trouble but causes me pain. Therefore I am reluctant to press the button to report the loss.

What we propose instead is to have an arrangement with *two* buttons. One of them — a yellow button — means the following: "I'm a bit worried because I lost the token, but don't reissue one yet; I'm just telling you I lost the token, therefore please freeze my account. If you see any attempts to use this token, it's not me, because I lost the token". Pressing this button can be undone. Pressing this button does not cause me all the pain of having the muzak, the voice menus, the interaction with the drone, the wait and then the irrevocability of having a new token sent to me whereas I might still find the old one. This is just "freeze my account; I may still find it, and in which case I will undo this". No interaction with human beings, and it's a low cost operation that can be undone.

I also still have a red panic button, which I can press after a while if I still can't find the token after looking under the sofa, after looking very carefully through all my luggage and so on. Pressing the red button means "Yes, I did lose the token. I have lost any hope of finding it in a reasonable time so please reissue it. I understand I will have to endure the pain but I've done all I could at this stage." This is an irrevocable action. It's the same as before. Once you have asked for a replacement, even if you find the old token, then you will still get the new one.

The core idea here is that pressing the yellow button is not a big deal, and therefore users will be encouraged to report the loss as soon as possible without having to face the bad consequences if they then happen to find the token again soon. The core idea is to *decouple the reporting from the reissuing* of the token. The two buttons, I stress, are metaphorical: we just need two mechanisms to say: "please freeze the account because I lost the token", but at low cost, and the other one, the more expensive "please reissue the token because I have given up".

Jonathan Anderson: Do you see the undoing of the yellow button as something that requires a manual intervention? Could you have a time lock system with the semantics of "Freeze everything for twelve hours. At the end of the twelve hours either unlock things or, if I haven't said anything more, then at that point consider the red button pressed"?

Reply: I'll discuss this over the next slide. I stressed that we are not talking about actual buttons, not physical buttons; certainly not buttons on the security token because I have just lost the security token. They are actions I can trigger once I have lost the token. It's just a mental image for saying you're raising an alert of some type or another.

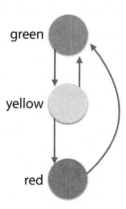

Fig. 1. State diagram with transitions (Color figure online).

In this state diagram (Fig. 1), I am normally in the green state where everything is fine. Then, if I lose the token, I transition to the yellow state by pressing the yellow button in some way. From there I have a grace period where, if anything bad should happen, my account is not in danger because I have reported the loss and so it's frozen; but, if I do find the token again, I can transition back from the yellow state up to the green by some explicit action through which say I have found it again.

However, if I don't find it and at some point I give up, then I will transition to the red button by saying "please reissue it because I can't find it", and it's arguable whether I would want to do that with a time out, but certainly I have the option of invoking that manually. The only way to get out of the red state is, implicitly, when the token is reissued. I end up in the green state for the replacement token.

Hugo Jonker: I'm assuming that you can also transition directly from green to red? You didn't put it in the state diagram, but if I land at the airport and I see someone run off with my suitcase I'm not going to press the yellow button.

Reply: Fair enough. Yes, the two buttons are independent. You can just press the red button. I accept the correction that I could add an arrow from the green to the red directly. That is a fairly uncontroversial case where I'm well prepared to pay the penalty of going through the call centre because the dilemma wouldn't apply in this case.

An implementation could be, for example, that the buttons are really just nonces that are printed on a piece of paper that is delivered with the token and that I, as they say, "keep in a safe place". Pressing the button could mean sending an SMS to some designated recipient, which would invoke the action of freezing the account. On doing that I would receive another token that would let me un-press the yellow button.

Note this subtlety: there are some buttons, like the doorbell, that you just press and they go "bing-bong" regardless of how long you press for, like a kind of edge-triggered action; and other buttons that are a level-based, not edge-based, action, like the light switch where you have to flick it one way to turn it on and then flick it the other way to turn it off. You could view the yellow one as a switch in this second sense. You set it to *alert* and then, after a few days, you could flick it back to *no more alert* because you found the token again. Whereas the red one is more like an edge-triggered button where you say there's an alert and it goes off and I can't undo it.

Ross Anderson: There is already an instance of this in the world: if you fly an aircraft you can call *mayday* if it's definitely an emergency or you can call *pan, pan, pan*, which is the equivalent of pressing the yellow button. There, of course, student pilots have reluctance to do either because even if you call "pan, pan, pan", you'll still get a bollocking from the flight instructor.

Similarly, there's a difficulty in having an easy-to-press yellow button: where for example is the nonce going to be? Is it going to be printed on the back of my bank card? But if the bank card is stolen along with my banking token then I basically have to fall back on the call centre.

My point is that implementations in the world of the yellow button and the red button are likely to have a certain cost associated with pushing it, whether an emotional cost or a transaction cost or both, and it's not at all obvious how you make the transaction cost or the emotional cost of pushing the yellow button substantially less then the cost of pushing the red button.

Reply: Yes, we are aiming to make the cost lower. It's going to be difficult to make it go to zero. Certainly, the yellow button's code will not be printed on the bank card if the bank card is the thing I'm going to lose. We said you could have something that you keep in your wallet, but you could lose that too, or you could have another copy of it, because you don't care if you have several copies, taped to something at home that you won't lose like your gas meter and then you always know where it is.

We think of these codes similarly to the revocation certificates for your PGP keys: if someone else finds it, they could always misuse it and revoke your key; but you could argue that that's the right thing to do because, at that point, someone else has got hold of your private key. If they revoke they're only doing you a favour. There is a bit of denial of service but it's not a disastrous thing.

Jonathan Anderson: And it's much less serious than somebody finding your revocation key because it means that somebody can lock out your Visa card for six hours or something. That's quite different from them being able to revoke it entirely. Of course, because it's a low-risk proposition you could allow lots of different ways to press the metaphorical button. You've got a nonce in your wallet and you can log in to your online banking and you've got an app on your phone. Maybe even your bank may be happy to give you an app that — even without authentication — if you possess the phone then it will let you lock out the Visa card for three hours while you figure stuff out.

Reply: I agree entirely.

We said that we would be talking about Pico as well. So far this is just a very general idea that applies in many contexts, from credit cards to aircraft, as we just heard.

We actually did think about this in the context of Pico and we are going to explore it, not simply because that's where we thought about it, but because Pico has a level of indirection that these banking tokens generally don't have. Most banking tokens are dedicated – they are issued by the bank – and if I bank with three different banks I have to have three different tokens. Then, if I have one for every different account, I end up with a key ring of tokens as big and heavy as the key ring of a prison warden.

It would be much better, from the view point of the user, to have just *one* token to deal with all the accounts. This is precisely what Pico does, but then the issue of freezing and revoking the loss of a Pico has to multiply out to freezing and revoking *all* these accounts. This is why this is a case that is interesting to explore. The Pico project has been presented at this workshop many times and previous speaker David Llewellyn-Jones mentioned things about Pico in another presentation, assuming that people more or less knew what it was.

If you have never heard of Pico then visit the Pico website[2], but what matters at this stage is that Pico is essentially a single sign-on system that you carry in your pocket. One reason to have it in your pocket instead of having it in the cloud is for privacy protection because your single sign-on system is the thing that knows all the places that you have accounts and when you login to each of them. If you don't like Facebook Connect to keep a log of that, then you might like to have the single sign-on in your pocket under your control.

---

[2] https://mypico.org.

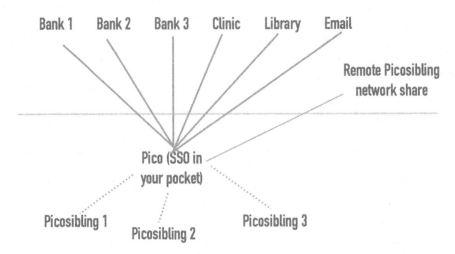

Fig. 2. One Pico interacts with multiple accounts and is unlocked by multiple Picosiblings. The entities below the horizontal line are local to the user, while those above are in the cloud (Color figure online).

This is, in a nutshell, the part of Pico that is relevant to this picture. In Fig. 2 the various accounts in the cloud are up there: Bank 1, Bank 2, Bank 3, Clinic, Library, Email and so on, and the Pico has a different persona for each one of them. For privacy reasons I may not want to be the same user, relinkable across all of them, and Pico supports that by having a separate account for each.

In this case, when I press the yellow or red button, I must freeze or revoke each of the accounts that the Pico knows about. When I press this button, *all* of them need to be contacted and obviously not by the Pico because I've lost it by then. Whatever the yellow button does, it has to talk to all these accounts; but when I do this freezing or revoking in bulk the evil global network observer may correlate all this network traffic and infer that this Pico was linked to this particular constellation of accounts. My act of revoking all the accounts at the same time reveals which accounts I had, which I was trying to keep private until now.

If I try to space them out in time so that they cannot be correlated I may negate the timeliness of the notification. Remember the splitting into yellow and red button was primarily to make the notification happen sooner (by removing the penalty of reporting until I was sure that I couldn't find the token again). So this basically is a solution that introduces, to some extent, a privacy problem.

If we look back at other features we introduced with Pico, which I presented in 2011 at this workshop [2], the original loss protection mechanism for Pico consisted of the Picosiblings, which were other body-worn devices that sent shares of the master secret that unlocked the Pico. There was also a special share that was not in one of my body-worn devices but was held in the network in a server controlled by me.

You see that the Pico has a link to a remote Picosibling network share, on the right, which is something that the Pico wants to contact every now and then, like once or twice a day, in order to stay up. If the Pico loses the connection to this special network share then the Pico locks up. This is so that, if I lose control of the Pico, then I can always tell my server to stop sending this share. This will disable the Pico even if I have no physical control over it any more.

Now, one of my students, Daniel Lowe, prototyped this last year. To unlock the Pico the local Picosiblings need to be heard but also the network share must have been received within a certain interval before that, say several hours. Given this architecture, I could simply freeze the network share. I just send my yellow or red button press to the network share (rather than to all the banks in the cloud) and that cuts off the Pico from working.

This solution here is okay for privacy, compared to the previous one, but has some security risks. One is that there is a delay between my pressing the yellow button and the next time that I notice that the network share is no longer there, but this delay is under my control. The other risk is that if the Pico has been lost and is in some dodgy foreign place and this place is full of people like our Sergei Skorobogatov, who open up chips and take their secrets out using a microscope, then I might not be safe from this attack even if switching off the network share means that the Pico will eventually lock itself. It might have been captured and depackaged and inspected before it locked itself properly. I might be worried about that from a security viewpoint.

Another solution that we thought of, a variant of the previous one, is to change the meaning of the network share as something that needs to be acquired at *every* log in. Then, when I revoke the network share, the Pico is immediately disabled as opposed to disabled after a few hours. That removes some of the security concerns I previously expressed. However it is possibly a worse trade-off because it introduces availability problems: sometimes the Pico will not work if I cannot reach my network server, whereas previously it would have been working. The system becomes less robust. Every log in will take longer. It's debatable whether this is the way to go.

Yet another solution we thought of is that we could instead dump this efficiency cost on the servers instead of the client. We could have, for privacy protection reasons, an append-only public log to which the press of the yellow or red button writes; but writes in an encrypted fashion. When I revoke, I press the yellow button and for each account I write a "please revoke" message in the log, which is encrypted to the public key of the intended recipients.

So the recipients have to monitor this log and decrypt all the messages in case one is for them. When one is for them they do the necessary action. But this means a lot of wastage for each server as the price to pay to have it efficient for the client. The issue here is that privacy and security are improved but there is more work for the servers and we have to figure out why they would want to do this extra work for us, especially if people are not prepared to pay for privacy.

There are many trade-offs for this universal authentication in various dimensions from privacy to efficiency, to security and so on. If we want to dump the

Detecting Failed Attacks on Human-Interactive Security Protocols

A.W. Roscoe[✉]

Department of Computer Science, Oxford University, Oxford OX1 3QD, UK
Bill.Roscoe@cs.ox.ac.uk

Abstract. One of the main challenges in pervasive computing is how we can establish secure communication over an untrusted high-bandwidth network without any initial knowledge or a Public Key Infrastructure. An approach studied by a number of researchers is building security though involving humans in a low-bandwidth "empirical" out-of-band channel where the transmitted information is authentic and cannot be faked or modified. A survey of such protocols can be found in [9]. Many protocols discussed there achieve the optimal amount of authentication for a given amount of human work. However it might still be attractive to attack them if a failed attack might be misdiagnosed as a communication failure and therefore remain undetected. In this paper we show how to transform protocols of this type to make such misdiagnosis essentially impossible. We introduce the concept of *auditing* a failed protocol run and show how to enable this.

1 Introduction

Human interactive security protocols (HISPs) achieve authentication by having one or more human users form part of a non-spoofable out-of-band (oob) channel between the devices that are involved. They do this without involving PKIs, shared secrets or trusted third parties (TTPs). The fact of humans' involvement severely limits the amount of data transferred on the oob channel, meaning that a compromise is required between the certainty of the authentication supplied by the protocol and ease of use. Therefore practical implementations frequently have a small, but not totally negligible, probability of a man-in-the-middle attack succeeding. For example if the humans have to compare six decimal digits, this probability cannot be below 10^{-6}. Protocols can be designed that essentially achieve this bound by preventing an attacker from performing combinatorial search to improve its chances [5,7,8,12,13].

A survey of the known approaches to creating such protocols can be found in [9]. They all work (in the sense of avoiding combinatorial attack) by the protocol participants becoming committed to one or more pieces of data such as a nonce, Diffie-Hellman token g^x or hash key before knowing that data. We give some examples as background (Sect. 2). In this paper we will only consider protocols that work in this way.

© Springer International Publishing AG 2017
J. Anderson et al. (Eds.): Security Protocols XXIV, LNCS 10368, pp. 181–197, 2017.
DOI: 10.1007/978-3-319-62033-6_21

Though such protocols only give an attacker Eve a single guess against each protocol run between Alice and Bob, she will get further attempts if they try again after seeing that they have a failed run. They are of course much more likely to try again if they believe the failure was due to a communication glitch, or a mistake on their part, rather than an abortive attack.

If it can be demonstrated to them that the strings they had to compare were different, then both they and the application which implements the protocol should know that an attack has occurred. However if the attacker can abort before they have this information it may be impossible for them to distinguish the two possibilities.

In this paper we show that on published protocols the attacker can prevent certain knowledge of an attack, but that all the protocols we consider can be transformed so that any meaningful failed attack is definitely detectable if the participants *audit* the values they transacted in the run.

In the next section we give background including a variety of protocols. In Sect. 3 we describe the mechanism behind our improvement, which depends on the addition of extra messages into the protocols based on the delayed decommitment of data from the protocol. Section 4 examines options for delayed decommitment, and potential attacks against them.

2   Background

This paper is set in the world of authentication protocols where either recipients need to authenticate the origins of messages, or where one or more people want to set up a secure network between a number of devices, but where there is no usable PKI or other pre-installed network of secrets to prove identities. Instead we assume that a high bandwidth network with no security guarantees at all is supplemented by out-of-band channels implemented by the human(s) using the devices. The assumption is made that these channels are authentic, in the sense that the humans know that they are correctly either transferring data between devices or correctly comparing pieces of data appearing on separate ones. We make no assumption, however that the out-of-band communications are private.

We assume that, in common with all the protocols in [9], the protocol succeeds (and authentication is assumed) if short strings generated on all the devices are equal in addition to all other messages conforming to the pattern expected of them. We will primarily concentrate on the case where this comparison is the final step of the protocol that confirms security. The reader will find other forms of protocol in [9].

It is easy to demonstrate that the strongest security guarantee that can be achieved with such a protocol is that an attacker can do no better than as a man in the middle who divides the group into two disjoint parts and runs the protocol separately with each, purporting to be the nodes missing for each (see Fig. 1), succeeding with probability $1/D$ where D is the number of short strings in the set from which the values compared via the humans are drawn. For the man in the middle will succeed in this strategy with at least this probability, on average, by using random values for the constants he has to introduce into the two partitioned runs, and without stronger guarantees on the network used to transport messages between the participants it is impossible to prevent such attempted attacks.

Protocols that meet this requirement are characterised by their use of techniques that prevent the man in the middle from choosing his constants more intelligently than by this random approach. For simplicity we primarily discuss the situation involving the pairing of Alice and Bob, but this discussion applies equally to situations like Fig. 1, at least for protocols capable of handing groups.

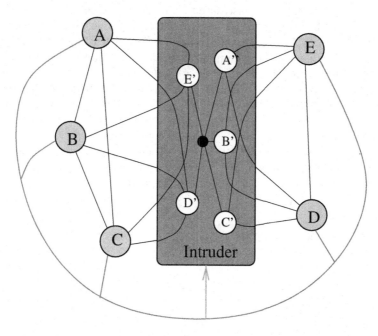

Fig. 1. Attacker replacing intended group of 5 with two groups of 5 that have fake nodes.

The most basic and challenging aim of these protocols is to authenticate: either one party to other(s) or all parties to each other. Most of them take advantage of this authentication to agree a key between the parties. The intruder's aim is to have them believe they have completed the protocol with each other when in fact they have different values for the "agreed" data. He will succeed in this just when he gets Alice's and Bob's short strings to agree though they have not run the protocol properly with each other. The best protocols are designed so that he cannot perform a useful search to make them agree with higher likelihood than when he chooses random values. For example if our attacker Eve has some information about the short string that Alice will use before Bob is committed to his value for it, Eve can potentially search for values of constants she sends to Bob (pretending to be Alice) that improve her chance of success. Most obviously if Eve already knows the value of the string Alice will use, she can look for values to feed to Bob that will generate the same value.[1]

More discussion of this issue, and examples of protocols susceptible to such attacks, can be found in [9]. The following are a few examples of protocols that are not susceptible in this way. We use a message-sending notation $A \longrightarrow_X B : M$ means that M is sent by A to B over the medium X. Two mediums are used: N is a high-bandwidth network with no security assumptions, typified by the internet. If A sends the message there is no guarantee that B gets it; if B apparently gets this message there is no guarantee that it comes from A (it might have been constructed by Eve); and even if the message gets through successfully it might have been overheard by Eve. In other words N is a *Dolev-Yao* channel [4]. E is the out-of-band, or empirical channel which is low bandwidth and implemented by human(s). It has the guarantee that if B thinks he has received M from A over E, then A really has sent this message to him.

The following protocol between A and B is adapted from the usual group version:

Symmetrised HCBK protocol (SHCBK), [7,8]
1a $A \longrightarrow_N B : A, INFO_A, hash(A, k_A)$
1b $B \longrightarrow_N A : B, INFO_B, hash(B, k_B)$
2a $A \longrightarrow_N B : k_A$
2b $B \longrightarrow_N A : k_B$
3 $A \longleftrightarrow_E B : digest(k_A \oplus k_B, INFOS)$

Here, $\oplus$ is bitwise XOR and $INFOS = (INFO_A, INFO_B)$ is the information A and B are authenticating to each other. k_A and k_B are cryptographic length, e.g. 256, strings of random bits and *hash* is a standard cryptographic hash function. $digest(k, M)$ is a function that chooses a b-bit short string representing a short "hash" of M with respect to k. It must ideally satisfy:

Definition 1 [7,8]. *A b-bit digest function: digest : $K \times M \to Y$ where K, M and $Y = \{0...(2^b - 1)\}$ are the set of all keys, input messages and digest outputs, and moreover:*

- *for every $m \in M$ and $y \in Y$, $Pr_{\{k \in K\}}[digest(k, m) = y] = 2^{-b}$*
- *for every $m, m' \in M$ ($m \neq m'$) and $\theta \in K$: $Pr_{\{k \in K\}}[digest(k, m) = digest(k \oplus \theta, m')] \leq 2^{-b}$*

In practice the final 2^{-b} is often replaced by some ϵ slightly greater than 2^{-b}, and the θ is only required in some protocols, not including the pairwise

---

[1] In a more extreme case, Eve may be in a position to control both runs' strings and use a birthday-style attack.

version above. Digest functions are closely related to universal hash functions: some methods of computing them are discussed in [10].

This protocol works because each of A and B is completely committed to the value of its final digest before it releases its contribution to the digest key. They therefore each know that Eve had no knowledge whatsoever of the digest key in time to have sent them material that could have been the result of a search for a value that will give a particular digest result.

We can characterise the two keys k_A and k_B as *independent randomisers* of the short string, thanks to the properties of $\oplus$ and the specification of a digest. Choosing either value randomly, and independently of however the other is chosen, maps the short string to a random value in its domain. In this protocol each party chooses a randomiser r and ensures that it itself is committed to the value of the short string before it tells anyone the value of r.

Nguyen and Roscoe [9] terms SHCBK a *direct binding* protocol because the agreed short string is a type of hash of the information Alice and Bob are trying to authenticate. This is analogous to the traditional use of signed cryptographic hashes in authenticating data: here the signature is replaced by the communication of the digest over the authentic oob channel, and the digest can be much shorter than a hash because of the care taken to avoid combinatorial attacks.

The following protocol, on the other hand, is termed *indirect binding* because the short string is chosen independently of the message and bound to it during the protocol. This particular protocol only transmits an authenticated message one way. Here, R_A and R_B are b-bit short strings chosen at random by the two agents.

Vaudenay pairwise one-way authentication protocol, [13]
$[A]\ c \parallel d := commit(INFO_A, R_A),$
1 $\quad A \longrightarrow_N B : INFO_A, c$
2 $\quad B \longrightarrow_N A : R_B$
3 $\quad A \longrightarrow_N B : d$
$[B]\ R_A := open(INFO_A, c, d)$
4 $\quad A \longrightarrow_E B : R_A \oplus R_B$
$\quad\ B$ verifies the correctness of $R_A \oplus R_B$

Here, $commit(M, R)$ is a pair $c \parallel d$ (following the notation of [13]) where knowledge of c commits the recipient to the values of M and R, through the said recipient may not yet know M and must not (even with the knowledge of M) be able to deduce the short string R. d reveals R and confirms (and if necessary reveals) M. Thus c is not a function of M and R, since if it were, a search through the relatively few possible values of R would reveal the real one. Rather it is in a one-to-many relationship with M and R, as possibly implemented by

- $c = hash(M, R, X)$ where X is a random nonce: a string of say 256 random bits.
- $d = (R, X)$

The purpose of R_B here is to make sure that if Alice sends Message 3 in response to a Message 2 faked by Eve before Bob has received Message 1, the chances of Eve's R_B equalling the real one are 2^{-b}. This normally prevents the final comparison being a success for Eve.

Note that R_A and R_B are independent randomisers for the short string, that B only sends R_B when it is committed to the final value of the short string (as well as $INFO_A$) and that A only reveals R_A when it is also committed to the final value of $R_A \oplus R_B$. Thus, though the appearance of this protocol is rather different from pairwise SHCBK, the *modus operandi* using a committed-before-reveal randomiser, and a pair of independent randomisers, is actually rather similar.

The two protocols above can be used to send or agree authenticated cryptographic material between Alice and Bob, but not in a way that is directly secret. Therefore the most obvious approach to building privacy for Alice and Bob is to make the authenticated material contain either an asymmetric "public" key or Diffie-Hellman style tokens such as g^{x_A} and g^{x_B}. Our final example is a direct binding protocol that uses cryptographic material in the authentication exchange: $g^{x_A x_B}$ becomes an authenticated session key between A and B. It is an interesting example chiefly because it is widely implemented [2]. The core of this protocol, closely related to ones by Hoepman [5,6], is:

ZRTP protocol (Zimmerman [14])
1    $A \longrightarrow_N B$: $hash(g^{x_A})$
2    $B \longrightarrow_N A$: g^{X_B}
3    $A \longrightarrow_N B$: g^{X_A}
4. $A \longleftrightarrow_E B$: $shorthash(g^{x_A}, g^{x_B})$

(The shorthash can equally be of the shared key $g^{x_A x_B}$.) This works in a way very similar to the shortened pairwise version of SHCBK mentioned above. The only difference is that the randomisation present in the authentication re-uses the Diffie-Hellman exchange that establishes the key. This is clearly efficient, but the properties of modular exponentiation and the b-bit *shorthash* need to be carefully managed and studied to provably achieve the same security bounds attained by the first two protocols. In other words, X_A and X_B are both used as randomisers for this protocol, and while intuitively this should work well it is not mathematically obvious, as it was with the previous protocols.

In each of these protocols, it is the scheme of commitment to the randomisers that avoids combinatorial attacks based on searching, and they all, seemingly inevitably, use a method of *commitment before knowledge*. [Of course the protocols also have to be immune to conventional attacks possible without such searching.] One assumption implicit in these protocols is that all the cryptographically important values and operations used in them, other than short values for human comparison, are strong enough to withstand any imaginable brute-force attack with probability so close to one that we can disregard the difference.

3   Attack Detection

Although these protocols prevent the attacker from searching against the short string on a single run of the protocol, they do not prevent repeated attempts to have a correct guess against multiple independent runs, whether the users try over and over again to bootstrap security in a single group of devices, or attempts are made against a variety of groups as they form until one succeeds. Realising this, we should think about how the attacker might execute a single attack. Again restricting for simplicity to the pairing of Alice and Bob:

1. When a run between Alice and Bob begins, initiated by Alice, the intruder Eve will play the part of Bob in that run and herself initiate a run with Bob, pretending to be Alice. These two runs will progress through a number of stages of interaction leading to the final comparison of short strings (which unbeknownst to them are the strings generated by the two separate runs) by Alice and Bob. Because we are assuming our protocol is optimal in the sense discussed above, Eve just introduces a random value when she has to contribute something like a key or nonce to either of her versions of the protocol. Of course the attack only succeeds if the separate short stings s_A and s_B in the two runs happen to co-incide.
2. At some point in the run between Alice and Eve (qua Bob), each of the two participants will have the data to allow them to compute their short string s_A. One of them will necessarily have this information before the other, inevitably the one to send the last message before they *both* know it. The same thing happens in the run between Eve (qua Alice) and Bob.
3. In organising her attack, Eve is free to interleave the messages she sends and receives to and from Alice and Bob, so that their own order of sends and receipts exactly follows what would have happened if they had really been running the protocol with each other. If she does this, Eve is bound to have first knowledge of the digest in one of the two runs and second knowledge in the other. Furthermore Eve will know *both* s_A and s_B before one of Alice and Bob knows his or her own short string. In some protocols (particularly the more symmetric group protocols) it may be possible for Eve to choose a schedule so that she knows both of these values before any of the honest participants do. In pairing protocols she will be playing the two roles in the two runs: one of these will be the one that gets knowledge of s first.
4. It follows that Eve will know whether her attack will succeed or fail before all of the devices that are being have the information that will allow them to know. If she is going to succeed, she will naturally press on and break into what Alice and Bob will both regard as a successfully completed session.

However if she is going to fail, the logical move for her will be not to send the messages remaining to Alice and/or Bob that will reveal the short string to them. For Eve knows that by sending them she will prove her presence in the interchange.

5. In that last case, Alice and Bob will never *both* have their short strings, and so will not be in a position to compare them. They will therefore lack conclusive evidence that an attack was taking place and may very well conclude that the failure of the protocol to complete is down to a communications glitch.

What would it take for Alice and Bob to be able to know that someone was attacking them? If it can be shown that some parties had progressed a long way in interacting with the two of them and then aborted runs which would have had differing short strings, this would represent conclusive evidence. Alice and Bob are still connected by their out-of-band channel, and so can compare notes on what has happened. Let us suppose we could achieve, following an aborted run, a state where each of Alice and Bob knows one of the following for certain:

– No conceivable intruder could have known the digest their own run was heading to at the point of the abort.
– Has direct evidence, through inconsistency of messages received, that an attack was attempted.
– Knows the digest value that he or she would have calculated and compared, and whether their device would have raised any further inconsistencies before the end of the protocol.

Then by conferring over the oob channel they can conclude one of the following *trichotomy* of outcomes.

(a) No intruder knew both short strings at the point of the abort, and therefore had no way of knowing at that point that any attack being carried out would succeed or not. An intruder would have no benefit from this other than denial of service.
(b) That the protocol failed even though the short strings would have agreed: this is almost certainly due to a communications failure.
(c) That Alice and Bob were heading towards different short strings, meaning that an attacker was almost certainly involved, or that some other sort of attack was taking place.

One might imagine that in the last eventuality Alice and Bob would take countermeasures such as

1. Upping the security level of any subsequent connection attempt (for example by increasing the length of the short string)
2. Notifying any servers associated with the applications running the protocol, so that they can take appropriate defensive or forensic action.
3. Changing the communications network being used.

We term a protocol that achieves this *auditable* because when things go wrong we can scrutinise the run and determine what when wrong.

The above trichotomy is unachievable in any of our example protocols thanks to our earlier analysis which showed that in the man in the middle attack the attacker can know both s_A and s_B before the moment when these values are known by Alice and Bob respectively, and can stop at least one of them knowing its value if they are not equal. What we will now demonstrate is a way of modifying the protocols so that they do achieve it: we introduce time-dependent data and time-outs into modified protocols. We can ensure that the new protocol behaves like the old one within some time limit T, and unless it completes before then either any intruder had no information about success before T or there is some later time T' at which Alice and Bob both know the short strings from their runs. There is no need to know exactly what the times T and T' are, merely that they exist. The best way to describe this is by modifying the three protocols set out above so that they have this property. We assume that there is an additional cryptographic primitive $delay(x, t)$ with the properties

- Anyone who knows $delay(x, t)$ can know x, but not until at least t units of time since its first creation.
- No-one can deduce anything about x from it before that point.
- In the same agent that created $delay(x, T)$, the boolean $intime(x)$ returns *true* if before T since the call of $delay(x, T)$, and *false* otherwise.

We will discuss potential implementations of $delay(x, t)$ in Sect. 4.

In the adapted protocol descriptions below the statement $[C] x := delay(k, T)$ is the creation of one of these time-locked means of calculating x by agent C. The strategy we follow is to make sure that Alice and Bob both have in their possession the means to calculate their short strings *perhaps at a later time* before Eve knows both s_A and s_B.

We suggest four strategies below for using $delay(x, t)$ in modified protocols.

1. Observe that $delay(x, T)$ has the interesting property of both committing the recipient to the value x before any but the sender knows it, and later releasing it. Therefore there is no *a priori* need to send the commitment and opening message openly any more. Of course such a protocol cannot complete before all the delayed data has opened.

   The simplest protocol which works in this context is

Delay commit protocol	
$[A]\ d_A := delay(k_A, T)$	
1 $A \longrightarrow_N B$	$: A, INFO_A, d_A, hash(A, k_A)$
2 $B \longrightarrow_N A$	$: B, INFO_B, k_B$
$[A]\ intime(k_A)$	
3 $A \longleftrightarrow_E B\ \cdot$	$: digest(k_A \oplus k_B, INFOS)$

It is fortunate here that the time limit on the *delay* need only be long enough for a small number of messages (here 2) to be sent and received by the nodes.

In particular it is advantageous that the wait does not need to encompass activity by the human user(s). Though we will not remark on this again it is true of all the protocols we develop. Having T small means that, even where A or B cannot open $delay(x, T)$ as fast as T, it still should not take them *too* long. See Sect. 4.

In the protocol above, A knows that she was committed to the final digest before the *delay* opened, meaning that the value received apparently from B cannot have aimed at creating any particular value of the digest. Similarly B knows that he is completely committed to the final value of the digest at the point he sends Message 2, and that he has randomised it. Therefore, although the attacker can send a fake Message 1 to B at any time (even after the *delay* has opened), there is nothing it can do to bias B's digest value.

Furthermore, if an attack is attempted where both digests are known to the attacker, then if A has not already abandoned the protocol on the time-out, she also knows (i) her own value of the digest (because she will have received Message 2) and (ii) that if there was no attack then B will also know his value of the digest without further communication once T has passed. This allows auditing.

2. Replace the existing commitment mechanisms (i.e. hashes and *commit*) by instances of *delay*. Time out the protocol unless all delayed data is released in the open by the protocol before the delayed version of it opens. These extra messages can have advantages in protocol design, but because of the necessity of checking the consistency of the commitment against the second communications the users will still have to wait for the *delay*s to open. This latter inconvenience (and a perhaps a lot of work) will be avoidable if a receiving party can check for this consistency without having to open the *delay*. If, for example, $delay(x, T)$ is created using a function that is much easier to compute directly than invert, it will be easier for the receiving party, upon receiving x directly, to re-create $delay(x, T)$ and test for equality[2] exactly as one would expect if sent a hash commitment for x followed by x itself.

   Depending on the means of opening a $delay(x, t)$, this (needed for both this approach and (1) above) might well be a lot of work. Generally we prefer to use $delay(x, t)$ in such a way that it does not have to be opened (as opposed to checked by recomputation) in a completed run of a protocol, only when auditing a failed run.

3. Accompanying each instance of a hash or *commit* in the original protocol with a corresponding *delay* (i.e. what was sent in the original protocol together with what was sent in the first approach above). This would achieve our aims completely provided suitable time-outs were included in the amended protocol, as above.

   This approach achieves our objectives, but we term it *weak* because its security depends on the correctness of the *delay* operator. We will discuss in the next

---

[2] If the value x has had to be salted to make the *delay* secure, it would then be necessary for the direct communication of x to include the salt as well.

section why it may be wise *not* to rely on *delay* so much. Therefore we prefer the following approach.

4. Develop a protocol which is auditable in the sense that we achieve the trichotomy set out above, but does not depend on the correctness of *delay* (in other words it would still be secure, but not auditable, if the intruder were able to extract x from $delay(x, T)$ immediately.)

The adapted protocols we present below are designed in line with this final option.

Auditable SHCBK

1a	$A \longrightarrow_N B$	$: A, INFO_A, hash(A, k_A)$
1b	$B \longrightarrow_N A$	$: B, INFO_B, hash(B, k_B)$
[A]	$d_A := delay(k_A, T)$	
2a	$A \longrightarrow_N B$	$: d_A$
[B]	$d_B := delay(k_B, T)$	
2b	$B \longrightarrow_N A$	$: d_B$
3a	$A \longrightarrow_N B$	$: k_A$
3b	$B \longrightarrow_N A$	$: k_B$
[A]	$intime(k_A)$	
[B]	$intime(k_B)$	
4	$A \longleftrightarrow_E B$	$: digest(k_A \oplus k_B, INFOS)$

In other words, after each of the two parties is completely committed to the final value of the digest it sends the other one the delayed reveal of its hash key, and is only prepared to do the digest comparison if it has received the unencrypted hash key from the other *before* any party can have extracted the data from the respective d_X. It follows that in order to know whether the usual man in the middle attack will work, Eve either has to wait for $delay(k_A, T)$ and $delay(k_B, T)$ to open or to get A to send the open k_A and B to send k_B. If she does the first she will know if her attack would have succeeded earlier, but it will not now because the booleans tested by A and B before Message 4 will be false. If she takes the second approach she will have to have at the very least sent data representing d_A to B and d_B to A as a continuation of her man in the middle attack. However if she does, gets the values of k_A and k_B and abandons the attack, all A and B have to do is wait. After time T they can endeavour to open the delayed values and one of two things will happen:

– The ds they hold open successfully, are consistent with the hashes they hold, and A and B can compare s_A and s_B and find that they are different.
– The ds do not open successfully or are not consistent with the Message 1 contents.

The second of these possibilities is unlikely, for if it happens then it would provide post-hoc evidence that the intruder was involved even if Eve had got lucky with the short strings: she would have had to have provided a d inconsistent with the Message 1 she sent to the same party *before* she knew if the two runs' short strings agreed.

In either case A and B can jointly deduce that an effort had been made to attack them. The revised protocol achieves the trichotomy above. Note that we can be confident that even if the *delay* function does not work at all, this protocol is still as secure as the original SHCBK presented above: for the original protocol fully reveals k_A and k_B at the points where the two delayed versions are revealed.

This approach readily extends to the group version of SHCBK of [7,8].

The following is an auditable version of ZRTP. Note that we have had to defer the release of g^{x_B} via hash commitment to make this possible.

Auditable ZRTP	
1 $A \longrightarrow_N B$	: $hash(g^{x_A})$
$[B]\ d_B := delay(g^{k_B}, T)$	
2 $B \longrightarrow_N A$	: $d_B, hash(B, g^{X_B})$
3 $A \longrightarrow_N B$	: g^{X_A}
4 $B \longrightarrow_N A$	: g^{X_B}
$[B]\ intime(g^{k_B})$	
5. $A \longleftrightarrow_E B$	: $shorthash(g^{x_A}, g^{x_B})$

The reason for including B's name in the hash in Message 2 is the same reason it is included in SHCBK: it prevents reflection attacks where A's own g^{X_A} is replayed to her in Message 2.

Finally we move on to the indirect binding Vaudenay protocol. To do this we, in much the same way as in the previous case, both delay R_B and allow its eventual send to be checked against an earlier commitment. Because R_B is short the best way of doing this is using the same sort of *commit* construct as for R_A, and in that context we might as well add in any information B wants to authenticate to A (which could of course be null).

The additional commitment in this protocol and the extra hash in Message 2 of Auditable ZRTP can be dispensed with if the form of *delay* allows it to be used as a convenient commitment scheme.

Auditable Vaudenay style protocol
$c_A \parallel dc_A := commit(INFO_A, R_A),$
1    $A \longrightarrow_N B : INFO_A, c_A$
$c_B \parallel dc_B := commit(INFO_B, R_B),$
$dy_B := delay(R_B, T)$
2    $B \longrightarrow_N A : INFO_B, c_B, dy_B$
3    $A \longrightarrow_N B : dc_A$
$[B]$ $intime(R_B)$
$[B]$ $R_A := open(INFO_A, c_A, d_A)$
4    $B \longrightarrow_N A : dc_B$
$[A]$ $R_B := open(INFO_B, c_B, d_B)$
5    $A \longleftrightarrow_E B : R_A \oplus R_B$

4   Options for Time Delay

The solution above depends on a construct that locks data away for a given period. It is recognised – see [1,11], where many ideas similar to the ones presented below can be found – that there are two basic options for this

- The use of trusted third parties.
- Creating a computation that simply takes at least a given time to perform by any party.

Neither of these is ideal: trusted third parties are potentially corruptible and is hard to guarantee that no-one can perform some computation quickly while relatively low-power computers such as smartphones must nevertheless be able to do the same calculations rapidly enough to audit a failed run.

This seeming fragility is one very good reason why we have been careful, in our *Auditable* protocols (i.e. those following the fourth design pattern set out earlier), not to rely on the *delay* construct to provide protocols' basic security. Of course the incentive for an attacker overcoming whatever delay mechanism is used is reduced if it is being used for auditability only.

We also remark that, in common with the traditional cryptographic one-way functions of hashing and public-key cryptography, it may well be necessary to salt a value that is being *delay*ed to prevent searching attacks by other parties. (This is also analogous to the nonce X used to prevent searching attacks against the c of commit schemes as referred to earlier.)

The most obvious way of creating the $delay(x, t)$ construct used in the last section appears to be using a trusted third party. Such a server S would perform the following service:

- When sent some data x encrypted under S's public key together with time t it will reply with a token y combined with a hash of (x, t).
- When sent y at least t beyond the point where it sent this reply, it reveals x.
- The values sent by S are signed by it.

In practice y might or might not contain the information S needs to recover the value of x without resorting to its own memory. That would affect whether the two instances of S used must be the same, or merely share keys with each other.

The usability of this, like the other forms of delay discussed below, will depend heavily on the context in which the HISP is being used. This particular one is unlikely to work well if Alice and Bob are likely to be cut off from any server when the protocol is run, but would be very suitable when they have to depend on the presence of a TTP for other reasons in their exchange. This would be true, for example, in the models of electronic transactions anticipated in [3].

Note that the form of time used in $delay(x, t)$ is relative: t is a delay from the present time, rather than an absolute time at which x will open. There is an advantage in this in that we would otherwise have to worry about how accurate the knowledge of the present time in each node might be. However the work required of the TTP above might be considerable if it was serving a lot of clients. The following alternative approach alleviates this.

We create a server TL that issues a series of asymmetric "time-lock" keys, each labelled with the time it was created and the time it will open, each signed by TL. When the appointed times for opening these keys, come round, TL issues them. So all this TTP has to do is post a series of signed keys.

For example our server might issue one key every 10 seconds, with a delay of one minute before the counterpart was issued. The key pairs might then be made available online for several days to enable auditing.

Agents can still implement $delay(x, t)$ using this service, but only if they can bound the divergence between their own system time and that employed by TL. This knowledge will enable them to pick an already posted key that will not be opened by TL for at least t units of time, and encrypt x under it.

The final option is to do without a TTP and make anyone who wants to open $delay(x, t)$ do a lot of work. Given that we expect these objects to be created a lot more often than opened it makes sense to want a version that is cheap to create. Given our application we want a method that will allow the sort of device running our protocols to be able (as part of the auditing process) to be able to open such an object in a short enough time to be of interest to the human users, and to take useful countermeasures against attackers (e.g. warning all users), even though an attacker may essentially unbounded computing resources to do this. As discussed in [1], this means that the computation must be sequential, in the sense that it is impossible to parallelise. It also means that we cannot afford to be too generous with the time delay T used in the protocol. In this respect our earlier remark that there is never a need for T to allow for human activity is positive. Several potential schemes are given in [1], based on a long sequence of operations. Two possibilities are

- A large prime p of the form $3m + 2$ is chosen[3], the number of digits determining a time delay t. $delay(x, t) = x^3 \bmod p$ is fast to compute, but to uncover x from this we have to compute $x^d \bmod p$ where d is chosen so that $p - 1$

---

[3] These are exactly the primes in which cubing x^3 is invertible. Squaring is not invertible for primes other than 2.

divides $3d - 1$. This will typically take $(log_2\, p)/2$ times longer to compute, namely a computational advantage proportional to the number of digits.[4] To achieve a sufficient delay it may be necessary to make p very large indeed; as an alternative we could repeat this operation with several increasing primes in turn. The primes in this example could be published and used by all nodes.

– $delay(x,t)$ is the combination of x encrypted under a secret RSA key (N, e) and d, where $d = d_0 + M\phi(N)$ and d_0 is a normal-sized inverse to e. In other words x^e is issued together with d such that $x^{ed} = x$, but where d is so large that this computation takes at least t.

While these computations have at their core the need to repeatedly square numbers in some modulus, it is hard to exclude, particularly in cases where pre-computations can be done for a particular modulus, special purpose hardware being used to speed up the individual multiplications, or there may be better algorithms employed than are widely known.

In any case it is likely to be very hard to *prove* that a particular calculation will certainly take a given time t, particularly when for auditing purposes we want relatively low power devices to be able to do the same calculation in a relatively small multiple of t. Of course the smaller we can make t, which will be determined by our confidence in the infrastructure implementing the protocol, the larger multiplier between user device and attacker speed we can tolerate.

Each of our alternative implementations of $delay(x,t)$ is subject either to the corruption of TTPs or to imponderables about the limits of computation and parallelisability. In the author's mind it is this which makes it highly advisable to use the approach to auditability we have, in which the basic security of the protocol is not compromised by it.

5   Conclusions

We have introduced the concept of a protocol being auditable, and shown how a variety of protocols can be made auditable by the addition of additional data fields and/or messages. All of these transformations involve the addition of time-dependent data to replace or supplement the mechanisms already present to commit agents to data before they know it. We have shown that this can be done straightforwardly if we can rely sufficiently on the security of the *delay* mechanism, and in a way that does not risk the security of the original protocols otherwise.

Finally we have given some examples of how *delay* might be implemented, observing that what method is preferable will depend on context. Indeed, one can imagine that a single protocol implementation might well use different *delay*s as alternatives (e.g. depending on the availability of TTPs.)

---

[4] The calculation of x^3 will clearly take more time, the more digits there are. Note that there are multiplication algorithms faster than the usual "schoolbook" one that can be expected to give significant advantages when p is very long.

One of the assumptions we have made in this paper is that when a message is received by a node over $\longrightarrow_N$ that is not consistent with the protocol, an attack is diagnosed. In order to make this reasonable, protocol implementers should ensure that accidental corruptions, mis-deliveries and abbreviations of messages are not accepted as "messages" at all. This will typically be achieved by using very explicit message formatting, e.g. in XML, and by including integrity information such as hashing to ensure that accidental issues relating to messages sent between trustworthy parties will essentially *never* lead to a node thinking it has received a message that was not sent to it in the form that was sent. Such precautions will not prevent an attacker from sending messages that look real, but should mean that agents can reject accidentally corrupted messages.

All the protocols we have considered so far in this paper have three properties:

– The oob channel is used simply for comparing two short strings.
– This comparison takes place at the end of the protocol.
– Each side of the protocol introduces something that randomises these strings.

Almost all the protocols described in [9] are of this type, and all of these can be made auditable using our techniques.

In this paper we have only investigated auditability in the contexts of HISPs. It is interesting to ask what other types of protocol it might be useful in. Two possibilities are Password Authenticated Key Exchange protocols (PAKEs), and in transaction-like protocols where the principals do not necessarily trust each other to complete protocols entirely. In either case we believe that the *delay* construct will be useful.

Acknowledgments. The author thanks Long Nguyen, Peter Ryan, Catherine Meadows and Thomas Gibson-Robinson for useful conversations on this work.

References

1. Time-Lock Encryption (2011). http://www.gwern.net/Self-decrypting
2. Wikipedia article on ZRTP. https://en.wikipedia.org/wiki/ZRTP
3. Bangdao, C., Roscoe, A.W.: Mobile electronic identity: securing payment on mobile phones. In: Ardagna, C.A., Zhou, J. (eds.) WISTP 2011. LNCS, vol. 6633, pp. 22–37. Springer, Heidelberg (2011). doi:10.1007/978-3-642-21040-2_2
4. Dolev, D., Yao, A.C.: On the security of public key protocols. IEEE Trans. Inf. Theory **29**(2), 198–208 (1983)
5. Hoepman, J.-H.: Ephemeral pairing on anonymous networks. In: Hutter, D., Ullmann, M. (eds.) SPC 2005. LNCS, vol. 3450, pp. 101–116. Springer, Heidelberg (2005). doi:10.1007/978-3-540-32004-3_12
6. Hoepman, J.-H.: The ephemeral pairing problem. In: Juels, A. (ed.) FC 2004. LNCS, vol. 3110, pp. 212–226. Springer, Heidelberg (2004). doi:10.1007/978-3-540-27809-2_22
7. Nguyen, L.H., Roscoe, A.W.: Efficient group authentication protocol based on human interaction. In: Proceedings of the Joint Workshop on Foundation of Computer Security and Automated Reasoning Protocol Security Analysis (FCS-ARSPA 2006), pp. 9–31 (2006)

8. Nguyen, L.H., Roscoe, A.W.: Authenticating ad-hoc networks by comparison of short digests. Inf. Comput. **206**(2–4), 250–271 (2008)

9. Nguyen, L.H., Roscoe, A.W.: Authentication protocols based on low-bandwidth unspoofable channels: a comparative survey. J. Comput. Secur. **19**(1), 139–201 (2011)

10. Nguyen, L.H., Roscoe, A.W.: Short-output universal hash functions and their use in fast and secure data authentication. In: Canteaut, A. (ed.) FSE 2012. LNCS, vol. 7549, pp. 326–345. Springer, Heidelberg (2012). doi:10.1007/978-3-642-34047-5_19

11. Rivest, R.L., Shamir, A., Wagner, D.A.: Time-lock puzzles and timed-release crypto (1996). http://bitsavers.trailing-edge.com/pdf/mit/lcs/tr/MIT-LCS-TR-684.pdf

12. Roscoe, A.W.: Human-centred computer security (2005). http://web.comlab.ox.ac.uk/oucl/work/bill.roscoe/publications/113.pdf

13. Vaudenay, S.: Secure communications over insecure channels based on short authenticated strings. In: Shoup, V. (ed.) CRYPTO 2005. LNCS, vol. 3621, pp. 309–326. Springer, Heidelberg (2005). doi:10.1007/11535218_19

14. Zimmerman, P.: ZRTP (2010). https://tools.ietf.org/html/draft-zimmermann-avt-zrtp-22

Detecting Failed Attacks on Human-Interactive Security Protocols (Transcript of Discussion)

A.W. Roscoe[⊠]

University of Oxford, Oxford, UK
Bill.Roscoe@cs.ox.ac.uk

This talk is about is detecting failed attacks, in other words, how to let protocols evolve, or how to evolve protocols so that at least in the particular class of protocol, if somebody does try to attack it, there's a very good chance you'll be able to detect this attack has happened, rather than perhaps suppose it was some innocent communications glitch.

I think that we've got an awful lot better at building cryptographic protocols in the 20 or so years that I've been working on this. However, in some types of protocols, you've got to accept some sort of probability of an attack succeeding. I think that Khalid and Ross's talk of the first part of the morning gave a good example of that. This might be because of the short CVV-like data, or you may not completely trust the party you're running the protocol with. Note that with there might be a man-in-the-middle you don't know if you are running with the person you do trust, or running with the person you certainly don't trust.

The philosophy I'm illustrating in this talk is after you develop a protocol, so it meets its primary objective, you might try to improve it so that it makes the environment yet more unpleasant or unattractive for potential attackers, in a way perhaps that might put them off trying to attack in the first place. The particular example of the protocols that I'm looking at have something in common with the protocol that we saw in the first talk of the morning in the sense that they also use weak values. That introduces a definite probability of attackability, and that is to say authentication protocols based upon using a human-based out-of-band channel.

The difference between the protocols I'm talking about and those in Ross's talk, is that in his, I believe all the values being transmitted were short In my talk you use a (weak) short string to authenticate a protocol which is otherwise run over a high bandwidth but completely insecure channel.

So we assume that a standard Dolev-Yao network is supplemented by a low bandwidth out-of-band channel between the human users of the devices involved in the protocol, and that this out-of-band channel is authentic. In other words if I receive a message from Bob over such a channel, then I know Bob really did send me exactly that message. However I have no guarantee whatsoever of privacy or secrecy. For example, Alice could post a message to Bob on her universally readable Facebook page, if they both trust the security of Facebook and secondly Bob is certain that this really is Alice's page as opposed to some spoof page. We will study protocols that, in this environment, authenticate that

© Springer International Publishing AG 2017
J. Anderson et al. (Eds.): Security Protocols XXIV, LNCS 10368, pp. 198–205, 2017.
DOI: 10.1007/978-3-319-62033-6_22

the devices that are connected by the humans really are running the protocol and sharing their keys (in secret) with each other.

It's interesting to note that this is not authentication by name, but basically authentication by the ownership of the other end of the channel. What you're authenticating here is that the party that you're sharing a key with is the same as the party that you share the out-of-band channel with. In particular, there's no essential reason why you have to know the name of a party at the other end.

Imagine you've got a protocol in which humans transmit b bits of information, encoded however you like. The intruder can run a man-in-the-middle attack on such a protocol by partitioning the group into two, and he runs a fake node for each of the real ones, so that each node is the a group of the right size with apparently the right identities.

The two runs are each going to generate b bits of information for transfer between the humans. But of course the only people who are actually going to be doing the transferring are the real humans as opposed to the fake nodes. The intruder wins, that is to say breaking authentication, if the b bits from one run equal the b bits from the other, because now all the humans will happily agree on this string of b bits, not knowing in fact that they were calculating two differently based strings of b bits that happen to be equal. If the intruder follows a random strategy for the pieces of information he introduces into these two man-in-the middle parallel sessions, he's going to have at least a 2^{-b} chance of success, no matter what we do in the design of these protocols.

Therefore, that gives an upper bound on how much security we can create with exactly b bits. If you design a protocol naïvely, it's almost certainly going to be easy for the attacker to do much better than that by doing some sort of combinatorial searching on the values that are passed in the protocol. However, there are protocols that achieve this 2^{-b} limit or very close to it. We can term such protocols *optimal*.

Optimal protocols were first of all developed around 2004–2005, and there are now many such protocols. Every one that I know of works on some variation of a commitment before knowledge principle, whereby the legitimate parties commit to one another in some way to values before they actually tell them what the values are. You can of course commit a value V to another party A, without A knowing V by sending $hash(V)$. Once A has received $hash(V)$ she's totally committed to the value V, because whenever she accepts a value that purports to be V she can hash it to check. More importantly, no intruder knows V from $hash(V)$ and therefore can do nothing constructive with V.

One example of an optimal protocol (designed by me and Long Nguyen just over 10 years ago) is the symmetrised hash commitment before knowledge (SHCBK) protocol, which was better than a previous (non-symmetric) version I had proposed. First of all, every node A sends to every other node in a group, an identity that they want to use for its particular run, information such as public keys that they want to have authenticated as attached to this identity in the group, plus the hash of a key, k_A. When a given node has received one of these from every member of the group, they are now themselves completely committed to a final digest value because they've received all of the information they're going to digest, and they're completely committed to the value of the key, k^*, that they're going to use to digest it by, even though they don't know it yet.

Frank Stajano: Is it resolved out of band what the membership of the group is?

Reply: Yes, we assume they all know and agree the group membership.

Having exchanged that commitment but not yet the value of the digest itself, they can now de-commit their keys. *As soon as I am completely committed to the value of the digest, I can tell everybody my key. When we've all got all the keys, we can Xor all the all together, and we form the k^*, which we use to digest all the INFO's, and then we compare that value over the out of band channel.* That's one of the many examples of optimal protocols that achieve what I set out earlier. You can find a good summary of the state of the art about five years ago in a survey paper I wrote with Long. No doubt more protocols have been invented since.

A digest function is like a short universal hash function, and it basically randomizes the stuff that you're digesting by the key in the appropriate way. The definition is not of the essence of this talk, so I won't dwell on it.

Ever since the time I first invented protocols of this type, I've been worried about what happened when an intruder did try to break into that protocol and failed. If you've got say three or four digits of digest that you're comparing, then clearly there's enough of a chance that the intruder will succeed, that it might be worth their while having a go. There's clearly nothing you can do about what happens if they succeed. The natural thought is that if they fail then everybody will notice that they were having a go because the digest will not agree, but if you think about it very carefully you realize that there's a problem in that argument. Namely, if the attacker carries out a standard man-in-the-middle attack on that protocol, or indeed any protocol in this class, he's able to tell if the two out-of-band communications arising in the pair of runs are equal or not *before* the honest parties have all the information that they need to determine this.

In other words, he will know whether or not it's worthwhile him carrying and giving them the information needed to compare before they have the information to allow them to determine that he was there. The logical move for such an attacker is to cut one or both protocol runs short, meaning the honest parties never get to see their connection was being hacked. Depending on the reliability of the communication medium they're using, they will probably just assume that some sort of communications glitch has got in the way. By this means, even though the attacker still only has a small chance of actual success, he's got a much lower chance of actually being caught. He can probably get lots of attempts before his presence is noticed, and each will give him an independent chance of success.

If you have a large network of people using this protocol, such as a payment system, then he's going to get some successes, but he's also going to get a lot of failures if he tries this in a widespread attack. It would be really nice if we could catch him on the first of his failures and thereby press the panic button as we saw in the last talk.

My solution is to make the protocol *auditable*. When a run goes wrong we can find out why. I would like to make it auditable in the following sense: if the protocol fails, Alice and Bob, by communicating on their out-of-band channel, would be able to discover that one of the following three conditions applied. First of all, no attacker could have had the information to know if an attack was going to fail or not. The second option is that the protocol failed despite the fact that it was heading to a successful conclusion. In other words, almost certainly there was a communications glitch. Thirdly, the out-of-band communication would have proved that an attack was going on because the digests would have been different. Another case in this third option is that inconsistent messages have been sent and detected during the auditing.

If this applied, a meaningful attack which had failed would be detected and counter-measures presumably taken. Of course, what counter measures there were would be context-dependent.

Bruce Christianson: Are these three cases mutually exclusive?

Reply: Yes.

Frank Stajano: Do these three things cover failed communication?

Reply: This would lead to options one or two. If the communication failed before they had the necessary information you would get option one. If it failed after they got the necessary information, you get option two. I'm assuming, by the way, that all the messages have enough error correction and formatting to ensure that if a poorly formatted message is received and accepted as a new message, then it is almost certainly generated by an attacker.

You can exploit the commitment before knowledge structure of this protocol to solve this in a number of ways, but they all depend on a particular sort of construct. If you put a time limit on the protocol's completion, it doesn't matter if the commitment scheme works just for all time or just until after this time limit. In other words, if I were to send you that hash at the start of the protocol that only conceals my k_A for a fixed amount of time, and then refused to complete the protocol if that time is finished before I am committed to my digest, then the fact it will open eventually wouldn't actually damage me. Let $delay(x, T)$ be a construct that releases x to anyone no sooner than T time after it's created.

I'll talk about a number of options for the delay later on. The first solution is to simply replace all the hashes with delays by T, because for the attacker to know in time whether his attack will fail, the trustworthy users will hold all the information they need to compare the out of band communications, they'll only be able to compare these things later. In other words, if an attack fails, the trustworthy users can wait until after the delays to discover whether or not that last condition holds.

Frank Stajano: Is the primitive $delay(x, T)$ implementable without a third party?

Reply: I'll give some options later on.

We could basically copy that earlier protocol. They send the same message as before, except now the hashes are delays, they're not hashed, and now everybody insists that they have all these messages, they're totally committed to their final digest before their own personal delay opens. At this point we have two options: the individual nodes could simply wait for the delays to open, which would be inefficient because they'd presume they have to do a lot of work and less implemented by third-parties. Alternatively, if you had a delay calculation that was both deterministic and fast, namely fast when calculating the delay as opposed to unraveling it, then the sensible thing to do actually would be as in the previous protocol, to send all the k_A's at this point and so all the nodes could simply recalculate all the delay terms and check that they were consistent, just as it would've recalculated all the hashes to check for consistency earlier on. As I say, that's the first solution.

If they didn't choose to wait for the delays to open, I think that's undesirable, because opening the delays as I say, in the absence of trusted third-parties, is likely to be a slow and expensive thing to do.

Frank Stajano: In the absence of a third party, the delay cannot be assigned reliably without having precise knowledge of the maximum computing capacity of an adversary, which is essentially unbounded.

Reply: I think what you have to rely on here to is the idea of sequential computation.

Frank Stajano: I have to rely on my users, who don't have a data center behind them, being able to get the delay in time, and someone who has a data center can do that in sequentially less time.

Reply: Having thought about this, I believe that one can potentially accept a couple of orders of magnitude less power. You almost certainly can't accept any less than that, and the only way that you can conceivably limit an attacker to little more than a couple of extra orders of magnitude is by making the computation sequential. In other words, ensuring that the attacker can't use a cluster to open this delay any faster than he could a single core.

Frank Stajano: There's still a lot more than a couple orders of magnitude between the power of someone with a data centre and the power of a normal user of the protocol.

Jonathan Anderson: The power of hardware is just parallelism, and if you're iterative hashing with ...

Reply: I don't think so. After all, the fastest processor speeds are no more than let us say four or five gigahertz, which is not that much different from the speed of the processor on your iPhone. The difference is, to some extent, in the architecture, and to a much greater extent that you've got a few thousand cores in your super-computer. If we can avoid the second of these, then I think there's considerable hope for this sort of thing.

As I say, I'm going to give some specific examples later on. As I say, I do personally worry that *delay* is not such a standard construct so not be as secure. Therefore, you might not want to rely on the basic security of *delay* for the basic strength of the protocol, only of the auditability. When I talk about protocol evolution, what I really mean is that you only use *delay* in order to enable auditability, not to generate the basic security or the protocol, unless you've done a lot more analysis on it than I have.

This argues for only sending delay terms in the modified protocol when, in the original protocol, the same data was sent openly, protecting the security proof even if the delay collapses into the identity function instantly. You then only send the contents of the delays openly when sufficient delayed data is present to audit. In the auditable version of SHCBK, this preserves the basic security, even if you believe that delay is somehow weak. The k_A are now swapped in three rounds: first committed via hash, second made auditable via delay, then openly.

We don't have to check such those delays are consistent with the K_A's, unless things go wrong, because we've already got a check from the hash round.

If you look up delayed encryption on the internet, which of course I did, you find a few but not very many papers on it. Obviously a trusted-third-party service has various options. The other option is, as I said, is essentially sequential computation. A TTP might, for example, issue asymmetric keys at various points promising that it will issue the duals to those keys at specified later times. Proposals for sequential computations frequently involve repeating squaring for inverting small exponents in multiplicative groups. It would be nice to use iterated hashes, except I haven't found a way yet of using iterative hashing, which is easy to compute. Easy to generate but hard to check, if you like. Whereas repeating squaring which is at the essence of basically many public key operations in any case, does appear at least if you believe the literature, to be essentially a sequential operation, and generates the examples at the bottom of our slide.

For example, take a very large prime p of the form $3M + 2$. A back of the envelope calculation suggests that defining the delay to be $x^3 \bmod p$ for p with $40,000$ bits might be good for a period of $30\,\mathrm{s}$ delay. One worry about very large multiplication like that is that you probably get into Karatsuba and Offman or FFT territory in a rather decisive sort of way. If the basic implementation does not use such optimisations and the attacker does, it would give him an extra advantage over you, so there may be advantages in bringing the size of the numbers to have to sort of more usual RSA territory. One option I thought of here, was what I termed *huge exponent RSA*.

The first thought I had was to use low exponent RSA in reverse, in other words to create the delay you say cube or raise to power of $65,537$, and then you issue the key to decrypt that with. Unfortunately, there are well known attacks on that that would give you the factorization, arising from knowing both the encrypting and decrypting keys. An alternative for this that I can't see an argument against, although I'm not a cryptographer, is to give out an unreasonably large public key for decrypting something created with an ordinary size secret key. In other words this is a public key where the exponent pe is far, far larger than is necessary, but where hopefully it's impossible for somebody without knowing the factorization of the base N to compute what the appropriate small key $p \bmod \phi(N)$ is.

Of course as you would expect, TTPs are not necessarily that desirable in this context, for one thing they might not be available. We might want to run such protocols where no TTPs are accessible, and secondly they might be corruptible. It's very difficult to legislate for the impossibility of doing a particular calculation fast, even if we don't know a way. I would argue for the principle of relegating the role of delay here to simply providing auditability, with no basic security flaw even if the delay can be overridden. It greatly reduces the benefit of such attacker activity, and is therefore much less likely to provide him with an incentive to do so. We've still got a protocol which was as strong as it was before, but now on assumptions about the security of the delay offers us auditability possibility.

What I did here was I preserved the structure and security of the original protocol, and I think that was the key to my believing that this work fitted well into the theme of protocol evolution. In the paper you will find this same approach applied to quite a number of other protocols from this class. I've tried it on various other ones as well and it simply works on all of them except ones which are decisively sub-optimal in some way.

In terms of future work, if we're going to employ this, we need to get some proper thought into these delay functions. As I say, there is some literature in this area, and I've referenced some of it in my paper, but that literature all envisaged very long delays, typically multiple-year style delays rather than the relatively short delay that I have in mind here. I don't in all honesty see why it should be any different in terms of its structure, but it does certainly deserve extra thought.

In respect of my work on this class of protocols in general, that's to say without auditability, I had a student work on a few years ago on human aspects. In other words, how accurately did humans carry out their role in comparing the digits of these protocols. Clearly there's also a role for the careful design of the implementation of these auditable protocols, and research on how humans actually do the auditing, if forced to do so by their devices.

Can we make other sorts of protocol auditable? Peter Ryan and I, when he was visiting us recently, have done some work on producing auditable PAKEs (password authenticated key exchange protocol), and we expect to produce a paper on that eventually. The use I made of the delay primitive in particular, the sort of delay primitive one can create without TTP, does really make one think, "What else could one use this for?" Could one use it, for example, in place of certain sorts of trusted third parties, where the role of this trusted third party is basically providing some escrow arrangement, because clearly this delay does offer a different form of escrow. I haven't personally thought very hard about this, but it's certainly a tempting thought. Thanks very much.

Audience: Could you use the third party as a compute server to entrust rather than trust it to be honest? You essentially give the third party the job of performing calculations and assume that the third party is faster than the first.

Reply: Certainly one could imagine using a fast, trusted third party in audit to do some of the auditing for you, I suppose, yes.

Bruce Christianson: There's something very similar that happens in some zero knowledge protocols, similar kind of thing going on where they say they want to be sure that once one party can drive the protocol to the conclusion of why, the other party can possibly much more slowly.

Reply: Peter and I have looked at some examples like that, yeah. Peter visited me for six weeks after, just after, I'd written this paper, so it provides and interesting key to our discussions over that period.

Malicious Clients in Distributed Secret Sharing Based Storage Networks

Andreas Happe[✉], Stephan Krenn, and Thomas Lorünser

AIT Austrian Institute of Technology GmbH, Vienna, Austria
{andreas.happe,stephan.krenn,thomas.loruenser}@ait.ac.at

Abstract. Multi-cloud storage is a viable alternative to traditional storage solutions. Recent approaches realize safe and secure solutions by combining secret-sharing with Byzantine fault-tolerant distribution schemes into safe and secure storage systems protecting a user against arbitrarily misbehaving storage servers.

In the case of cross-company projects with many involved clients it further becomes vital to also protect the storage system and honest users from malicious clients that are trying to cause inconsistencies in the system. So far, this problem has not been considered in the literature. In this paper, we detail the problems arising from a combination of secret sharing with Byzantine fault-tolerance in the presence of malicious clients, and provide first steps towards a practically feasible solution.

Keywords: Distributed systems · Secret sharing · Malicious clients · Byzantine fault-tolerance

1 Introduction

Cloud data storage often is a scalable and cost-efficient alternative to in-house storage servers, in particular for user groups that traditionally lack professional dedicated IT support such as consumers and SMEs. But besides obvious advantages, outsourcing storage into the cloud also poses various security risks that do not exist in offline or in-house solutions, in particular concerning the confidentiality and integrity of the stored data.

For this reason, initial solutions encrypted data locally before transferring it to a single cloud provider. For better availability and to prevent vendor lock-in, advanced solutions distribute data between multiple clouds, e.g., by storing multiple replicas. However, encryption might not always be an appropriate solution — in particular when storing highly sensitive data such as electronic health records. This is because encryption can only hide the data computationally, and it is virtually impossible to reliably estimate how cryptanalysis and an adversary's computational power will develop in the far future (just think of DES which was assumed to offer sufficient security 40 years ago, and which can easily

---

This work was in part funded by the European Commission under grant agreement number 644962 (PRISMACLOUD).

J. Anderson et al. (Eds.): Security Protocols XXIV, LNCS 10368, pp. 206–214, 2017.
DOI: 10.1007/978-3-319-62033-6_23

be broken nowadays). Modern cloud storage systems based on secret sharing scheme thus also offer the option to distribute the information in an redundant yet information theoretically secure way, e.g., [8].

In parallel to this development of cloud storage and due to the increased availability of high-bandwidth Internet connections, also the usage changed: from pure archiving systems to data sharing and collaborative development systems. Therefore, protocols handling concurrent user requests have been developed, e.g., to avoid that two users writing different versions of the same file at the same time cause an inconsistency in the system. As a result, Byzantine fault tolerant (BFT) algorithms that can cope with arbitrarily malicious storage servers have been presented.

In this work we now consider the next evolutionary step of cloud storage: multi-client secret sharing based storage systems that allow for secure collaboration *even in the presence of malicious users*. This becomes necessary because of the increasing number of participants working on joint projects — e.g., in case of cross-company projects — where it must be assumed that an adversary will eventually gain access to some user's login credentials, and that he will then try to boycott the project by causing an inconsistent state in the system.

In this document, we first describe selected complications that must be addressed by such protocols in Sect. 3 and then sketch mitigation strategies in Sect. 4.

1.1 Related Work

Various secret sharing based storage systems have been proposed and implemented (cf. [15]). We will briefly summarize the most relevant ones and discuss their shortcomings when dealing with multiple potentially malicious clients.

Multiple cloud storage solutions [14,16] implement a proxy pattern: clients communicate with a central server that in turn splits up data and distributes it over multiple backend cloud storage providers. This creates a single point of trust and failure within the proxy and thus fails our availability and privacy needs.

RACS [1] utilizes erasure-coding to distribute data upon multiple cloud storage providers. It's use-case is prevention of vendor lock-in. Security and privacy is of no concern, i.e., data is not encrypted. Parallel access to stored data through multiple RACS instances is achieved through usage of Apache Zookeeper, which implements the Zab primary-backup protocol for synchronization. This allows for parallel client access but does neither protect the data's security nor can it cope with malicious Zookeeper nodes.

DEPSKY-CA [3] is a Byzantine fault-tolerant storage system. In its system model, servers do not communicate with each other, clients must synchronize access to files through a low-contention lock mechanism that uses cloud-backed lock files for synchronization. While being obstruction-free this mechanism is not safe in face of malicious clients. Similarly, Belisarius [9] integrates robust versions of secret sharing with BFT protocols, but explicitly forbids malicious clients.

Summarizing, existing proposals and solutions are dealing with information dispersal mechanisms for remote data storage, they are using secret sharing to protect confidentiality and some of them deal with Byzantine robustness. To the best of our knowledge, however, none of them supports full concurrency for a multi-user environment while allowing for malicious clients.

2   Preliminaries

In the following we briefly recap the necessary background on secret sharing and Byzantine fault tolerance.

2.1   Secret Sharing and Information Dispersal

In threshold secret secret-sharing schemes, a *dealer* splits up data d into n shares, such that at least $k \leq n$ of these shares are needed to reconstruct the original data. Conversely, an attacker with access to less than k cannot gain any information about d. Basic secret sharing schemes assume that at reconstruction time, shares are either correct or missing. *Robust* secret sharing schemes are able to detect and cope with maliciously altered shares. Conversely, *verifiable* secret sharing schemes can be used to detect dealers who are creating and distributing inconsistent shares, by enabling storage nodes to (jointly) verify that they received consistent shares.

As an extension to basic secret sharing schemes, *verifiable secret sharing* (VSS) offers protection against malicious dealers. That is, in a VSS scheme the share holders can efficiently verify that they received consistent shares without violating the confidentiality of the shared message, cf., e.g., [11].

2.2   PBFT Standard Implementation

This section gives an overview of the PBFT protocol [4], which is the most prevalent BFT protocol for storage solutions. For clarity of presentation, we present the protocol in its vanilla form, and omit any possible performance optimization.

PBFT assumes a system consisting of n nodes (or *replicas*), which are connected through authenticated and private channels. At most $f = \lfloor \frac{n-1}{3} \rfloor$ nodes may be faulty. Exactly one replica is designated as primary. The system moves through a sequence of *views*, where the primary replica might be changed with every view-change in order to cope with malicious primaries. The view-concept introduces the concept of bounded synchronicity into an otherwise asynchronous system.

In the following we describe the normal mode of operation of PBFT. For error handling mechanisms we refer to the original literature [4].

Normal Operation and Transaction State-Machine. In PBFT a client sends the operation to the designated primary node. The primary associates an unique counter and broadcasts the operation and the counter to all other replicas as PREPREPARE message. Upon receiving this message all replicas broadcast a PREPARE message including a hash of the operation and its sequence number. If more than $2f + 1$ prepare messages (including one's own) are received by a replica, it broadcasts a COMMIT message. After $2f + 1$ matching COMMIT messages have been collected by a replica and all transactions with lower sequence numbers have been performed, the requested operation is executed and the result sent to the original client. After $f + 1$ matching results the client knows the operation's result. The archetypal message flow diagram as well as state diagram describing a single operation/transaction can be seen in Fig. 1.

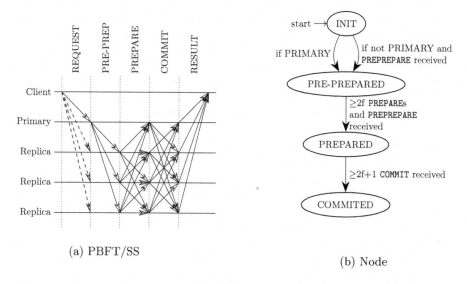

(a) PBFT/SS

(b) Node

Fig. 1. Black arrows describe the message flow of the vanilla PBFT protocol. The dashed blue arrows show the extension discussed in Sect. 3. (Color figure online)

3   Integration Issues with Secret Sharing

Integrating secret sharing into the PBFT model is far from trivial: the PBFT protocols sketched above rely on the fact that all replicas contain the same data, which is not the case for a secret sharing based storage where each node receives a distinct share which does not allow for reconstructing the original data.

Consequently, the core PBFT protocol must be altered to allow for per-replica shares. This leads to various issues, including:

Matching client-requests: In the original PBFT protocol, the client transmits operation requests to the primary which in turn distributes them to all other replicas. As the operation requests might also include data, this is not applicable in the new setting, as no replica is supposed to learn the original data.

A natural modification of the original scheme thus seems to be to split up the operation into secret-shared data and plaintext (such as type of operation, etc.). The client would now transfer the same metadata and distinct shares directly to each single replica and let the replicas match this data to the primary's PREPREPARE message; the possible protocol flow is depicted in Fig. 1. The main challenge in this approach now is how this matching of can be done reliably, in particular if the client sent duplicate, incomplete, or inconsistent requests to the system.

Clients providing inconsistent shares: A malicious client might send inconsistent shares to the replicas within a single valid operation request. Now, in the original PBFT protocol, a digest over the initial client message — containing the operation (comprising the data), a timestamp, and the an client identifier — is utilized as identifier and checked for consistency.

For PBFT/SS, this approach could only be applied to the metadata, but not to the data itself, as digests of different shares will not match, and thus consistency cannot be assured in this way.

It is thus required to efficiently detect inconsistent shares within a request that is valid from a PBFT point of view.

Clients submitting "consistent garbage": A malicious client can, while confirming to the PBFT protocol, provide consistent shares that contain destructive payloads, e.g., by overwriting sensitive files with consistent shares of random bits. This is a generic problem and needs to be addressed in any meaningful multi-client system.

Besides these client-related issues, integrating secret sharing into PBFT also causes numerous further problems, including:

Verifying operation results: In non-secret-shared PBFT clients can verify an operation's result by comparing the replica's return values. Similar to before, because of different replica starting with different input, an operation cannot be verified by simply checking return values for equality.

Checkpointing protocol: Replicas periodically perform protocols where a check sum over the replicas' data is utilized to detect anomalies. Secret-sharing prevents simple hashing schemes as replicas do not contain the same data.

State-transfer, recovery and pro-activity: Those are important aspects of long-running systems. Protocols needed for those functions again have to be augmented to be able to cope with secret-shared data.

4   Our Approach

We now address the mentioned issues regarding malicious clients in byzantine secret-shared storage networks. We always detail the simplest solution, further performance improvements are mentioned if applicable.

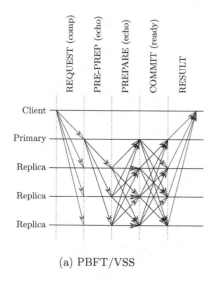

(a) PBFT/VSS

AsyncVSS		BFT
Phase	Message	Message
Sharing	send	REQUEST
Sharing	echo	PRE-PREPARE
		PREPARE
Sharing	ready	COMMIT
Reconstruct	-	after COMMIT phase, before operation execution

(b) Mapping *AsyncVSS* onto BFT

Fig. 2. Integration of VSS with the modified BFT protocol.

4.1 Matching Client-Requests

Implicit matching of client requests over their shared meta-data (e.g. type of operation, file names, timestamp) can be performed relatively easy as all needed meta-data is part of the plain-text message portion, i.e. is not secret-shared. Clients submit their operations over authentic and integrity-protected channels: if malformed or non-matching meta-data is detected, a malicious client is indicated.

The client-provided meta-data is utilized as simple identifier, i.e. can easily be generated by using a digest over each request's metadata. To improve performance, clients can implement an explicit id scheme, i.e. unique client-assigned identifiers (e.g. random number) per matching requests. This identifiers are then used to match the requests. If a malicious client submits non-matching identifiers or reuses them, the resulting transactions never complete and are detected by either a timeout mechanism or during the eventual execution of the view-change protocol.

As this leads to increased processing and memory utilization node-side, rate-limits might be required to counter denial of service attacks. A simple solution—e.g. rate limiting each client through an exponential backoff algorithm based upon the per-client mismatch detection rate—should be sufficient for the initial system prototype.

4.2 Clients Providing Inconsistent Shares

To detect inconsistent shares sent to the replicas, a verifiable secret sharing scheme (VSS) can be used. This allows the replicas to detect the inconsistency, but imposes computational and messaging overhead. However, to reduce the messaging overhead non-interactive VSS schemes [11] could be integrated into the PBFT protocol in order to simulate an asynchronous VSS [10]. Initial work on integration of the *AsyncVSS* protocol [2] has shown that VSS-protocols can be piggy-backed upon our existing BFT/SS protocol. *AsyncVSS* is an asynchronous computational-secure protocol requiring a minimal replica count of $>= 3f + 1$ thus providing a good match to our similar BFT requirements. Figure 2a shows the resulting protocol, Fig. 2b matches *AsyncVSS* phases and messages to BFT messages used in our storage protocol. No new BFT messages were required as all *AsyncVSS* messages were integrated into our BFT/SS protocol. Another benefit of this approach is, that the VSS information—i.e. that a client provided matching shares—is generated exactly before the replicas would execute and commit the corresponding operation. Replicas are thus able to detect malicious data before they would execute the corresponding operation.

Further efficiency improvements can be derived from the realization that a single operation usually comprises many secret shared blocks.[1] Batch techniques for VSS can be used to minimize the computational and messaging overhead [6].

Alternatively, servers could employ versioning to perform "speculative" acceptance: operations produce new versions while the old data version is kept until a client certificates that the data was received correctly. This approach is well known in the BFT world, e.g. the "Zyzzyva" family of BFT algorithms [5] improves the performance of PBFT algorithms by utilizing speculative operation execution. Other byzantine systems allow for unconditional command execute and depend upon subsequent (probabilistic) error detection [12]. In both situations, an error detection mechanism must be embedded in order to allow for rollback actions.

However, versioning impacts security mechanisms, and therefore needs to be handled with care. The following section details issues that arise from utilizing speculative execution and versioning.

4.3   Clients Submitting "consistent garbage"

An issue inherent to every storage solution are malicious clients that submit formally correct but semantically destructive operations. Typical examples are malicious users purposefully deleting compromising documents or the recent wave of encryption-based ransomware programs [13]. The mentioned versioning approach can be reused to mitigate the risk associated with evil clients. If malicious alterations are detected, a non-altered prior version of the document can be restored.

As only non-malicious clients can attest that an operation was semantically correct, there's a trade-off between storage and availability of older data versions. Versioning adds a "speculative" phase to stored documents' life cycle. This phase starts after each data alteration operation and ends after a quorum of clients did

---

[1] Secret sharing is usually applied on a several-byte level, while typical file sizes are in the range of MBs.

perform read operations upon the same data without any subsequently reported integrity violations.

Also the selection of trustworthy clients needs to be solved on a per-deployment base, examples includes selection through policy or achieving a quorum of consistent clients.

Versioning allows for performance and efficiency improvements as additional meta-data is implicitly available at the storage-server. This metadata (i.e. Change or Commit information) allows detection of causal dependencies between operations and might be utilized to introduce weaker—but more efficient—consistency models such as causal consistency (instead of the currently used sequential consistency model [7]).

5 Future Work

Metadata privacy is a challenging question which could be explored in further research. The main issue arises from trade-offs between metadata privacy, performance, and the possibility of multi-user access, especially in face of malicious users. Fully private metadata management places all metadata tasks at the client and thus severely limits exploitation of parallelization – preventing performance benefits – at the server level. Increased client-side state automatically increases opportunities for client-side attacks and thus poses new challenges in a fully Byzantine setting.

References

1. Abu-Libdeh, H., Princehouse, L., Weatherspoon, H.: Racs: a case for cloud storage diversity. In: 1st ACM Symposium on Cloud Computing, pp. 229–240. ACM (2010)
2. Backes, M., Kate, A., Patra, A.: Computational verifiable secret sharing revisited. In: Lee, D.H., Wang, X. (eds.) ASIACRYPT 2011. LNCS, vol. 7073, pp. 590–609. Springer, Heidelberg (2011). doi:10.1007/978-3-642-25385-0_32
3. Bessani, A., Correia, M., Quaresma, B., André, F., Sousa, P.: Depsky: dependable and secure storage in a cloud-of-clouds. ACM Trans. Storage (TOS) 9(4), 12 (2013)
4. Castro, M., Liskov, B.: Practical byzantine fault tolerance and proactive recovery. ACM Trans. Comput. Syst. 20(4), 398–461 (2002)
5. Kotla, R., Alvisi, L., Dahlin, M., Clement, A., Wong, E.: Zyzzyva: speculative byzantine fault tolerance. In: ACM SIGOPS Operating Systems Review, vol. 41, pp. 45–58. ACM (2007)
6. Krenn, S., Lorünser, T., Striecks, C.: Batch-verifiable secret sharing with unconditional privacy. In: ICISSP, pp. 303–311 (2017)
7. Lamport, L.: How to make a multiprocessor computer that correctly executes multiprocess programs. IEEE Trans. Comput. 100(9), 690–691 (1979)
8. Loruenser, T., Happe, A., Slamanig, D.: ARCHISTAR: towards secure and robust cloud based data sharing. In: 2015 IEEE 7th International Conference on Cloud Computing Technology and Science (CloudCom), pp. 371–378. IEEE (2015)
9. Padilha, R., Pedone, F.: Belisarius: BFT storage with confidentiality. In: International Symposium on Network Computing and Applications, pp. 9–16. IEEE (2011)

10. Patra, A., Choudhury, A., Pandu Rangan, C.: Efficient asynchronous verifiable secret sharing and multiparty computation. J. Cryptol. **28**(1), 49–109 (2013)
11. Pedersen, T.P.: Non-interactive and information-theoretic secure verifiable secret sharing. In: Feigenbaum, J. (ed.) CRYPTO 1991. LNCS, vol. 576, pp. 129–140. Springer, Heidelberg (1992). doi:10.1007/3-540-46766-1_9
12. Popescu, B.C., Crispo, B., Tanenbaum, A.S., Bakker, A.: Design and implementation of a secure wide-area object middleware. Comput. Netw. **51**(10), 2484–2513 (2007)
13. Savage, K., Coogan, P., Lau, H.: The evolution of ransomware (2015)
14. Selimi, M., Freitag, F.: Tahoe-lafs distributed storage service in community network clouds. In: BdCloud 2014, pp. 17–24. IEEE (2014)
15. Slamanig, D., Hanser, C.: On cloud storage and the cloud of clouds approach. In: ICITST-2012, pp. 649–655. IEEE Press (2012)
16. Spillner, J., Bombach, G., Matthischke, S., Muller, J., Tzschichholz, R., Schill, A.: Information dispersion over redundant arrays of optimal cloud storage for desktop users. In: UCC 2011, pp. 1–8. IEEE (2011)

Malicious Clients in Distributed Secret Sharing Based Storage Networks (Transcript of Discussion)

Andreas Happe[(✉)]

AIT Austrian Institute of Technology GmbH, Vienna, Austria
andreas.happe@ait.ac.at

Malicious clients in distributed storage networks. The presentation will be split up into two parts. In the initial part, we're going to talk about distributed storage networks that use secret-sharing, and in the second part I'm going to introduce malicious clients, their possible attack vectors and how to protect against those attack vectors.

Why are we doing this research area? Well, our basic assumption is we have a couple of companies. Each of the companies have their own data center. The basic idea is to create a shared storage network where each data center can back up data to. Through that, we want to gain high-availability, because if the data is shared between data centers, a single data center could burn down, but the data's still to be delivered. To do that, we need multiple user access, we need availability, also we need privacy—because if the data center backups data, it would be mandatory that only that data center can access this data. Also it's important for the other data center to have some sort of plausible deniability, that in case of a data leak, it wasn't us, it was somewhere other where the data was stolen.

To build a system like that, we're using two technologies. The one thing is PBFT, which stands for practical byzantine fault tolerance. This is a distribution mechanism that allows us to distribute operations upon multiple data centers and make sure that all operations are executed in the same order and achieve the same result.

Data-sharing is a data splitting technique that we are using to split up the data so that each data center has encrypted data to persist later on. It's quite important to note, that all data splitting and the re-combination of shares are performed at the the client's side, so the client does the encryption as well as the decryption. This places high importance on the client: it's not the server who does that stuff, it's always the client who performs the data-sharing. As soon as we hand over plain-text data to a server we assume that the data's compromised.

A common question that we're getting is, why are we not we using symmetrical encryption for that? So for example: we could just encrypt the data with a symmetric key and then transfer a copy of the data to each data center. The main reason we are trying to implement that with secret sharing and PBFT is

A. Happe—This work was in part funded by the European Commission under grant agreement number 644962 (PRISMACLOUD).

J. Anderson et al. (Eds.): Security Protocols XXIV, LNCS 10368, pp. 215–218, 2017.
DOI: 10.1007/978-3-319-62033-6_24

that we can either gain a better level of security by being information theoretical secure, or we can get the highest level of efficiency. In addition, if we just encrypted a data, we still have to solve the whole data synchronization problem. We can do that by design, by a combination of PBFT and secret-sharing—our approach will be more beautiful than the other one.

What is secret sharing? Secret sharing is just a family of algorithms that splits up plaintext data into n shares. You can use a configurable subset k of those n shares to reconstruct the original data. For example, in this case, we split up the data and one part goes to each data center. As we do not need all shares for recombination this gives us availability. For example if the first share might be on a data center that gets corrupted, we can still rebuild the data without that data center.

On the other hand, it also gives us privacy, because as soon as the attacker has access to fewer then k parts, he cannot gain any useful information of the plain text data. We're changing computational security with another trust model as our trust is based on the assumption that the data centers do not collaborate and just combine the data. This is also aided by the the synchronization model. Well again, it's used to execute the operations on all services in the same order and verify that they yield the same result. It also makes sure that a single, corrupt server or initial server can not impact the overall availability. In the typical PBFT protocol, the client sends the operation to a special server, which is the primary. The primary performs the ordering and transfers the operations to all other server replicas.

The protocol goes through multiple phases which are more or less here so that a malicious primary or a malicious replica cannot corrupt the protocol. After the Commit phase, the operation is executed and the client gets the result. That's the basic version of the protocol but that's not a good fit for secret sharing because if you look at the initial command, the client would transfer all data to the primary and if the primary gets our shares, the primary can reconstruct the data. So we altered the protocol. The first step has been exchanged so that the client performs the secret sharing operation and each server just gets the encrypted part of the data. The rest of the protocol resumes the same, that's except at the end of the commit phase: the problem is that PBFT normally compares the results, but in the secret-shared case those results are completely different.

The client would have to do some sort of auditing of the operation result and in this case would have to download the data of the corresponding data servers. That was the initial prototype that works as is. Now we try to incorporate malicious clients into the model. As I already mentioned, the clients are splitting up on the data. They combine the data. They are responsible for tracking malicious changes. They are quite important and powerful.

We identified 3 simple attack vectors that clients could be using. The first is that they are just flooding the network with corrupt data. It's simple to achieve. The second attack vector would be that clients submitting correct PBFT transactions but they would add garbage instead of valid secret-shared data.

Think of data as just an array of bytes. Each server just receives an individual array of bytes, and have no means of detecting if those are part of the data created by secret sharing, or if it's just random garbage.

The third attack vector would be the client using correct PBFT and correct secret-sharing, but the original data is just garbage. Which sounds kind of weird but then if you think about all those locky ransomware stuff it's exactly this attack class.

What we're currently working on is: the initial problem is quite easy to solve because PBFT takes care of that for us. It's the basic assumption of PBFT that it can cope with randomly automated messages. That's not a problem at all.

For the second vector, where we have correct PBFT but the data within the PBFT commands is corrupted, we can exchange the secret sharing protocol with something called verifiable secret sharing. And that gives us exactly the attributes that we need, that is, that the server can differentiate between data that has been part of validly secret-shared data and random garbage. We're using a thing called computational secure secret-sharing, mentioned in the paper over there, mostly because it's protocol can be piggybacked on top of our PFTT protocol so we don't have any communication overhead for doing that.

If I get back to our protocol, that's the original protocol adapted for secret sharing, and we can add the information for verifiable secret sharing just to each phase. The client has to do more computations in the initial request phase, but the replicas can just piggyback the additional data on top of the already existing commit or prepare messages, so we don't have an additional messages based on that. Also, what's quite nice is, that we would execute the commands at the end of the commit phase. Exactly at that time we have the verification information and know the secret sharing was performed correctly, so it's just in time we can execute it.

For the third case, this is the corrupt data case, we don't have a real solution, because we cannot magically detect the corruption correctly. We try to have some versioning, so all information is versioned and stored and if a client later detects an errors caused by an malicious operation, the server can issue a rollback command and can move back to a prior version of the data. Which sounds nice but has lots of problem, because here we have to store malicious data on the server.

We have a more complex consistency model when dealing with errors. To store data and metadata, we lose some privacy, so that's also not a good option. Also, we have a very big trust issue, because why should the server trust the second client—that tells me that the operation is malicious—more than I should trust the initial client that added the operation to the server in the first place? There are also advantages with versioning, we wouldn't have to think of verifiable secret-sharing at all. We could use an easier PBFT protocol and rollback in case of errors. We also could get some performance benefits out of it, but that's an ongoing discussion.

Yeah, that pointed to, we are currently working on improving the performance of verifiable secret-sharing with an batch verification scheme. The VSS code that we added to solve the second attack vector only works on a byte level. So the whole verification overhead is added for each transferred byte. We're currently working on a batch-based models so we can have the overhead on an transcational level.

On the versioning, I am not even sure that we should even do it because it adds lots of different error cases, as well as an reduced consistency model. Then for transactional data the versioning would add lots of complexity. That's an ongoing question. I'm not sure whether to do the versioning or not. That would be it for my part, so if you have any ideas that you'd like to discus. Or any questions? Thanks.

Jonathan Anderson: On versioning, you could look to systems like Ori, or for that matter Git or ZFS and things.

Reply: Yeah, yeah. Versioning has to be performed serverside on the active replicas. Initially the replicas had no idea of meta-data and data so their information was perfectly private and they we liked it that way because of privacy concerns. Also the storage owner, the storage center, can claim plausible deniability. Regardless of how we implement it, we need to have the distinction between a perfectly private and safe solution.

Reconsidering Attacker Models
in Ad-Hoc Networks

Radim Ošťádal, Petr Švenda$^{(\boxtimes)}$, and Vashek Matyáš

Masaryk University, Brno, Czech Republic
ostadal@mail.muni.cz, {svenda,matyas}@fi.muni.cz

Abstract. Our paper aims to move the research of secrecy amplification protocols for general ad-hoc networks to more realistic scenarios, conditions and attacker capabilities. Extension of the current attacker models is necessary, including the differentiation based on types of attacker's manipulation with a node, monitoring capabilities and movement strategies. We also aim to propose suitable secrecy amplification protocols that can reflect the new attacker models in different examined scenarios, utilising genetic programming and manual post-processing.

Keywords: Ad-hoc networks · Attacker models · Genetic programming · Secrecy amplification · Wireless Sensor Networks

1 Background

Ad-hoc networks of nodes with varying capabilities (including quite limited ones) often handle sensitive information and security of such networks is a typical baseline requirement. Such networks consist of numerous interacting devices, price of which should often be as low as possible – limiting computational and storage resources, also avoiding expensive tamper resistance. Lightweight security solutions are preferable, providing a low computational and communication overhead. When considering key management, symmetric cryptography is the preferred approach, yet with a low number of pre-distributed keys. While all results[1] we present can be applied to general ad-hoc networks, we present them directly on wireless sensor networks (WSNs) as typical representatives.

Attackers in such an environment can be categorised into different classes with respect to link key management. The global passive attacker is able to monitor all communication of the entire network. Monitoring might include the initial exchange of the keying material in an open form. The active global attacker comes from the classic Needham-Schroeder model [7]. She is able to alter and copy any message, replay messages or inject any forged material. She might drop part of the communication at her will. The node-compromise model [3] assumes that the attacker is able to capture a fraction of deployed nodes and to extract all keying material from a captured nodes. No tamper resistance of nodes is assumed

---

[1] Paper's supplementary materials can be found at http://crcs.cz/papers/spw2016.

© Springer International Publishing AG 2017
J. Anderson et al. (Eds.): Security Protocols XXIV, LNCS 10368, pp. 219–227, 2017.
DOI: 10.1007/978-3-319-62033-6_25

because of their low production cost. The weakened attacker model was defined in [2]. In this model, an attacker is able to monitor only a small proportion of the communications within a network during the deployment phase. Once the key exchange is complete, she is able to monitor all communication at will.

Substantial improvements in resilience against node capture or key exchange eavesdropping can be achieved when a group of neighbouring nodes cooperates in an additional secrecy amplification (SA) protocol after the initial key establishment protocol. SA protocols were shown to be very effective, yet for the price of a significant communication overhead. The overall aim is to provide SA protocols that can secure a high number of links yet require only a small number of messages and are easy to execute and synchronize in parallel executions in the real network. Different types of SA protocols were studied – node-oriented protocols, group-oriented protocols and hybrid-design protocols. We provide the basic comparison regarding the overall success rate and a number of sent messages in Figs. 1 and 2.

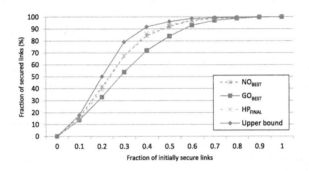

Fig. 1. An increase in the number of secured links after secrecy amplification protocols in the random compromise pattern. The best performing node-oriented protocol [14] is denoted as NO_{BEST}. The best performing group-oriented protocol [10] is denoted as GO_{BEST}. The best hybrid protocol [8] is denoted as HP_{BEST} and its optimised version as HP_{FINAL}. As can be seen, a strong majority of secure links ($> 90\%$) can be obtained even when the initial network had one half of compromised links.

Genetic programming was utilised to discover the best known node-oriented protocol so far, presented in [14]. Evolution was also the primary tool for a proposal of new kind of group-oriented SA protocols. This example might illustrate the fact that even when the evolved solution achieves good results, there might be other practical issues limiting the usability of the outcome. Group-oriented protocols suffer from the complicated synchronization of parallel executions and also from a complex security analysis due to the high number of nodes involved. Such complexities limits a practical use of group-oriented algorithms. For the hybrid-design solution, the genetic programming was used together with manual post processing. The whole process is described in [8]. In the same way, we would like to develop suitable protocols to counter the new classes of attackers with different capabilities.

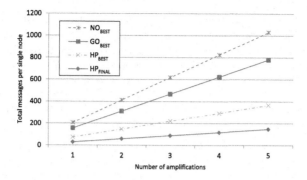

Fig. 2. Total number of messages per single node required to perform the best node-oriented and the best group-oriented secrecy amplification protocols (7.5 neighbours on average assumed). The hybrid protocol even with five amplifications (repetitions) sends considerably less messages than node or group oriented protocols with a single execution.

2   New Attacker Models

Previous research mostly expected the global passive attacker together with the node-compromise attacker model, sometimes weakened to the real world attacker model. We define the following new classes of attackers, differentiating the node-compromise attacker model from the following cases based on different kinds of manipulation with a node:

Key exfiltration model: The attacker is able to extract a part of the keying material from the compromised node (might be even all keys). After the key exfiltration, the node continues working in the original – uncompromised – manner.

Passive node control model: The attacker compromises the node, extracts all keying material and installs her malware. The node is under attacker's control, but the control remains passive – besides the monitoring purpose, the malware does not affect any behaviour of the node.

Active node control model: The attacker compromises the node in the same way as described in the previous point, but the attacker actively influences the behaviour of the node. She could discard some messages, change their content or even generate new messages at her will. In the context of the secrecy amplification protocols and link key security, she is able to influence steps of a particular protocol, initiate new amplification or attempt to make the protocol fail completely. Another example could be the disruption of an SA protocol by manipulating with relative distances from parties relevant in group-oriented and hybrid protocols.

According to the attacker capabilities, we distinguish global and local attackers. A global attacker was described in the previous section, and its passive version was used in multiple pieces of research. As far as we know, the local attacker was never considered regarding the link key security and SA protocols.

Local attacker with limited eavesdropping capabilities. This one might be even split into several subcategories. The examples of influencing parameters are the range that the attacker is able to monitor (e.g., the three times the range of legal node) and speed of the attacker movement. We could also consider several local attackers and their possible cooperation.

Besides the extension of the studied attacker model, our primary objective is to provide suitable secrecy amplification protocols that can counter different attacker models in various scenarios.

3   New Secrecy Amplification Protocols

We do not expect the existing secrecy amplification protocols to perform perfectly when new attacker models and the new attacker strategies are assumed. We would like to employ the genetic programming to develop suitable SA protocols and also the manual post-processing to identify the similarities among protocols to construct the SA protocol suitable for most of the scenarios.

We also consider the new way how to evaluate the success rate of SA protocols, in other words, how to compute the fitness function for genetic programming. Only the fraction of non-compromised link keys was used so far. We present the additional views:

- Percentage of secure communication. Legal nodes periodically communicate with their neighbours. The fraction of communication that is not eavesdropped by the attacker is used to evaluate the success of an SA protocol.
- Compromising ratio of messages that are sent from the node to the base station. Nodes emit those messages at regular intervals.

We use the KMSforWSN framework for the simulation of different parametrizable attackers and the evaluation of SA protocols. The KMSforWSN framework was introduced in [4]. It is a tool for an automated evaluation of KMS properties in WSNs built on top of MiXiM [6], a WSN framework for the OMNeT++ simulator [13].

We extended the architecture with two new modules to reflect the different attacker models and also to implement the secrecy amplification capability. The overall changes to the architecture are necessary as the original purpose covered only the key establishment protocols as well as different approaches for the success rate measurements.

We will also use the optimization framework developed originally for the evolution of intrusion detection systems in WSNs [11]. The framework is prepared to work together with the OMNeT++ environment and is also capable of distributing the tasks to BOINC, a distributed computing platform [1]. We expect to use BOINC on tens of CPUs to evaluate several candidate solutions in parallel.

4   Parametrisable Attacker and Experimental Results

The main decisions to define a particular attacker are to select the attacker type and attacker capabilities (global or local). Even after this, we still can define the number of parameters for such an attacker. Those include but are not limited to:

- Initial compromise pattern regarding the attacker movement strategies. Several patterns were defined in [5] – random attacker strategy, outermost attacker strategy, direct centre attacker strategy and centre drop attacker strategy. Additional movement strategies will be defined.
- Number of local attackers. Several local attackers might work together. Collaboration could be only in the exchange of compromised keys, but also, the coordinated movement strategies have to be considered.
- Eavesdropping range is radius where the local attackers are able to intercept the communication, in meters (e.g., the three times the range of legal node).
- Initial location of attackers might be selected randomly or predefined (e.g., at the boundary of the network [0,0]). There is also a possibility for a cooperation of several attackers.
- Movement patterns of attacker during the execution of a SA protocol. Those range from simple random walk up to coordinated patrolling.
- Movement speed of attackers in meters per the second unit.

The experiment is performed and evaluated on a network with 100 nodes randomly distributed on a playground of 115 m x 115 m. Definition of the channel properties and a physical layer setting are based on measurement done for TelosB motes in outside environment, available in [12]. All result are the average of ten random executions. The average density of the network is 7.34 neighbours per node. We use the node-oriented protocols for the comparison of different attackers. Detail evaluation of Pull, Push, Multi-hop Pull (M-Pull), Multi-hop Push (M-Push) and Best NO could be found in [9].

For the first experimental comparison of different attackers, we chose the key exfiltration model. Within this model, we have two cases: (1) Random keys are compromised – this corresponds to previously inspected random key compromise pattern. (2) Random nodes are compromised – all link keys from the compromised node are exfiltrated. Regarding the attacker capabilities, we compare the global attacker and local one with following parameters: 1, 3 and 5 cooperating attackers, eavesdropping range of 30 m, the initial position of all attackers on coordinates [0, 0], random movement pattern and speed of 5 m/s. The initial compromise rate of the network is 50% of all link keys, and the process of sending all nonces takes 100 s. Every attacker walks randomly 500 m in total.

The results are summarised in Table 1. The 100 s assigned for SA protocol to distribute nonces are not sufficient for the four-party protocols (Multi-hop Pull, Multi-hop Push and Best NO). The nonce packet loss ratio increases up to 12%. Nevertheless, it influences the success ratio only slightly due to high redundancy of protocols. Amplification protocols achieve better results for the random key compromise pattern than for the random node compromise pattern in general. The concentration of compromised links around particular node makes it harder to re-secure such links. Multi-hop protocols together with Best NO achieve quite constant success rate for local attackers, regardless of the random key or random node compromising. Again, the reason is high redundancy, compare the number of messages of Pull protocol and its multi-hop version. Push protocol is the best one for both compromise patterns for a local attacker considering the negligible difference in success rate compared to Best NO and number of messages they send.

The Push protocol gives significantly better results than the Pull protocol for both random key and random node compromise patterns. The Push protocol is better probably due to a particular protocol implementation and the timing for nonce distribution. The Push protocol initiates the protocol in a randomly generated time (0–100 s), and the intermediate node resends the message immediately. To the contrary, the Pull protocol generates the two messages with the same nonce, and every message is sent in a different randomly generated time (again 0–100 s). In the second case, the local attacker has a higher probability of intercepting at least one message.

Table 1. Success ratios for attackers with different properties.

Protocol	Pull	Push	M-Pull	M-Push	Best NO
Original compromise ratio	50.00	50.00	50.00	50.00	50.00
Messages sent per node	55.35	88.93	1074.33	811.01	1158.26
Nonce loss ratio	00.47	00.69	10.95	07.47	12.17
Random key compromise					
Local attacker (1)	97.86	99.17	98.63	98.76	99.23
Local attacker (3)	94.96	97.86	97.78	98.01	98.94
Local attacker (5)	93.08	96.12	96.80	97.20	98.19
Global attacker	84.17	84.41	89.22	89.34	92.42
Random node compromise					
Local attacker (1)	97.35	99.03	98.32	98.65	99.26
Local attacker (3)	87.03	96.03	96.41	97.47	98.40
Local attacker (5)	79.77	90.50	93.26	94.83	95.68
Global attacker	50.00	50.00	50.00	50.00	50.00

The experiment runtime varies according to the complexity of the protocol. The Pull and Push protocols are simulated in one minute; their multi-hop versions take eight minutes and the most complex protocol Best NO is simulated in ten minutes. All measurement are done on a double core CPU @ 2.4 GHz. Optimisation of the source code will be necessary to run the genetic evolution as thousands of generations (multiplied by a simulation runtime of a single scenario) will be required.

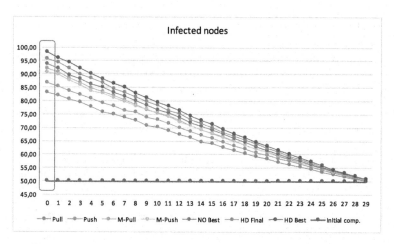

Fig. 3. Success rate of SA protocols for a different number of malware infected nodes. A decrease in percentage of secured links is linear. One can obtain reasonably secure network (more than 85% of secure links) even in case of 7 malware infected nodes considering the hybrid designed protocols are used.

5   Conclusions and Future Work

Our goal in this work was to initiate a discussion about realistic attacker capabilities and behaviour. We showed a large difference between the previously assumed random key compromise pattern and the more realistic attacker with the random node compromise pattern. Our future work will focus on parametrisation of attacker behaviour and her capabilities as presented in Sect. 4.

We also present preliminary results for other two attacker models. Figure 3 shows partial results for the node compromise attacker together with the passive node control model. The active node control model requires a further inspection. The basic results of this model showed that the attacker is not able to improve her success by neither the manipulation with a nonce message nor by dropping the entire message.

Other results suggest that the most beneficial strategy for an attacker is to stay in one place and not to move at all. The cause for these surprising (preliminary) results in our opinion lies in the execution dynamics of a secrecy amplification protocol. In a real network, a secrecy amplification protocol is not executed instantly as nodes need to synchronize send and receive multiple messages (another example of the difference between simplistic and realistic simulation). The moving attacker will, therefore, change her physical position relatively to start of a protocol execution, resulting in an ability to eavesdrop transmissions between a different set of nodes. As a secrecy amplification protocol is composed of multiple (and often functionally redundant) steps, a moving attacker may initially be able to prevent a change of particular compromised link into a secure one (when a local attack can still overhear and compromise newly transmitted key shares). Yet she would fail to do so few seconds later, when the remaining steps of protocol are executed and a moving attacker is already out of reception range for these nodes.

For a realistic simulation, the definition of standard network operations and message flow during a network lifetime will be required. Several other methods were suggested in Sect. 3. Those are areas for future work.

References

1. Anderson, D.P.: BOINC: a system for public-resource computing and storage. In: Proceedings of Fifth IEEE/ACM International Workshop on Grid Computing, pp. 4–10. IEEE (2004)
2. Anderson, R., Chan, H., Perrig, A.: Key infection: smart trust for smart dust. In: 12th IEEE International Conference on Network Protocols, pp. 206–215. IEEE (2004)
3. Eschenauer, L., Gligor, V.D.: A key-management scheme for distributed sensor networks. In: 9th ACM Conference on Computer and Communications Security, Washington, DC, USA, pp. 41–47. ACM (2002)
4. Jurnečka, F., Stehlík, M., Matyáš, V.: Evaluation of key management schemes in wireless sensor networks. In: Mauw, S., Jensen, C.D. (eds.) STM 2014. LNCS, vol. 8743, pp. 198–203. Springer, Cham (2014). doi:10.1007/978-3-319-11851-2_16
5. Jurnečka, F., Stehlík, M., Matyáš, V.: On node capturing attacker strategies. In: Christianson, B., Malcolm, J., Matyáš, V., Švenda, P., Stajano, F., Anderson, J. (eds.) Security Protocols 2014. LNCS, vol. 8809, pp. 300–315. Springer, Cham (2014). doi:10.1007/978-3-319-12400-1_29
6. Köpke, A., Swigulski, M., Wessel, K., Willkomm, D., Haneveld, P.T., Parker, T.E.V., Visser, O.W., Lichte, H.S., Valentin, S.: Simulating wireless and mobile networks in OMNeT++ the MiXiM vision. In: Proceedings of the 1st International Conference on Simulation Tools and Techniques for Communications, Networks and Systems & Workshops, p. 71. ICST (Institute for Computer Sciences, Social-Informatics and Telecommunications Engineering) (2008)
7. Needham, R.M., Schroeder, M.D.: Using encryption for authentication in large networks of computers. Commun. ACM 21(12), 993–999 (1978)
8. Ošťádal, R., Švenda, P., Matyáš, V.: A new approach to secrecy amplification in partially compromised networks (invited paper). In: Chakraborty, R.S., Matyas, V., Schaumont, P. (eds.) SPACE 2014. LNCS, vol. 8804, pp. 92–109. Springer, Cham (2014). doi:10.1007/978-3-319-12060-7_7
9. Ošťádal, R., Švenda, P., Matyáš, V.: On secrecy amplification protocols. In: Akram, R.N., Jajodia, S. (eds.) WISTP 2015. LNCS, vol. 9311, pp. 3–19. Springer, Cham (2015). doi:10.1007/978-3-319-24018-3_1
10. Smolka, T., Švenda, P., Sekanina, L., Matyáš, V.: Evolutionary design of message efficient secrecy amplification protocols. In: Moraglio, A., Silva, S., Krawiec, K., Machado, P., Cotta, C. (eds.) EuroGP 2012. LNCS, vol. 7244, pp. 194–205. Springer, Heidelberg (2012). doi:10.1007/978-3-642-29139-5_17
11. Stehlik, M., Saleh, A., Stetsko, A., Matyas, V.: Multi-objective optimization of intrusion detection systems for wireless sensor networks. In: Advances in Artificial Life, ECAL, vol. 12, pp. 569–576 (2013)
12. Stetsko, A., Stehlik, M., Matyas, V.: Calibrating and comparing simulators for wireless sensor networks. In: 2011 IEEE 8th International Conference on Mobile Adhoc and Sensor Systems (MASS), pp. 733–738. IEEE (2011)

13. Varga, A.: Using the OMNeT++ discrete event simulation system in education. IEEE Trans. Educ. **42**(4), 11 (1999)
14. Švenda, P., Sekanina, L., Matyáš, V.: Evolutionary design of secrecy amplification protocols for wireless sensor networks. In: Second ACM Conference on Wireless Network Security, pp. 225–236 (2009)

Reconsidering Attacker Models
in Ad-Hoc Networks
(Transcript of Discussion)

Petr Švenda[✉]

Masaryk University, Brno, Czech Republic
`svenda@fi.muni.cz`

Our scenario assumes a network of lightweight communicating nodes. These nodes form an ad-hoc network of devices that are limited with respect to computation power, with respect to storage, and also with respect to the amount/frequency/speed of communication. If some sensors are attached to the nodes, the sensor network is formed. These nodes are deployed and the basic key establishment is executed. We focus on links between the nodes and keys used to protect these links.

There are many different schemes for how to establish secure links, and our work has tackled this issue for the last ten years in different flavours. An important shared factor is that an attacker can interfere with the initial link key establishment and compromise some links as a result. Therefore, our basic assumption is that we have a network with some links compromised (link key is known to an attacker) with the rest being secure. The question is how we can improve the ratio between these two parts.

The attacker scenario is dependent on the key distribution scheme used, with different resulting network compromise patterns possible. The first part of the question is how to evaluate an attacker scenario. One can come up with a manual expert evaluation or the attacker's actions can be simulated in a suitable network simulator. The latter is our approach.

The secrecy amplification was introduced by Ross Anderson, Haowen Chan, and Adrian Perrig in 2004, and the basic idea is very simple. The network nodes are deployed and will realize who is their direct communication neighbour (usually by means of wireless radio communication). The nodes will exchange link keys in plaintext with their neighbours and start to use this to secure subsequent communication. But because an attacker is either eavesdropping on the original link transmissions or capturing selected nodes and extracting their keys, she is able to compromise some links. Not all, but some of them. Our basic assumption is that part of the network is compromised and we need to live with that fact.

Secrecy amplification protocols try to turn some of these compromised links back to secure ones again. If we know which particular links are compromised, we can generate a new key and send it via an uncompromised path to a target node. But we usually don't know which particular links (and therefore paths) are compromised. We can try all possible paths, but there are way too many of them, especially if we like to save battery and communicate infrequently.

A secrecy amplification protocol, therefore, specifies how to select a subset of all possible paths to be used to distribute fresh keys.

As we still don't know if the selected path is secure or compromised, it would be a mistake to replace old key (which is possibly secure) with fresh one (which might be compromised during transport). Instead, we combine old and fresh key together and derive the new key from both. If at least one key (either old or fresh one) is secure, resulting one will be secure as well.

There are three main groups of secrecy amplification protocols. The original one is called node-oriented. These are protocols for two parties (which are trying to establish new key) with multiple additional intermediates. If there is one intermediate, a protocol is executed for all triples of direct neighbours. Some were designed manually, others with the combination of a network simulator and genetic programming.

There is a second group that addresses one particular issue with the node-oriented protocols. The node-oriented protocols work pretty well but require a huge amount of messages to be send. The group-oriented protocols try to keep the number of transmitted messages low, yet achieve a high number of secure links. The difference is in the way how the keys are propagated. Instead of triples, the whole group of neighbours is participating in the protocol. The disadvantage is the need for more precise synchronization.

Therefore, we worked on something we call hybrid protocols which take the better elements from both previous types. The result is a simple protocol with a low number of messages transmitted. The question is how well this works and if we can achieve a high number of secure links. It turns out that it is working surprisingly well.

How many links you can actually improve by running a secrecy amplification protocol? Let's evaluate on the basic graph for the network with 7.5 neighbors on average. What you can see here is that secrecy amplification protocols in this particular setting can improve from 60% of initially secured links to close to 97%. That's quite an improvement and it's working even better in dense networks with 20 neighbours on average.

We compared many different secrecy amplification protocols in united settings inside the simulator and the result is that you really can turn quite a compromised network into a quite secure one. The important question is: How realistic is this? Initial work, starting with the first attempts, were done on a very simplified network simulator. These simulators were built to just simulate the exchange of the keys and monitor resulting compromise. They were not contending with effects like transmission layer collisions – effects like that were abstracted. The positive aspect of these simulators was their high speed, making them usable for automatic generation of protocols. One can try millions of candidate amplification protocols and select ones that work well.

In this work, we pushed forward with respect to how realistic the simulation is. We implemented everything inside the OMNeT++ simulator, so we can realistically simulate the packet collisions. This makes the results obtained more trustworthy and also allows us to inspect different attackers actions. We simulate how the attacker is moving through the network, what she can eavesdrop and which nodes are becoming compromised. We also implemented selected protocols on real hardware to verify if they will actually run on real nodes. The overall requirements for amplification protocols are low, and they can run pretty fast. It can be used and it improves the network security significantly.

The secrecy amplification protocol is not executed just once but multiple times instead. This means that attacker is forced to actively spend time to monitor, interfere with, and capture these additional transmissions of the fresh keys. Otherwise, she would slowly lose the fraction of compromised links she achieved at the beginning. The message overhead for the secrecy amplification for the hybrid protocols is already low but you can further piggyback on regular transmissions.

Most of the papers published in this area basically assumed a random compromise model in the sense that attacker is either randomly compromising the keys or randomly eavesdropping the transmissions in the network. The question is – is this the realistic attacker? We utilized a more realistic simulator that can simulate a more realistic attacker with some real limitations, moving along the defined path to see the performance of amplification protocols in different scenarios. We simulated attacker strategies in two phases.

The first phase is the attacker strategy during the initial compromise. This is the place where the nodes are deployed and the initial keys are exchanged. The second phase is the period where the secrecy amplification protocol is executed. An attacker can have different strategies in different phases.

Attacker strategies are simulated with an extension to the OMNeT++ simulator. The success rate is equal to the fraction of secure links after execution of the secrecy amplification protocol. Our baseline setting is that after the initial key distribution, a network has half links its compromised and the other half secure.

We simulate different parameters of the attacker strategy: number of eavesdropping nodes, their start position, how and how fast they are moving. The effect of the number of eavesdropping nodes and its start position will not surprise you. The more nodes the better for an attacker, and if the eavesdropping nodes are close to the border of the area, fewer links are compromised.

The more interesting results are obtained when different movement patterns of an attacker are considered, which gave us something we didn't expect. The different movement patterns have an impact, but the best possible outcome is for attacker which stays at the same place where it started during the initial compromise. Related is the speed of an attacker – the slower the movement, the better the result. The impact is that the secrecy amplification protocols force an attacker to stay in the single place during the whole secrecy amplification protocol to keep at least a portion of the previously compromised links.

The use of different metrics than the fraction of secure links may influence this situation. If the number of messages that will be successfully transmitted to the base station is counted, or latency is evaluated, and the attacker may choose not to maintain maximum compromised links but rather focus on links along the important routing paths. The realistic simulation of these network parameters is vital.

Audience: Are you using only the fraction of the secure links? It seems like it doesn't necessarily correspond to the real world objectives that attackers might have.

Reply: Of course, you can have other different metrics, like delaying the messages delivered to the base station and others. We can simulate these as well. The issue is that the number of potential scenarios is so high that from my perspective it doesn't really make sense to simulate all those scenarios. What makes sense is to provide a tool where the user running a network can set up his own scenario and then let it run.

Jonathan Anderson: I guess you didn't talk very much about the initial key establishment protocols, but what do those look like?

Reply: It can be something as simple as an exchange of the keys in plaintext. If the two nodes are in a communication range they can generate and exchange the key in plaintext, and then the attacker strategy is to be close and eavesdrop the communication. The attacker can't eavesdrop all the communication in the network because the nodes in the distant areas are reusing the same radio channel. Or you can have something like some randomized key pre-distribution scheme, where you are putting multiple randomly selected keys into each node's keyring. An attacker strategy is then to capture the nodes and extract the keys. As a result, links are randomly compromised through the network.

David Llewellyn-Jones: Did the results scale with the size of the network?

Reply: Yes. The results are basically independent of the size of the network because the nodes are usually talking just to direct radio neighbours. This is why we show the results for, for example, seven neighbour nodes on average. If you increase the size of the whole network, it will not change the result at all, as the secrecy amplification protocol runs locally among the neighbour nodes only. There is no need to communicate between the distant nodes.

Author Index

Printed in the United States
By Bookmasters